The Gingrich Senators

THE GINGRICH SENATORS

SEAN M. THERIAULT

OXFORD
UNIVERSITY PRESS

OXFORD
UNIVERSITY PRESS

Oxford University Press is a department of the University of Oxford.
It furthers the University's objective of excellence in research, scholarship,
and education by publishing worldwide.

Oxford   New York
Auckland   Cape Town   Dar es Salaam   Hong Kong   Karachi
Kuala Lumpur   Madrid   Melbourne   Mexico City   Nairobi
New Delhi   Shanghai   Taipei   Toronto

With offices in
Argentina   Austria   Brazil   Chile   Czech Republic   France   Greece
Guatemala   Hungary   Italy   Japan   Poland   Portugal   Singapore
South Korea   Switzerland   Thailand   Turkey   Ukraine   Vietnam

Oxford is a registered trademark of Oxford University Press
in the UK and certain other countries.

Published in the United States of America by
Oxford University Press
198 Madison Avenue, New York, NY 10016

[Insert Cataloguing Data]
ISBN 9780199307463

Contents

Acknowledgments　　　　　　　　　　　　　　　　　　　　　　　vii

Part I. An Introduction to the Gingrich Senators

1. The Partisan Senate　　　　　　　　　　　　　　　　　　　　　3
2. Newt Gingrich and the House of Representatives in the 1980s　　19

Part II. The Gingrich Senators as Party Polarizers

3. The Gingrich Senators and Party Polarization in the U.S. Senate　　35
4. The Constituencies of the Gingrich Senators　　　　　　　　　41
5. The Effect of Personal Characteristics and Proximity
   to Newt Gingrich on the Gingrich Senators　　　　　　　　　64
6. Getting In and Staying In the U.S. Senate　　　　　　　　　　73

Part III. The Gingrich Senators as Partisan Warriors

7. Compatriots in the Battle? The Other Republican Senators　　　91
8. The Gingrich Senators as Partisan Warriors on Roll-Call Votes　　113
9. The Gingrich Senators as Partisan Warriors beyond
   Roll-Call Votes　　　　　　　　　　　　　　　　　　　　　130

Part IV. The Future of the Gingrich Senators

10. The 2010 Elections, the 112th Congress, the Tea Party
Senators, and Gingrich's Presidential Campaign 155

11. The Future of the U.S. Senate 171

Notes *177*

Bibliography 221

Acknowledgments

ON DECEMBER 4, 2012, the U.S. Senate rejected a United Nations Treaty that drew its inspiration from the Americans with Disabilities Act. In his advocacy for it from his wheelchair on the Senate floor, Bob Dole (R-Kansas), a former five-term senator and the 1996 Republican presidential nominee, argued that the treaty was an attempt to make the rest of the world as hospitable as the United States for people with disabilities, including disabled veterans like himself. One-hundred-fifty-four countries—including Russia, Mongolia, China, and Paraguay—signed the treaty, which was negotiated by President George W. Bush and supported by President Barack Obama. In the end, the treaty was rejected when 38 senators voted against it. Although Republicans John Barrasso (R-Wyoming), Dick Lugar (R-Indiana), and Kelly Ayotte (R-New Hampshire) voted for it, they were joined by only one of the 21 Gingrich Senators (Republicans who were first elected to Congress after 1978 and had previously served in the House). None of the five senators who received significant financial backing from Senator Jim DeMint (R-South Carolina) in the 2010 elections supported it.

The lessons of the 2012 election, so it would seem, had been forgotten. Six current House Republicans and two former House Republican had lost their Senate bids in part because of their strident partisanship. Seven of the eight would-be Gingrich Senators had done worse than Republican presidential candidate Mitt Romney in their states. Several of the losses kept Republicans scratching their heads in the weeks after the election. Current House Republican Rick Berg lost an open seat to Heidi Heitkamp, the former North Dakota attorney general, in a state that Mitt Romney won by 20 percentage points. And despite his having won two statewide House contests since his opponent had even been on the ballot, Denny Rehberg lost to Jon Tester even though Romney's margin over Obama was 14 points in Montana.

If I had any concerns that the 2012 election would make this book obsolete even before its publication, I could put them to rest. The Gingrich Senators and their ideological soulmates and fellow partisan warriors, the Tea Party Senators, were not going to let a few alarming election results blow them off course. Party polarization and the partisan war would be as relevant after the election as before, even if it meant that one of the best pieces of American law, the Americans with Disabilities Act, and the very face of the Senate Republicans for much of the second half of the twentieth century, Bob Dole, would be sacrificed on its altar. Thankfully, Elizabeth Dole (R-North Carolina) had enough foresight to wheel former Majority Leader Dole off the Senate floor before his former colleagues voted against him and the treaty.

Luckily for me, this project has never had to overcome secret holds, filibusters, a screwy legislative process, or antischolarly warriors who would do to my research agenda what has been done to the Senate—unless, of course, you count all those negative reviews and frequent hate email I get when I talk about the Gingrich Senators. I have been fortunate to receive assistance, critiques, and helpful suggestions from a community of political science scholars that still operates more like the Senate of the 1950s than the Senate of today. For that, I am most grateful.

This project benefitted tremendously from generous financial support from the President's Office of the University of Texas at Austin, the W. Glenn Campbell and Rita Ricardo-Campbell National Fellows Program at the Hoover Institution (Stanford University), and the J. J. "Jake" Pickle Regents Chair in Congressional Studies (at the University of Texas). I thank the professionals at Oxford University Press who shepherded this project to completion: Dave McBride for having confidence in the project, Sarah Rosenthal for putting all the pieces together, and Marc Schneider for guiding the production of my book.

I thank Sarah Binder, Jon Bond, Doug Harris, Greg Koger, Keith Poole, and Michael Rocca for their generous sharing of data. In a book that has attempted to go beyond an analysis of roll-call votes, they made my task much easier and my final product much better. What they supplied in Excel spreadsheets was matched by the blood, sweat, and tears that I forced from my undergraduate research team. While I may have introduced them to the rigors of social science research, they have introduced me to a career filled with vicarious triumphs as they now walk the halls of the U.S. Capitol, the floors of the Texas House of Representatives, and teach in classrooms throughout Texas, the United States, and the world—even Bulgaria! They are now lawyers, political advisers, bureaucrats, teachers, elected officials, and mentors. Nothing in my professional life brings me more pride than their accomplishments and no words in this book mean more to me than naming them:

Tony Gius, Chelsea Bordovsky, Joanna Griswold, Jennifer Ponder, Courtney Mitchell, Shivani Mathur, Nick Coates, Alvaro Corral, Paige Cory, Brandon Chase, Kopia Keculah, Naela Sobhiye, Brandon Chase, Lauren Lucas, Hilary Lane, Sadie Weiner, Genevieve Woodard, Maria Brain, Dave Gillette, Jennifer Spencer, Lautaro Millman, Cole Dabney, Gordon Rooney, Jackie Wood, Andrew Childs, Matt Lamb, Geneva Castellanos, Andrew Ketner, Charles Maddox, Shelby Carvalho, Kritika Dube, Catharine Hansard, Howard Shin, David McNamire, Laurie Walker, Michelle White, Alenjandro Barrientos, Jose Galvan, Abel Mulugheta, John Powers, Emily Self, Joshua Teahen, Chris Kirby, Shannon Lemex, Monica Idnani, Zachary Garber, Joseph Guerra, Juan Gargiulo, Janette Martinez, Billy Calve, Natalie Butler, Kelly Depew, Owais Durrani, Nathaniel Norris, Justin Perez, Lartrell Ransom, Paola Tostado, and Cortney Sanders.

David Oshinsky, Frances Lee, Scott Adler, Tracy Sulkin, David Canon, Kathryn Pearson, Randy Strahan, Dan Palazzolo, Dave Lewis, Greg Koger, Jason Roberts, Jamie Carson, Michael Rocca, Wendy Schiller, Sarah Binder, Tom Mann, Norm Ornstein, Will Howell, Barbara Sinclair, Eric Schickler, David Mayhew, Jacob Hacker, John Sides, Gerald Gamm, Scott Ainsworth, and Barry Burden have heard, read, or been subjected to my argument— most on more than one occasion. Their keen intellect and helpful advice was needed and very much appreciated. Jon Bond read an earlier version of this book—my hope is that the plot now is commiserate with the character development. No one has been more unconvinced of my argument than Jen Lawless. I hope that seeing it in book form will do what hearing it and read- ing it in manuscript form didn't do. In the end, I may not have fulfilled their high standards, but I am grateful that their healthy skepticism was combined with helpful comments and suggestions to hone my argument and improve my book.

Just as the Gingrich Senators had their Newt Gingrich, so have I had my mentors who changed who I was and how I did my job. Barry Weingast and Dave Brady continue to both motivate and mentor me. Although my days "on the Farm" at Stanford have been traded in for the "40 acres" of the University of Texas (UT), I remain in their debt not only for their guidance as a graduate student but even now as a tenured faculty member. Paul Sniderman's friend- ship, advice, and support have been more generous than I deserve. He inspires me with his work ethic, intellectual rigor, and scientific integrity. Larry Dodd, whose old classes at UT I now teach, has become a true friend and trusted adviser. Almost 15 years ago, Dave Rohde drew the short straw. After read- ing his book on the House leadership, I had found a scholarship that would become for me the epitome of what I would attempt to do as a researcher. Though I cannot possibly measure up to that high standard, Dave has always been willing to read chapters, to offer advice, and to pour a glass of our favorite Australian Shiraz at the perfect moment. I was truly humbled when he broached in conversation the penultimate chapter of my second book *Party Polarization in Congress*. Even though that conversation continues, it has found a nice plateau in the publication of this book.

The University of Texas community has provided me with the environment to foster my productivity. My colleagues at Texas, especially Joshua Blank, Clare Brock, Stephen Jessee, Annelise Russell, JoBeth Surface Shafran, Bat Sparrow, Trey Thomas, Michelle Whyman, and Sam Workman, have vastly improved this book. I am particularly thankful for Pat Hickey, Jonathan Lewallen, and Megan Moeller, who have heard more about the Gingrich Senators than any human being should. Juliet Hooker always offered up a conversation or a glass of wine—or a trip!—to refresh my brain. More than four years ago, my life at UT immeasurably changed when Bryan Jones showed up. Bryan brought with him an intellectual curiosity without bounds, an openness to looking beyond changes in policy, a sermon about the outputs of Congress, and a cadre of graduate students that share his dedication to research, a knack for working on interesting problems, and a social ease that makes going to work a pleasure. Bryan's support of me—and this project—is more than I deserve.

My parents continue to inspire me to be a better person and to tell my story in a language that is accessible to those who do not live, eat, and breathe politics. Alas, as Newt has his Callista, I have my Anthony, to whom I dedicate this book. I remain indebted to him for his support, companionship, and love.

Most men here are alike in the deep sense that they are Senate men, joined in a common pride in the meaning and traditions of their forum. To outside attack from any source, not excluding the White House, they will certainly turn a common face, and they are at the end members of the Senate even before they are members of political parties.

—William S. White, *Citadel: The Story of the U.S. Senate* (1956)

PART I

An Introduction to the Gingrich Senators

I

The Partisan Senate

IN HIS FIRST address to Congress on February 24, 2009, President Barack Obama made health care reform the centerpiece of his legislative agenda: "So let there be no doubt: Health care reform cannot wait; it must not wait; and it will not wait another year."[1] At the time most people thought the president would achieve his goal. He was personally popular, enjoying a 64 percent approval rating.[2] Furthermore, Americans expressed general frustration with the increasing costs of health care. Around the time of his address, 79 percent of Americans were "dissatisfied" with the current costs and nearly 90 million Americans lacked health insurance at some point in the preceding two years.[3] Such data gave the Democrats confidence that major health care reform was possible because the Republicans had sufficient incentives to compromise or else they would be steamrolled by public opinion and large Democratic majorities in Congress.

Although the president's approval rating dipped to 59 percent in July, the political dynamic between the parties had not significantly changed, especially because the bill that was developing seemed to have the same features as the bill that Governor Mitt Romney (R-Massachusetts) implemented in Massachusetts, which, in turn, was based on Senator Bob Dole's (R-Kansas) bill from the 1990s. On July 17, 2009, it did. Speaking on a conference call to Conservatives for Patients' Rights, Senator Jim DeMint (2011, 75) said, "If we are able to stop Obama on this, it will be his Waterloo. It will break him, and we will show that we can, along with the American people, begin to push those freedom solutions that work in every area of our society." DeMint's salvo created a firestorm.

Three days later, Obama ridiculed the remark while visiting a children's hospital in Washington, D.C., arguing, "This isn't about me. This isn't about politics. This is about a health care system that is breaking America's families, breaking America's businesses and breaking America's economy."[4] Several of DeMint's Republican colleagues sided with the president in this tussle. Senator Kit Bond (R-Missouri) commented, "I think he was way off-base in his attack on the president." Senator George Voinovich (R-Ohio) added that he thought that half of the Republican opposition to health care reform—in his words, "probably 50/50"—was a consequence to deny the president a victory, whereas the other half was based on policy grounds.[5] Interestingly, both Bond and Voinovich had already announced their retirement from the Senate at the end of 2010. DeMint's party leaders did not rebuke him, but neither did they endorse his comments.[6] DeMint (2011, 74) recounts, "Several of my Republican colleagues chastised me for making all Republicans look like obstructionists. I was, once again, the skunk at the party in Republican Conference meetings."

While Republicans may have thought that DeMint's remark was ineloquent or impolitic, it was prophetic as the Republican Party leadership made sure that their members would not compromise to help Obama on his signature issue. Throughout most of the summer, the health care debate centered on a group of six senators—three from each party—who served on the Finance Committee: its chair, Max Baucus (D-Montana), and ranking member, Chuck Grassley (R-Iowa), were joined by Republicans Olympia Snowe (R-Maine) and Mike Enzi (R-Wyoming) and Democrats Kent Conrad (D-North Dakota) and Jeff Bingaman (D-New Mexico). At various times during the summer, the group seemed to be close to a deal, and at other times, their efforts were completely stymied.

Grassley was always considered the key participant in the talks. Snowe would have been unlikely to sway many of her Republican colleagues, and any bill supported by Enzi would enjoy near-unanimous support from Republicans. The Democrats had reason to believe that Grassley would negotiate in good faith. He and Baucus had championed many causes over the years from their seats on the Finance Committee. Most recently, in 2007, Grassley had sided with the Democrats to expand the children's health insurance program, which was vetoed by Bush and sustained by congressional Republicans before Obama and large Democratic majorities wrote the bill into law. In April 2009, Grassley declared, "I am doing everything I can to make the [health care] reform effort in Congress a bipartisan one."[7] On June 12, Minority Whip Jon Kyl (R-Arizona) undercut Grassley's efforts: "Senator Grassley has been given no authority to negotiate anything by all of us Republicans on [the Finance C]ommittee."[8]

Shortly thereafter Grassley became one of the fiercest critics of the Finance Committee's bill, leading some to question his motives during the committee's negotiations, especially when he continuously described Obama's bill as "pulling the plug on grandma" in town hall meetings during the August recess.[9] Grassley may have had a variety of explanations for his sudden switch in positions: a potential primary opponent in his 2010 reelection effort, a fundamental breakdown in talks, or even the August town hall meetings where his constituents voiced their opposition. The influence of Jim DeMint's call to arms and the effect of Kyl's undercutting of his authority, however, cannot be easily dismissed for two simple reasons. First, Grassley had previously complained about the leadership meddling in the Finance Committee's affairs: "Not as much gets done out of the Finance Committee that would get done if the leadership would leave us to our own pursuits."[10] Second, shortly after Grassley started criticizing the reform effort, Senate Majority Leader Mitch McConnell (R-Kentucky), John McCain (R-Arizona), and Mel Martinez (R-Florida) hosted a fundraiser for him in Miami even though his name did not appear on the initial invitation.[11]

When Grassley turned against the Finance Committee's bill, the partisan script for health care reform was written. It is possible that Republicans would have come around to opposing Obama's efforts on health care reform anyway, but DeMint surely helped that process along with his early strident opposition. The Republican Conference went from criticizing him to lining up behind him in a matter of months.

DeMint's assault on Obama's health care proposal went beyond an ideological dispute. In invoking Napoleon's Waterloo, DeMint purposefully transformed the debate from one about policy disagreement to an all-out partisan war. Although the president and DeMint's fellow Republicans were unwilling to engage initially in the warlike rhetoric, by the time the bill was enacted into law, no one serving in Congress was on the sidelines of the battlefield—all members and senators were fully engaged. This debate over "Obamacare," though perhaps the largest, was only one of many recent battles that the parties have waged.

Not surprisingly, most Americans have recoiled at what their Congress has become. After a recent poll showing congressional approval in the single digits, Senator John McCain concluded that the only congressional supporters these days included "blood relatives and paid staff."[12] In an article titled "Our Broken Senate," Norman Ornstein, the dean of political pundits, argued that "the Senate had taken the term 'deliberate' to a new level.... In many ways, the frustration of modern governance in Washington—the arrogance, independence, parochialism—could be called 'The Curse of the Senate.'" He concludes that the problem with the Senate is the "the culture" and that "is not going to change anytime soon."[13] Some of the most pointed criticisms come from senators as they are on their way out of the institution. When

Senator Evan Bayh (D-Indiana), whose father was also a senator, announced his retirement in 2010, he complained:

> For some time, I've had a growing conviction that Congress is not operating as it should. There is much too much partisanship and not enough progress; too much narrow ideology and not enough practical problem-solving. Even at a time of enormous national challenge, the people's business is not getting done.... I love working for the people of Indiana. I love helping our citizens make the most of their lives. But I do not love Congress.[14]

Two years later when Olympia Snowe announced that she would retire at the end of 2012, she commented, "Unfortunately, I do not realistically expect the partisanship of recent years in the Senate to change over the short term."[15]

I. The Development of the Senate

The Senate, so it would seem from Bayh's and Snowe's assessments, has entered a new era. That the Senate has changed and that politicians, pundits, and political scientists have offered their descriptions of it is not new. Even at its inception, the Senate was the subject of attention, scorn, and even admiration. While the anti-Federalists were concerned about the aristocratic nature of the Senate's design, the Federalists proffered a strong defense of the need for both its existence (to offer the citizens an additional level of protecting their liberty) and its institutional design (to offer a degree of insulation from the impulse of the people).

As the nascent country was taking its first steps, the Senate was already evolving. Although George Washington thought that the body would simply rubber-stamp his early decisions to get the national government running, the Senate quickly asserted its independence. In August of his first year as president, Washington was doubly rebuked by the Senate. For the first time, the Senate rejected a presidential nomination when Georgia's two senators worked to defeat Washington's choice for the naval officer position in the Port of Savannah. Three weeks later, Washington hand-delivered an Indian treaty to the Senate in hopes of obtaining quick ratification. Instead of rubber-stamping the presidential request, the Senate sent his treaty to committee so it could obtain more information before passing judgment on it. This action was a personal blow to Washington, who, on the way out of the chamber that day, is said to have remarked that he would never again set foot in the Senate.[16] He was true to his word. Since then few sitting presidents have gone to the Senate, and when they have they rarely fared better than Washington.[17]

Despite suffering President Washington's rage on these two occasions, the Senate's reputation for wise and prudent decisions—even if a bit delayed—persisted and developed over time. In the mid-nineteenth century, as the House of Representatives suffered through battles to get itself barely organized and as the executive branch suffered through a series of weak presidents, the Senate time and again forestalled armed conflict between the states by resolving—at least temporarily—the various slavery crises. The Senate was the main stage for the development and enactment of the Missouri Compromise of 1820, the Compromise of 1850, and the Kansas-Nebraska Act of 1854. Its heroes—Henry Clay, John C. Calhoun, Daniel Webster, Sam Houston, and Stephen A. Douglas—continue even today to be the models of revered American statesmen.

Though the "Gilded Age"—a term coined by Mark Twain to describe the graft and corruption rampant in American politics in the late nineteenth century—tarnished the Senate's reputation, the passage of the Seventeenth Amendment providing for the popular election of senators was just the cure the progressives wanted. Even as President Franklin D. Roosevelt took the governmental reins in passing his New Deal programs, the Senate thwarted his scheme to pack the Supreme Court. Roosevelt's subsequent strategy of purging the Democrats who crossed him enjoyed no more success than the legislation that triggered it.

Since the New Deal and World War II, the Senate has gone through at least three different phases: the Textbook Senate, the Individualized Senate, and, now, the Partisan Senate. These phases are probably not as distinct as the commas that separate them would suggest. The Individualized Senate, for example, was not a nonpartisan institution, and, from time-to-time, even the Partisan Senate operates in a way that would make Henry Clay, Stephen Douglas, and Robert Taft proud. Nonetheless, a short description of the first two phases provides a context for understanding the third phase, which is the subject of the remainder of this book.

A. The Textbook Senate

The Textbook Senate operated in the era of the "Textbook Congress," which was "an institutional bargain that gave prominence to committees and the jurisdictional imperative" (Shepsle 1989, 239). With the New Deal and World

War II operating in the background, the Textbook Senate took form with the Legislative Reorganization Act of 1946, which reduced the number of Senate committees from 33 to 15 and solidified their jurisdictional boundaries.[18] With only minor adjustments along the way, these committees and jurisdictions are still in operation today. Senators were said to relate to one another through readily established folkways that encouraged respect not only for one another but, more importantly, for the institution. The six folkways, according to Matthews (1960), were:

1. Apprenticeship—"New members are expected to serve a proper apprenticeship" (92).
2. Legislative Work—"Senators should be work horses in lieu of show horses" (94).
3. Specialization—A senator should specialize on "the relatively few matters that come before his committees or that directly and immediately affect his state" (95).
4. Courtesy—"Political disagreements should not influence personal feelings" (97).
5. Reciprocity—"A senator should [help out a colleague] and that he should be repaid in kind" (99).
6. Institutional Patriotism—"Senators are expected to believe that they belong to the greatest legislative and deliberative body in the world" (101).

This list is similar to the list of House norms that operated during a similar time period (Asher 1973). The one exception is that the House list did not include loyalty to the institution as did the Senate list. It was this institutional patriotism that set the Senate apart. Not only were its members engaged in the craft of legislation, but they were doing so while serving in an institution that they genuinely revered.

The Senate folkways were maintained by an "Inner Club," whose membership included those who "express, consciously or unconsciously, the deepest instincts and prejudices of 'the Senate type.' The Senate type is, speaking broadly, a man for whom the Institution is a career in itself, a life in itself and an end in itself" (White 1956, 84). When the folkways were violated, the offending senator would frequently be brought back into the fold through informal sanctions. If the senator persisted in breaking the folkways, they risked being ostracized.[19]

The Textbook Senate is portrayed as a genteel and well-functioning institution. Senators in this era, while they may have disagreed—and, at times, they disagreed terrifically—did so with the decorum that one would expect from members of this august institution. It is the Textbook Senate that has provided the benchmark for measuring all future Senates. The encomium that William White, who also studied the U.S. House of Representatives, wrote at the beginning of his 1956 book on the Senate, *The Citadel*, typifies the Senate and its admirers during this time period: "For a long time I have felt that the one touch of authentic genius in the American political system, apart, of course, from the incomparable majesty and decency and felicity of the Constitution itself, is the Senate of the United States" (White 1956, ix).

B. The Individualized Senate

The Republican senators who were brought into office on Eisenhower's coattails in 1952 faced a far different electorate in their 1958 reelection efforts. The Soviet Union's launch of Sputnik in 1957 damaged the United States' reputation abroad; and the economic recession at home soured the mood of the American public even more. Fearing that they would face certain defeat as a team, the Republican senators opted to run as individuals rather than as members of the Republican Party. The strategy, at least as measured by the results on election day, failed as Democrats gained 3 open seats and defeated 10 Republican incumbents.

The large class of Democratic freshmen, many of whom had won with little help from their party, were reluctant to abide by the established Senate folkways. They had won their elections by campaigning for progressive change and they were not about to let the Senate's Inner Club keep them from fulfilling their promises. The members of the Inner Club, too, recognized the power of the new progressive senators and were less willing to reprimand them for fear of bringing down the entire modus operandi of the institution in its wake.

As the senators became increasingly responsible for their own elections and reelections to enter into and stay in the Senate, the strong sense of community began to break down (Cain, Ferejohn, and Fiorina 1987). Beginning with the class of 1958, senators were less willing to specialize, less willing to serve apprenticeships, and more willing to use the rules of the Senate to thwart the will of the majority. In the 84th Congress (1955–1956), only 15 senators offered more than two amendments on the Senate floor. By the 99th Congress (1985–1986), 60 senators did (Sinclair 1989, 80). Freshman members in the same two congresses went from offering, on average, 2.5 amendments per member to 12.7 (Smith 1989, 136). While the 84th Congress did not have a single filibuster, the 99th Congress had 22 (Koger 2010, 107). As the floor became more prominent in shaping legislation, the plum committee assignments became less concentrated. While 52 percent of Northern Democrats held positions on the top four Senate committees (Appropriations, Armed Services, Finance, and Foreign Affairs) in the 84th Congress, more than 81 percent did during the 99th Congress (Sinclair 1989, 76).

As power decentralized, the Senate became a more equitable place. The distinction between the Inner Club and the rest of the membership became less defined. While senators and would-be senators relied on their party's assistance in elections, they were no longer dependent upon the party for electoral success. They assumed much more responsibility for their campaigns and were subsequently less tied to the institution or their parties upon their elections. According to Sinclair (1989, 210), the Senate of the 1980s, "compared to the Senate of the 1950s, [was] an institution in which influence [was] much more equally distributed and members accorded very wide latitude; it [was] an open, staff-dependent, outward-looking institution in which decision making [took] place in multiple arenas."

C. The Partisan Senate

That the Congress has recently become more partisan is one of the most obvious and, subsequently, most noted trends in American politics. While scholars and pundits alike debate the extent to which Congress mirrors (Abramowitz 2010), causes (Hetherington 2001), or simply exacerbates (Fiorina 2010) the polarization in the electorate, no one disputes that Congress is more polarized than it used to be. The Senate has not been immune from this growing partisanship. Most analyses show that the Senate has become polarized almost as much as the House (Fleisher and Bond 2004; Theriault 2006, 2008; McCarty, Poole, and Rosenthal 2006; and Brady, Han, and Pope 2007), despite the fact that the causes of polarization are more easily explained in the House of Representatives.

A first explanation, popular especially among political pundits and politicians, is that the purposive creation of safe districts through redistricting has led ideologically purer districts to elect more conservative Republicans and more liberal Democrats (Carson, Finocchiaro, and Rohde 2007; Hirsch 2003; though also see McCarty, Poole, and Rosenthal 2006 for the counterargument). With fixed state borders, the Senate is immune to the manipulation of constituencies that may cause party polarization in the House. Second, several scholars suggest that voters have geographically segregated themselves quite independent of district-boundary manipulation (Oppenheimer 2005; Bishop 2008). Voters can more easily move across House district lines than state borders to live by their political soulmates. A third set of scholars think that the evolving legislative process exacerbates the divide between the parties (Roberts and Smith 2003; Theriault 2008).[20] Unlike in the House of Representatives, where the majority party leaders can more easily manipulate floor proceedings, the more egalitarian Senate requires that much of its work on the Senate floor be accomplished through unanimous consent agreements. Because of these polarization theories and because of the greater access to and variation within them, most party polarization studies focus exclusively on the House (see, e.g., Jacobson 2000; Stonecash, Brewer, and Mariani 2003; Sinclair 2006; and Mann and Ornstein 2006).

Despite the greater theoretical underpinning of House polarization, few doubt that the Senate, too, has become hopelessly polarized. When Bayh and Snowe announced their retirement from the Senate, it is my contention that they were criticizing the institution on two different, though related, underlying dimensions. First, the senators serving today are more ideologically polarized than their predecessors. While the Senate has always had extreme conservatives and extreme liberals, today's Senate seems to have more of both than it did before. As the senators have become more ideologically polarized, the number of senators in the middle has shrunk, which has impeded the compromises necessary for solving public policy problems.

Providing evidence for this first criticism is relatively straightforward. Any number of roll-call voting analyses can show the distinct patterns separating Democrats from Republicans. Party votes as calculated by *Congressional Quarterly*, liberalness scores as determined by Americans for Democratic Action, and ideology as measured by political scientists Keith Poole and Howard Rosenthal all show that the parties are as divided as they have been in at least 100 years—perhaps as divided as they have ever been.

While some may think that the growing ideological divide between the parties is reason enough to criticize the institution, a second criticism seems to bother Snowe, Bayh, their fellow senators, political pundits, and congressional scholars even more. It goes beyond voting differently on the Senate floor. The second criticism is the increasing partisan warfare in the Senate, which taps into the strategies that go beyond defeating your opponents into humiliating them, go beyond questioning your opponents' judgment into questioning their motives, and go beyond fighting the good legislative fight to destroying the institution and the legislative process in order to serve not only your ideological goals but, more importantly, your electoral goals.

This warfare certainly has party polarization at its roots. Polarization may be necessary for warfare, but it is not a sufficient cause of it. Parties that are divided over policy can have a serious and honest debate, which can even become heated. In the first half of the famous idiom, the opposing sides can "agree to disagree." Quite apart from the serious policy disagreement, though, the debate between the opposing sides can degenerate into a shouting match where the policy proscriptions are lost in a fight over legislative games and where the combatants question the motives, integrity, and patriotism of their opponents. Under such a situation, the second half of the idiom—"without being disagreeable"—is never realized.

This partisan warfare dimension is harder to quantify. Roll-call votes reveal issue positions, but they cannot reveal strategies and motives. What I call "partisan warfare" is what Frances Lee (2009) characterized as "beyond ideology" in her book of the same name. Lee argues that only so much of the divide between the parties can be understood as a difference in ideology. The rest of the divide—by some accounts, the lion's share of the divide—is motivated by some other goal. Lee (2009, 193) defines this behavior as "partisan bickering" and offers the following description:

> If partisanship has roots in members' political interests, then political parties actually exacerbate and institutionalize conflict, rather than merely represent and give voice to preexisting policy disagreements in the broader political environment. In their quest to win elections and wield power, partisans impeach one another's motives, question one another's ethics and competence, engage in reflexive partisanship, and—when it is politically useful to do so—exploit and deepen divisions rather than seeking common ground.

I argue that it is this portion of the divide that causes the angst of those who long for the Textbook Senate. Lee restricts her evaluation of the combat that is beyond ideology to an examination of roll-call votes, which is an appropriate first step. Partisan warfare, though, can operate in contexts beyond the "yeas" and "nays" on the Senate floor. In fact, it is frequently other actions in the legislative and electoral processes that are better exhibits of partisan warfare. DeMint's declaration of the demise of health care reform being Obama's Waterloo is only the first of many examples of partisan warfare. DeMint did not offer a conservative argument to critique the president's developing bill; he rejected the entire enterprise, because if Obama was stopped on this one issue his entire presidency could be brought down. In this book, I begin to sketch out what partisan warfare looks like and how we can measure it.

More often than not, congressional scholars have opted to merge these two dimensions for a couple of reasons. First, there is no doubt that they are related. The distinction between party polarization and partisan warfare can easily be masked as the same or at least similar enough to collapse into one dimension. Second, partisan warfare, especially in comparison to party polarization, is much harder to isolate, operationalize, and analyze. Nonetheless, real analytic leverage can be brought to our understanding of how the current Senate operates and how it is evaluated if these dimensions are pulled apart. This book is my attempt to accomplish that goal. While it may be convenient to collapse these dimensions, real analytic leverage can be gained if they remain distinct. The feeling behind Bayh's and Snowe's words makes much more sense in light of warfare than it does if only polarization is considered.

II. The Plan of the Book

The transition between the Textbook Senate and the Individualized Senate had a clear date and a clear group of champions: the progressives elected in the 1958 election (Sinclair 1989). In this book, I argue that the transition to the Partisan Senate from the Individualized Senate had an equally clear group of champions though the transformation was more gradual. I call the instigators of this transformation the "Gingrich Senators." By definition, the members of this group share three characteristics: they are Republicans; they served in the House before moving to the Senate; and they were elected to Congress after 1978, which was the year when a suburban Republican from Atlanta, Newt Gingrich, entered the House and began his slow and steady rise to become the Speaker of the U.S. House. Jim DeMint is a Gingrich Senator. Kit Bond, George Voinovich, and Olympia Snowe are not. Both here—and throughout the book—I do not want to put too much emphasis on the causation of Gingrich himself. I refer to these senators as "Gingrich Senators" because it is easier than referring to them by their more proper name: "Republicans who were first elected to the House after 1978 and subsequently served in the Senate." The 40 Gingrich Senators are listed in table 1.1, which includes not only their names but also their states and the congresses they served in the House and Senate. The table also lists their House and Senate extremism scores, which are based on the roll-call votes that they have cast in the respective chambers.[21]

While the Gingrich Senators share some characteristics—for example, they are all white men—the table shows some obvious differences. First, the Gingrich Senators have represented 25 different states. They represented not

Table 1.1 The 40 Gingrich Senators

| Name | State | Senate | | House of Representatives | |
		Tenure	Ideology[1]	Tenure	Ideology[1]
Allard	Colorado	105–110	0.613	102–104	0.597
Allen	Virginia	107–109	0.407	102	0.474
Blunt	Missouri	112–present	*	105–111	0.602
Boozman	Arkansas	112–present	*	107–111	0.521
Brown	Colorado	102–104	0.543	97–101	0.456
Brownback	Kansas	105–111	0.459	104	0.546
Bunning	Kentucky	106–111	0.630	100–105	0.505
Burr	North Carolina	109–present	0.579	104–108	0.445
Chambliss	Georgia	108–present	0.518	104–107	0.427
Coats	Indiana	101–105, 112–present	0.407	97–100	0.297
Coburn	Oklahoma	109–present	0.907	104–106	0.815
Craig	Idaho	102–110	0.512	97–101	0.487
Crapo	Idaho	106–present	0.493	103–105	0.523
DeMint	South Carolina	109–present	0.831	106–108	0.704
DeWine	Ohio	104–109	0.192	98–101	0.343
Ensign	Nevada	107–112	0.554	104–105	0.635
Graham	South Carolina	108–present	0.473	104–107	0.477
Gramm[2]	Texas	99–107	0.561	98	0.548
Grams	Minnesota	104–106	0.526	103	0.530
Gregg	New Hampshire	103–111	0.429	97–100	0.412
Heller	Nevada	112–present	*	110–112	0.646
Hutchinson	Arkansas	105–107	0.457	103–104	0.412
Inhofe	Oklahoma	104–present	0.689	100–103	0.475
Isakson	Georgia	109–present	0.504	106–108	0.500
Kirk	Illinois	111–present	0.333	107–111	0.453
Kyl	Arizona	104–present	0.616	100–103	0.527
Mack	Florida	101–106	0.407	98–100	0.520
McCain	Arizona	100–present	0.371	98–99	0.302
Moran	Kansas	112–present	*	105–111	0.494
Portman	Ohio	112–present	*	103–109	0.447

Table 1.1 (*Continued*)

Name	State	Senate		House of Representatives	
		Tenure	Ideology[1]	Tenure	Ideology[1]
Roberts	Kansas	105–present	0.399	97–104	0.407
Santorum	Pennsylvania	104–109	0.373	102–103	0.294
Smith	New Hampshire	102–107	0.747	99–101	0.545
Sununu	New Hampshire	108–110	0.423	105–107	0.634
Talent	Missouri	108–109	0.305	103–106	0.455
Thomas	Wyoming	104–110	0.525	101–103	0.396
Thune	South Dakota	109–present	0.509	105–107	0.358
Toomey	Pennsylvania	112–present	*	106–108	0.795
Vitter	Louisiana	109–present	0.623	106–108	0.550
Wicker	Mississippi	110–present	0.444	104–110	0.487

* Ideology scores are not computed until the senator completes at least one Congress.

[1] Ideology is measured by the average DW-NOMINATE scores.

[2] Gramm was first elected as a Democrat to the 96th Congress. In January 1983 he resigned his seat, switched parties, and won reelection as a Republican. The data analysis includes only his service as a Republican.

only the most conservative states, like Oklahoma, Kansas, and Idaho, but also some Democratic states such as Pennsylvania, Illinois, and Minnesota.

Second, some Gingrich Senators had brief congressional careers, such as George Allen and Rod Grams, while others had long careers like Pat Roberts and Jim Inhofe. Third, while some Gingrich Senators became important senators—such as Jon Kyl, the minority whip, and John McCain, the 2008 presidential candidate—others had relatively undistinguished careers (pick any name from table 1.1 that is new to you). Fourth, some, such as Judd Gregg and Lindsey Graham, are known for their personal integrity, while others such as Larry Craig, David Vitter, Tim Hutchinson, and John Ensign have gotten caught, quite literally, with their pants down. Finally, although none could be described as moderates in the tradition of Susan Collins (R-Maine) or Scott Brown (R-Massachusetts), the Gingrich Senators' extremism scores range from those of Mike DeWine to Tom Coburn. All of this diversity within the ranks of the Gingrich Senators demonstrates that not all of them are cut from the same cloth, neither are they equally extreme nor equally combative.

For example, Rick Santorum had a relatively moderate voting record, but he was a field commander in the partisan war. Others, like Craig Thomas and Saxby Chambliss, had more conservative voting records, but they were not particularly bellicose. Jim DeMint, David Vitter, Sam Brownback, and Phil Gramm typify what it means to be a Gingrich Senator—a party polarizer and a partisan warrior. Despite the differences among them, as a class, they remain distinct from their Senate colleagues.

I assert here—and will demonstrate throughout this book—that the Republicans who served in the House before Gingrich's election and the Democrats who served in the House before, during, and after Gingrich are not any different from their non-House veteran colleagues. The Gingrich Senators, almost single-handedly at first, propelled party polarization and escalated partisan warfare in the Senate. Their behavior, of course, reverberated around the institution and affected both their fellow Republicans and their Democratic colleagues.

At about the same time that Newt Gingrich entered the House, so did Representative Richard Gephardt (D-Missouri).[22] Although no one argues that Gephardt's style was as confrontational as Gingrich's,[23] the timing of their service, the importance they played in their respective parties, and the hyperpartisan House in which they both served suggest that there could be a similar polarizing phenomenon in the Democratic Party. To test for its existence, I will frequently compare the Gingrich Senators to the Gephardt Senators. As with the Gingrich Senators, I use the term "Gephardt Senators" to mean "Democrats who were first elected to the House after 1978 and subsequently served in the Senate." The Gephardt Senators, though at times acting differently than their fellow Democrats, are never as distinct as the Gingrich Senators' actions compared to their fellow Republicans.

From the outset, I want to state clearly two caveats about my Gingrich Senator argument. First, I do not believe that the transformation of the Senate began and ended with the Gingrich Senators. The Republican Party does not operate in isolation in the Senate. Certainly, the Democrats elected during the Republican Party's collapse at the end of the Bush administration in 2006 and 2008 were not like their predecessors, though their behavior is not as distinct as that of the Gingrich Senators, nor can their political background so easily characterize them. My argument is simply that the Gingrich Senators, either implicitly or explicitly, were a major source of the transformation. Along the way, their fellow Republicans as well as the Senate Democrats were more than willing to meet them on the battlefield.

Second, I do not intend to put this transformation in a negative light. For years, political scientists lamented the lack of strong political parties. Because of the individual enterprises by which congressional candidates became members of Congress, party leaders had very little control over their fellow partisans once they showed up in Washington. Reformers bemoaned the irresponsible parties that flourished throughout most of the twentieth century. What political observers called "responsible parties" in the 1950s have become the polarized parties of today. At every step of the transformation, conservatives have encouraged the Gingrich Senators while many liberals have stared in awe at what they have been able to accomplish. A chamber filled with individual members that former Senate Majority Leader Trent Lott (2005) likened to "herding cats," has made coordinating strategy for either political or policy reasons exceedingly difficult. Nonetheless, a pack mentality, which will be described later in the book, flourishes among the Gingrich Senators. While Democrats scorn the effect that these senators have had on politics, they have also marveled at the degree of unity among them. In this book, it is the factual record that I document and seek to explain. I leave it to the reader to determine if the transformation was a positive development for, specifically, the U.S. Senate or, more generally, for American politics. I will have fulfilled this goal if both Norman Ornstein and Jim DeMint think that I have faithfully presented the evidence for the Gingrich Senators as both party polarizers and partisan warriors.

My investigation of the Gingrich Senators is broken up into four parts. In the next chapter, I describe Newt Gingrich and the strategies that he introduced into the House of Representatives. I show how Gingrich transformed not only the Republican Conference but the entire House of Representatives. The second part of the book explores more deeply the first dimension of the Partisan Senate—party polarization. In chapter 3, I outline how much more distinct the roll-call votes of the Gingrich Senators are from their colleagues in the Senate. In chapter 4, I find that part—only about one-quarter—of their voting record can be explained by their more conservative constituencies. Most of the analysis shows that the Gingrich Senators remain distinct even after their constituency is factored into the analysis. In chapter 5, I find that very little of their voting record can be explained by the personal characteristics that they share or their personal connection to Newt Gingrich. The overall lesson in the chapter is that it was the Gingrich Senators' service in the House and not their proximity to Gingrich that largely influenced their Senate voting behavior. In the last chapter of part 2, I show how the Gingrich Senators have had longer careers in the Senate than their counterparts despite their more conservative voting records. It seems as though they have been able to buy a more conservative voting record by raising substantially more money for their reelection campaigns than the other Republicans in the Senate.

Part 3 of the book examines the second dimension of the Partisan Senate—partisan warfare. First, I explore the Gingrich Senators' relationship with their fellow Republicans in the Senate (chapter 7). In the following two chapters, I provide evidence—both from roll-call votes (chapter 8) and other sources (chapter 9)—for their role as partisan warriors. They have had a profound effect not only within their own group but also across the American political landscape. Furthermore, their effect goes beyond mere roll-call votes. Negotiations, nominations, and the legislative process in the Senate have all been fundamentally transformed by the Gingrich Senators.

Part 4 of the book contains two chapters that examine the future of the U.S. Senate. Chapter 10 examines the 2010 elections, the 112th Congress (2011–2012), and the Tea Party Senators. Chapter 11 examines what the future holds for the U.S. Senate and, for those who fear these prospective developments, how they may be forestalled.

2

Newt Gingrich and the House of Representatives in the 1980s

THE FRAMERS OF the Constitution intended for the House to be different from the Senate. Different constituencies, different term lengths, and different electoral mechanisms were to provide the Senate with more insulation from the impulse of the people. As the institutions developed, their differences grew. Early in its development, the Senate dropped the use of a previous question motion, which meant that unanimous consent agreements were the only way for the chamber to move its legislation along. This move instilled in each senator the power to bring the Senate to a standstill. The relative informality and late-developing leadership structure of the Senate has ensured that all senators are equal, although the old adage that some senators are "more equal" than others still rings true.

At times these differences have caused some friction between the House and the Senate. A crowd-pleasing line used by House members is: "The Democrats (or Republicans) aren't the enemy. The Democrats (or Republicans) are the opposition. The real enemy is the Senate."[1] The vitriol does not only go in one direction. Hillary Clinton, while still serving in the Senate in 2006, famously commented on the House: "When you look at the way the House of Representatives has been run, it has been run like a plantation, and you know what I'm talking about. It has been run in a way so that nobody with a contrary view has had a chance to present legislation, to make an argument, to be heard."[2] That House service would affect how senators do their job is not surprising, especially among the Republicans who were serving in the 1980s and later, when their caucus was being transformed from a go-along-to-get-along permanent minority to a burgeoning majority party.

In this chapter, I sketch out this transformation and measure its effect on the House members who subsequently served in the Senate. I describe how Newt Gingrich transformed, initially, the House Republican Conference and then the House of Representatives in the 1980s and 1990s.[3] Then I show

how the Republicans who came into the House after Gingrich's first election looked and acted differently from the Republicans who entered the House before Gingrich's first election. The Republicans who entered the House even after Gingrich became Speaker solidified this transformation.

I. The House of Representatives in the 1980s

The Democrats in the House wrestled with the same ideological split that helped transform the Senate. As a consequence, Democrats knew that it was frequently easier to negotiate with Republicans than to forge a Democrats-only enacting coalition. Though frustrated with being a "permanent minority," as some pundits and political scientists called it, the Republicans seriously engaged the legislative process because doing so brought about policy rewards. These dynamics fostered legislation that typically won large bipartisan majorities.

Nothing upset this delicate balance more than Ronald Reagan's election as president in 1980. Although the polls heading into the election showed a much closer race, Reagan's popular vote margin was nearly 10 points greater than his opponent, incumbent President Jimmy Carter. Furthermore, Reagan won 489 of the 538 electoral college votes. On Reagan's coattails, the Republicans were able to pick up 12 seats and majority control in the U.S. Senate. While the Republicans gained 34 seats in the U.S. House of Representatives, they were still a minority by more than 50 seats. Because the Democrats maintained a majority amid an election that brought many more Republicans to Washington, D.C., the House became the battleground between Reagan's new conservative compatriots and the Democratic old guard.

The 1980 elections brought not only a new occupant to the White House but also a new Republican leader to the House. Bob Michel (R-Illinois), who was then Minority Whip, defeated a more vociferous and combative Guy Vander Jagt (D-Michigan), who chaired the National Republican Campaign Committee, on a close 103–87 vote. Although he could be counted on to give a tough speech critical of House Democrats, Michel never let politics get in the way of his warm relationship (and regular golf game) with Speaker Tip O'Neill.

Reagan's overwhelming victory and his popularity in the early days of his term dealt a blow to the congressional Democrats. When he became the Minority Leader, Michel assumed the responsibility of carrying the president's legislative initiatives through a House where his Republicans still toiled in the minority as Senate Majority Leader Baker (R-Tennessee) and his fellow

Republicans were banging committee gavels for the first time since the 1950s. Michel masterfully kept the Republican Conference largely united while picking off enough Boll Weevil Democrats to secure House passage for many of Reagan's important economic policies in the House. Within eight months of his inauguration, Reagan signed into law the biggest tax and spending cuts up to that point in American history. The legislation cut income taxes by 25 percent and cut domestic social programs by more than $130 billion. These policies presented the American electorate with the first real alternative to the New Deal (Pierson 1994). The conservatism that broke into the national dialogue with Barry Goldwater's 1964 presidential campaign was finally getting a chance to shape national policy. The New Deal ethos that had dominated national policymaking—even through the Eisenhower and Nixon administrations—was being sacrificed on the altar of race, rights, and taxes (Edsall and Edsall 1992).

By year's end, though, the United States had entered its most severe economic downturn since the Great Depression more than 50 years before. As the economy fell, the Democrats in the House regained their footing. In 1982 the Democrats pushed through a substantial tax increase and a decrease in the defense budget, and they overrode a presidential veto on an appropriations bill that Reagan labeled a "budget buster." Furthermore, Democrats in the House stopped other items on Reagan's agenda including implementing prayer in school, stopping court-ordered busing, revamping the clean water and clean air laws, and dismantling the Departments of Energy and Education. As a consequence of the ongoing recession, the Democrats gained 27 seats in 1982 House elections. Due to the mix of states that were in play that year, the Republicans gained an additional seat in the Senate. These mixed election results only deepened the partisan battles in Congress. The House Republicans were especially frustrated because their policy successes diminished after the low-hanging fruit had been picked in Reagan's first two years, and they could not soften the blow by banging the committee gavels.

As Reagan's legislative record stalled, Michel came under increased pressure from the supporters of his former foe, Vander Jagt. One of Vander Jagt's key lieutenants was Newt Gingrich, who was first elected to Congress in 1978 after two previous unsuccessful attempts. Gingrich, whom Vander Jagt appointed to a leadership position in the National Republican Congressional Committee even before he was sworn in as a member of the House, formed an informal group—the Conservative Opportunity Society (COS)—as a mouthpiece for the more conservative, more confrontational members of the House Republican Conference. The group included Robert

Walker (R-Pennsylvania), Vin Weber (R-Minnesota), and Dan Lungren (R-California), as well as future Gingrich Senators Judd Gregg, Dan Coats, Connie Mack, and Jon Kyl. Perhaps it was Weber, first elected in 1980, who best articulated their sentiment that the Republican leadership had "been too reluctant to confront in the past. A party that has been in the minority has a tendency to become a little bit cowed, but I'm hard-pressed to see where compromise has advanced the Republican agenda."[4] Over the winter recess in 1983–1984, the COS became more formalized when it gave its members specific tasks. While Gingrich was responsible for policy, Walker became the group's parliamentarian, taking on the moniker of "minority objector" to gum up the Democrats' legislative strategies, and Weber coordinated the group's actions with the White House and other Republicans on Capitol Hill.[5]

Gingrich's penchant for confrontation started even before Reagan's election and the establishment of the COS. While the Republicans were nearly outnumbered 2–1 in his first term, Gingrich called for the expulsion of Representative Charles C. Diggs Jr. (D-Michigan), who had been convicted on 29 felony counts for illegally diverting more than $60,000 from his congressional employees' salaries for his personal use.[6] A month after his conviction was handed down, Diggs won reelection. Immediately upon his seating in the next congress, the Ethics Committee started an investigation. Gingrich, in his first couple of months in the House, tried to bypass the committee's investigation by immediately fighting to expel Diggs after he cast a vote to raise the debt limit. House rules recommended that convicted felons refrain from voting on the House floor unless they were reelected. Despite Diggs's reelection a couple of months before, Gingrich tried to reinterpret the rules to deny Diggs his right to vote. The only way Gingrich could prevail was for the House to expel Diggs, something it was reluctant to do as indicated by its overwhelming approval (322–77) of a motion by Democratic Majority Leader Jim Wright (D-Texas) to refer Gingrich's measure to the Ethics Committee. The Republican Leader at the time, John Rhodes (R-Arizona), supported Wright. On July 30 the House again defeated an attempt to remove Diggs by tabling the measure (205–197)—this time, only 12 Republicans voted against expulsion. The following day, Diggs was unanimously censured, 414–0. At the conclusion of the Congress, he retired.

With the founding of the COS, Gingrich had an organization to help him criticize the Democratic leadership and bring down the 30-year Democratic majority that persisted in the House. One of the first head-on and public confrontations the COS had with the Democrats came in spring 1984. As "minority objector," Walker had coordinated the COS to use "Special Orders," which are the speeches members can give about any topic they choose at the end of the legislative day, to criticize and ridicule the Democrats. Gingrich asserted that the speeches were going to be "like Chinese water torture" on the Democrats.[7] The speeches were particularly effective because the C-SPAN audience had no idea that the speeches were being made to a nearly empty House chamber. On May 8, their rhetoric and vitriol reached a new level when they read into the *Congressional Record* a report published by the Republican Study Group that criticized Democratic foreign policy over the previous 15 years. After Walker exhausted his one-hour allotment, Gingrich followed. He singled out 51 Democrats who believed that "America does nothing right and communism ... rushes into vacuums caused by 'stupid' Americans and its 'rotten, corrupt' allies."[8] Gingrich had broken House protocol by not alerting the 51 Democrats that he was going to criticize them on the House floor.[9] The viewers on C-SPAN, who did not see the empty chamber but only the COS members leveling serious and harsh charges against the Democrats, were amazed that the charges went unanswered.

Two days later, Speaker Tip O'Neill escalated the confrontation by using the powers that the Speaker was given to control the C-SPAN cameras when they started broadcasting in 1979. Without the COS's knowledge, he ordered that the cameras pan the House floor during "Special Orders" to show that the room was essentially empty. The COS was furious. On May 15, Gingrich, on the House floor, defended the COS's tactics and lambasted O'Neill and the Democrats for deviously panning the empty chamber. When multiple Democrats asked Gingrich to yield the floor, he refused, only relenting when O'Neill, himself, asked him to yield the floor. O'Neill retorted, "You [Gingrich] deliberately stood in the well before an empty House and challenged these people and challenged their Americanism. It's the lowest thing I've ever seen in my 32 years in Congress."[10] O'Neill was rebuked for using derogatory words toward another member. It was the first time a Speaker had received such a punishment since 1797. At the episode's conclusion, Gingrich folded his papers and sat down to a standing ovation by most Republicans— Republican Leader Michel did not join in the applause.[11]

The COS's inside legislative strategy expanded to an external strategy when Gingrich took over GOPAC, a Leadership PAC started by Delaware Governor Pete DuPont, in 1986. DuPont had focused his efforts on recruiting Republicans to run at lower levels of government service in an effort to build a farm team for future congressional runs. Gingrich combined DuPont's electoral strategy with his own of confrontational legislative politics. Under the GOPAC label, Gingrich produced audiotapes to give Republican candidates strategies and talking points to run more effective campaigns. These tapes became legendary as scores of listeners filed papers to run for elective office. Most—including future Gingrich Senator Rick Santorum—cited these tapes as being critical for their political development. In a 2011 Republican primary presidential debate, Santorum commented:

> When I was first running for office, Newt Gingrich was the guy whose tapes I've listened to as a young man and tryin' to at 30 years old, deciding to run for Congress. He laid out a vision for conservative governance that I adopted and ran with in a very, very tough congressional district outside of suburban Pittsburgh, so tough that no one gave me a chance of winnin' it.
>
> Fact, election night the Wall Street Journal called the Republican National Committee to find out the name of the guy that won. And they didn't even know my name at the RNC.[12]

He credited the audiotapes not only for help on the issues but also, as he said in an earlier interview, for the "strategy and tactics on how to win a political election" (Corkery 2011, 28). Under Gingrich, GOPAC also provided significantly more funds for many House candidates.

Now utilizing the double-barreled approach of campaign strategies and legislative tactics, Gingrich focused his crosshairs on the biggest game in the House, Jim Wright, who had succeeded O'Neill as Speaker of the House. The hatred between Gingrich and Wright was legendary. While Gingrich called Wright the "least ethical speaker in this century," Wright commented that he viewed Gingrich "as a fire hydrant toward a dog."[13] Gingrich seized an opportunity to ratchet up his rhetoric against Wright when the *Washington Post* disclosed that the Speaker had signed a book deal that provided him with a 55 percent royalty rate (which is, trust me, far higher than normal royalty rates). Even Gingrich's friends and some in the COS suggested that he should back off. Despite being in the hunt alone, Gingrich would not relent. In time his persistence paid off when Common Cause joined the growing chorus calling for an investigation into Wright's sweetheart deal. A formal investigation began shortly thereafter.

As bits of evidence were leaked, Gingrich's strategies were winning new followers in the Republican Conference in the House. At the same time, Minority Whip Dick Cheney's (R-Wyoming) resignation from the House to become President George H. W. Bush's Secretary of Defense in early 1989 introduced a hotly contested intraparty squabble. Michel made it clear that his candidate in the whip race was Ed Madigan (R-Illinois), who very much followed the Michel philosophy of going along to get along. The divide between Gingrich and Madigan had much more to do with style than ideology (Harris 2006). Gingrich prevailed by two votes. When the contest was over, Gingrich's confrontational politics was no longer practiced only by a fringe group of conservative firebrands. It now enjoyed the stature of the second most important position in the Republican Conference.

Gingrich did not waste time in using his powers as whip to ruffle more feathers. On April 17, 1989, the Ethics Committee completed their 10-month investigation into Wright by finding 69 instances where the committee had "reason to believe" that he had violated the House rules over the previous ten years.[14] The drumbeat calling for Wright's resignation was too loud to ignore. On May 31 he gave up the Speaker's gavel and his seat in the House of Representatives. By bringing down the Speaker, Gingrich's stock among his fellow Republicans rose considerably.

Under Reagan, the Republicans pushed through tax cuts and increases in defense spending while the Democrats stood in the way of cutting domestic programs. Midway through President George H. W. Bush's term in office, the deficits that were generated by this mix of policies became a major economic issue. Although the public demanded an economic package that would curb the growth in debt, Bush's hands were tied because of the "No New Taxes" pledge he made during his 1988 presidential run—a pledge he continued to reiterate as president. Eventually, public pressure became too great to ignore. In a summit with congressional leaders at the White House, Bush reached an agreement that would control the deficit, but only at the expense of breaking his pledge. The participants of the summit announced their agreement in a Rose Garden ceremony on September 30, 1990. Newt Gingrich, who participated in the summit, skipped the ceremony because he was still "studying the plan."[15] No one was surprised that Gingrich skipped the event because he made his displeasure clear throughout the negotiations by "ostentatiously reading books and magazines during bargaining sessions … exasperating even fellow GOP negotiators."[16]

A day after the Rose Garden ceremony, Gingrich, as well as Weber, Hunter, and Walker (who were all not only old COS members but also now in the Republican leadership), announced their opposition. Gingrich argued that "it will kill jobs, weaken the economy and that the tax increase will be counterproductive."[17] Although the conservative firebrands walked away from the agreement, Michel and his allies continued to fight for it. Three days later it was defeated on the House floor, 179–254. The Republicans split 71 in favor and 105 opposed.

From the ashes, the Democratic leadership forced through a more liberal plan. The Democrats in the Senate, on the other hand, knew that the final solution required a bipartisan bill. After much negotiation, they passed a plan that enjoyed a bare majority of support from both Democrats and Republicans. After the conference committee largely adopted the Senate language, the bill passed both chambers. Bush signed the legislation into law, officially breaking his "No New Taxes" pledge. Gingrich and the other members of the COS, as well as a large majority of Republicans in the House, voted against the bill at every stage. Michel was one of only 47 Republicans to support the conference committee report.

Coming out of this showdown with the president and the Senate Republicans, Gingrich became the de facto leader of the House Republicans. *Congressional Quarterly* describe his role in the process: "Gingrich, a skilled guerrilla fighter not known for his ability to put together coalitions beyond his fiercely loyal conservative adherents, suddenly looked as if he might have been elevated to an uneasy new level of leadership." In the same article, they quoted Jack Buechner (R-Missouri), who had earlier supported Madigan in the race for Whip, saying that "Newt's the new torchbearer."[18] Gingrich would only achieve the title formally when Michel retired in 1994. Following the Republican Tsunami the same year, Gingrich became not only the head of the Republican Conference in the House but also the Speaker of the entire House.

With Michel's retirement, the transformation of the Republican Conference in the House was complete. Going along to get along was a strategy that few House Republicans even recognized let alone practiced. The partisan war in the House was fully engaged in the run-up to the 1994 elections. In announcing the Contract with America, which became the rallying cry for the Republicans in the election, Gingrich declared, "We will cooperate with anyone, and we'll compromise with no one."[19] As evidence of the completeness of the Republican Conference transformation, only two House Republicans running for reelection did not sign the contract. When Gingrich assumed the Speaker's chair, his priorities did not change. According to Dan Meyer, his chief of staff, "Being speaker of the House is his third most important job. The first was defining the movement, the direction we are going; the second was being leader of his party; the third was being speaker of the House."[20] Gingrich's tenure as Speaker was short-lived. After the Republicans lost seats in the 1998 election, Gingrich tendered his resignation from the speakership and from the House altogether. By then, though, the die of the new Republican had already been cast. The Republican Conference in the House, and the entire House of Representatives, had been transformed into an image very much like that personified by Newt Gingrich and his supporters in the COS, who even a dozen short years prior constituted a tiny minority of a minority party.

II. The Systematic Effect of Gingrich in the House of Representatives

Institutions and collectives of individuals can be exceedingly difficult to change. One would be hard-pressed to argue that the Republican Conference of the 1970s was moderate in ideology and tone *because of* Bob Michel's leadership. Equally, one would be hard-pressed to argue that the Republican Conference of the 1990s was as conservative or confrontational *because of* Newt Gingrich's leadership. Just as Michel could not have been the Republican leader in the 1990s, neither could Gingrich have been the Republican leader in the 1970s. They both epitomized the time in which they were leader. In both cases, it is safe to say that these leaders were chosen *because of* the sentiments of their conference at the time. Nonetheless, no one would dispute that the member of Congress who most pushed—or, more accurately, pulled—the Republican Conference to the right was Newt Gingrich (Strahan 2007).

Without a doubt, the Republican conference in the House transformed from one in the image of Bob Michel to one in the image of Newt Gingrich. This transformation is most easily visualized by comparing the DW-NOMINATE scores within parties of the entering classes of members to the House of Representatives (see figure 2.1). The average ideologies for the Democrats who entered the House in the 80th Congress (1947–1948) was -0.16. The Democratic classes did not vary much with the exception of the 90th Congress (1967–1968), which was more moderate than those congresses surrounding it. The Democrats who entered the House at the same time as Obama entered the White House had an average ideology score of -0.22.

The stability among the Democratic classes is not present with the Republican classes. The DW-NOMINATE score for the Republicans who began their House service in the 80th Congress was 0.25. For the next 32 years (16 congresses), each successive class of entering Republicans had a similar score. In only the 84th (1955–1956) and 91st (1969–1970) Congress classes did the Republicans' score even rise above 0.3. In fact, the time trend for the Republicans from the mid-1950s through the 1960s was slightly negative.

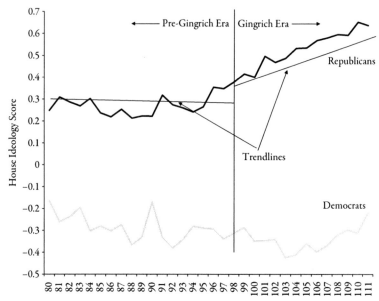

FIGURE 2.1 House Ideology Scores for Classes of House Members, 80th to 111th Congresses (1947–2010).

Each class of Republicans entering Congress was, on average, 0.001 less conservative than the class before it.

Beginning with the 96th Congress (1979–1980), the scores began to rise steadily. Newt Gingrich, of course, was part of this entering class. In no congress after Gingrich entered the chamber did the Republican's entering class average less than 0.30. Since the 96th Congress, each class that has entered the House was, on average, 0.021 more conservative than the previous class. Even though Gingrich rose to the Speaker's rostrum in the 104th Congress (1995–1996) and left after the elections to the 106th Congress (1999–2000), those events do not significantly alter the time trend. The key inflection point is the 96th Congress—Gingrich's first in the House.

To ensure that figure 2.1 is not playing visual tricks with the data, I performed a statistical test to find the point of disjuncture in the Republican entering class DW-NOMINATE scores. It shows that the cleanest break in the data comes with the Congress that includes for the first time Newt Gingrich. Using the 96th Congress as the breaking point yields the model with the best fit.[21]

Both qualitatively and quantitatively, the Republican Conference in the House of Representatives began to change in 1978. The late 1970s were a tumultuous time in the House of Representatives and in the country. The

Iranian hostage crises, stagflation, and the oil shocks led to much trepidation in the electorate and among elected officials. In the 1980 presidential contest, Republican Ronald Reagan presented himself as a strong leader in troubled times. His 1984 reelection theme of "Morning in America" struck the right note. The Republican conference in the House of Representatives may have become more conservative in the late 1970s because the new president cast conservatism in a new light, or it could have been because of a little-known, two-time loser from the suburbs of Atlanta who finally won his 1978 House race.

What the data reveal is that those Republicans who were associated with Newt Gingrich were more conservative than the Republicans who had no obvious connection to him. I use three different variables to characterize House Republicans' association with Gingrich: COS members,[22] those members who supported Gingrich in the Minority Whip race against Ed Madigan,[23] and those members who received money from Gingrich's Leadership PAC.[24] Those members with an association to Gingrich are more conservative than those Republicans who did not have an obvious association to him. The heavy line in figure 2.2 shows how the Republican House average in the 95th Congress (1977–1978), the last congress before Gingrich was elected, was

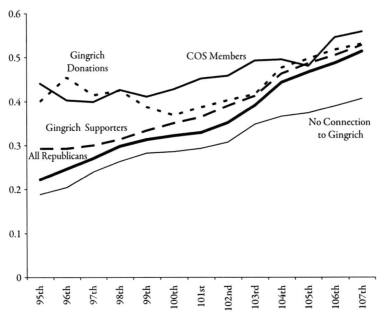

FIGURE 2.2 Polarization Scores by Association to Gingrich in the House, 95th to 107th Congresses (1977–2000).

similar to the ideology of those without a Gingrich connection to the 107th Congress (2001–2002), when it is almost the same ideology as the Gingrich supporters supported.

Ideology only tells half of the story of how Gingrich transformed the House Republican Conference. When the Republicans chose him over Madigan, they were endorsing a strategy of confrontation. The COS early on adopted a strategy of using Special Orders and one-minute speeches to ridicule, embarrass, and criticize the Democrats and their House leadership. Special Orders and one-minute speeches, of course, can be used for other purposes, but the number of these types of speeches that a member gives may suggest an underlying strategy. All members have constituents that they want to recognize and issues that they want to address on the House floor during nonlegislative debate. Members wishing to use this format as part of their confrontational strategy will rise to give more of these addresses than their colleagues. Rocca (2007) finds that these addresses were an important part of Gingrich's overall confrontational strategy. Those Republicans without a connection to Gingrich gave an average of 12 of these speeches each congress from the 101st Congress (1989–1990), Gingrich's first congress as Minority Whip, to the 103rd Congress (1993–1994), the last congress before the Republicans became a majority party (see figure 2.3). Members of the COS

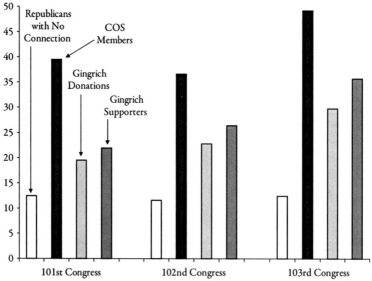

FIGURE 2.3 Special Orders and One-Minute Speeches by Association to Gingrich in the House, 101st to 103rd Congresses (1989–1994).

gave an average of 40, 37, and 49 of these speeches in those same three congresses. The Gingrich supporters and those he supported gave between 21 and 36 speeches in each of these three congresses. These data suggest that Gingrich led not only an ideological fight in the House of Representatives but also a partisan war. Both aspects were soon to be replicated in the Senate.

III. Conclusion

The Republican Conference in the House of Representatives underwent a radical transformation from the late 1970s to the early 1990s. By the time that Republican Leader Bob Michel stepped down in 1992, he enjoyed the respect, but not necessarily the strategy, politics, or conservatism, of his newer Republican colleagues. Shortly after his first election to the House in 1978, Newt Gingrich became a leader. At first, he was only the leader of a small group of Republican mavericks who wanted to tear down the House and rebuild it in their own image. Over time, his influence and his followers grew. In 1989 he became the Republican whip. Four years later he would be the first Republican to bang the Speaker's gavel since the 1950s. The Republicans who entered Gingrich's House looked and acted differently than the Republicans who entered the House before Gingrich.

The Senate was not immune to this transformation. When the members who entered Gingrich's House migrated to the Senate, they slowly, but surely, changed the Senate. In the next part of the book, I highlight how they were party polarizers in the Senate. In part III, I outline their behavior as partisan warriors.

PART II

The Gingrich Senators as Party Polarizers

The evidence from part 1 shows the dramatic effect that Newt Gingrich had on the House Republican Conference and the House of Representatives as a whole. Many politicians, political pundits, and political scientists have made that claim and with much more evidence and in a much more compelling way. That Gingrich's style of politics had an influence on the Senate is rare, and the route by which the influence became felt is novel to this book. I argue that the Gingrich Senators as party polarizers and partisan warriors have fundamentally transformed the Senate from Sinclair's individualized institution into a partisan one.

In part 2, I describe, argue, and analyze how the Gingrich Senators made the Senate more polarized. While the Democratic senators' ideological voting, today, has remained similar to their 1970s counterparts, the Republican Conference has become much more extreme. The 40 Gingrich Senators can account for almost the entirety of that change.

3

The Gingrich Senators and Party Polarization in the U.S. Senate

AS STORIES OF rancor, partisanship, and legislative gamesmanship in the Senate became newspaper headlines, the long-serving senators, still infused with institutional patriotism, were quick to blame the House. Senator Alan Simpson (R-Wyoming) commented, "The rancor, the dissension, the disgusting harsh level came from those House members who came to the Senate. They brought it with 'em. That's where it began." Thad Cochran (R-Mississippi) claimed, "It's just a matter of age. I'm not going to use the word 'maturity.'" As George Voinovich (R-Ohio), a former governor, added, there are "too many" former House members and not enough "other people."[1] In fact, former governors, other former executive branch officials, and former mayors, who are now serving in the Senate, have even formed an informal caucus to counteract the pervasive combative partisan strategies employed by former House members. This group's leader, Senator Mark Begich (D-Alaska), the former mayor of Anchorage, maintains that it is easier to negotiate with these executive-minded legislators than engage in political games with his colleagues who came from the House.

This chapter describes the extent of Senate party polarization. First, I show how the lion's share of that polarization has come as a result of the Gingrich Senators. Second, I put the distinctivenss of the Gingrich Senators into perspective by comparing the difference between the Gingrich Senators and other Republicans to the difference between Northern and Southern Democrats in a different era. Third, I test the robustness of the claim that the Gingrich Senators can account for the growing divergence between the parties in the U.S. Senate.

I. Party Polarization in the Senate

When Newt Gingrich took the Oath of Office upon entering the House in 1979, the Senate was still adjusting to the second wave of liberal reformers who were elected in the wake of the Watergate scandal. The 1974 entering class of senators reinforced the transformation of the Senate from its mid-century Textbook Era into the Individualized Senate that had begun under the 1958 entering class. At the same time, the roots of the Partisan Senate were beginning to take form. While the total polarization in the Senate was the lowest that it had been since before World War II, the amount of overlap between the parties was shrinking as the old conservative Southern Democrats were being replaced by either conservative Republicans or more moderate Democrats (Fleisher and Bond 2004; Theriault 2006). Only two Republicans—Jacob Javits (R-New York) and Charles Mathias (R-Maryland)—had a more liberal voting record than the most conservative Democrat.[2]

Since the 96th Congress (1979–1980), the Senate has become more polarized with each succeeding Congress (see figure 3.1 to see the divide between the parties from 1973–2010). For the 96th Congress the total polarization score, which is simply the average of all the individual senators' extremism scores, was 0.27. By the end of the first two years of the Obama administration in 2010, the score jumped to 0.41, a more than 50 percent increase. Not only was there no overlap between the parties in the 111th Congress (2009–2010), but the parties were completely separated—and by a not-insignificant distance (0.08, which represents slightly more than 5 percent of the entire ideological continuum in the U.S. Senate).

Although Gingrich did not enter the House until 1979, the data analysis throughout much of this book begins in the early 1970s to incorporate a broader perspective on the transformation of the Senate. Starting with the 93rd Congress (1973–1974) has three benefits. First, it allows an analysis of the Watergate Babies, who are those Democrats elected to the Senate in 1974 in the voters' rebuke of President Richard Nixon. Including this class permits a true test as to whether the polarizing phenomenon of House experience is truly present only in one party. Second, most scholars who study party polarization argue that the current polarization between the parties started in the early 1970s in both chambers (Collie and Mason 2000; Fiorina 2010; Fleisher and Bond 2004; Jacobson 2000; Roberts and Smith 2003; Stonecash, Brewer, and Mariani 2003). Third, by beginning before the Gingrich Senator era, we can assess the unique contribution of those former House members who were elected to Congress before Newt Gingrich's first election. The selection of this time period permits a true test of whether Gingrich's election in 1978 is the critical breaking point of House experience leading to more polarized behavior in the Senate.

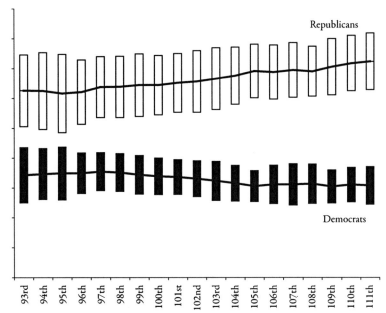

FIGURE 3.1 Ideology by Party in the U.S. Senate, 93rd to 111th Congresses (1973–2010).

A. The Gingrich Senators

By definition, the first Gingrich Senator could have been elected in 1980 to serve in the 97th Congress; but the first one, Phil Gramm, was not elected actually until 1984. Gramm started his congressional career as a Democrat.[3] After using his perch on the Budget Committee to help pass Reagan's tax cuts early in his first term, the Democrats refused to reappoint him to the Budget Committee. He then left the party, resigned his seat, ran for it as a Republican, and was overwhelmingly reelected. A year later, he ran for and won the seat being vacated by Senator John Tower (R-Texas).

Two years after his victory, Gramm was joined by John McCain, who at the time was a two-term House incumbent. Two years later, Connie Mack and Dan Coats, who replaced Dan Quayle when he was elected vice president, joined Gramm and McCain. The number of Gingrich Senators continued to grow with each election cycle, reaching numeric strength at 25 senators after George W. Bush's successful reelection in 2004. Not surprisingly, the number of Gingrich Senators has risen and fallen with the fortunes of the Republican Party, increasing the most in the 1994 and 2004 elections. The number of Gingrich Senators decreased in the 2006 and 2008 elections when

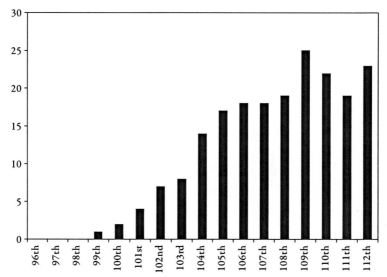

FIGURE 3.2 The Number of the Gingrich Senators, 96th to 112th Congresses (1979–2012).

Republicans lost a net of 15 seats. (Figure 3.2 shows the number of Gingrich Senators from 1979 to 2012.)

B. The Ideology of the Gingrich Senators

An analysis of ideological scores shows that the definitional components of what makes a Gingrich Senator are not additive. Those Republicans who were first elected to Congress prior to Gingrich's first election and who did not previously serve in the House have an average extremism score of 0.30. To put this score in context, the highest possible extremism score is 1.0, so those non-House Republicans elected to the Senate before 1978 are, roughly speaking, 30 percent as extreme as they could have been. The House veterans who were elected to the Senate prior to Gingrich's congressional service have an average score of 0.23. The non-House veterans elected to the Senate during the same time period as the Gingrich Senators have an average score of 0.33. The Gingrich Senators, in contrast, have an average extremism score of 0.51, which is 54 percent greater than any of the other categories of Republican senators. Figure 3.3 shows how distinct the Gingrich Senators are by placing all four Republican groups, as well as their Democratic counterparts, on the same extremism continuum. Table 3.1 puts these four groups (as well as the four parallel groups of Democrats) in a table that divides senators according

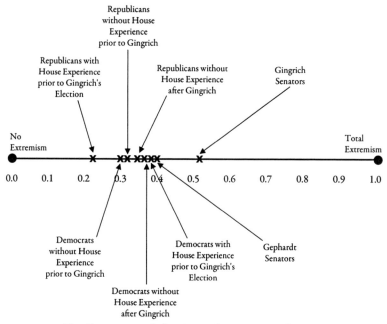

FIGURE 3.3 The Extremism of the Gingrich Senators Relative to Other Senate Groups.

to House experience and the date of their first election to Congress (either the House or Senate). I also report the Gingrich (Gephardt) Senator Effect, which is the difference between the Gingrich (Gephardt) Senators and the average of the other three groups. The Gingrich Senator Effect for extremism is 78 percent, meaning that the Gingrich Senators are 78 percent more extreme than the average of the other three Republican groups.

Only two Gingrich Senators—Mike DeWine (0.192), a former House member who served one term as Ohio lieutenant governor in between his

Table 3.1 The Extremism Scores for the Gingrich and Gephardt Senators and Their Partisan Counterparts, 93rd to 111th Congresses (1973–2010)

	Republicans			**Democrats**	
	No House Experience	House Experience		No House Experience	House Experience
Pre-1978	0.30	0.23	Pre-1978	0.30	0.36
Post-1978	0.33	0.51	Post-1978	0.35	0.40
Gingrich Senator Effect		78%	Gephardt Senator Effect		19%

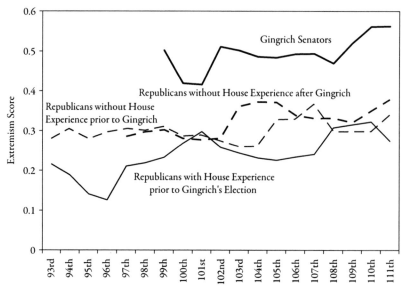

FIGURE 3.4 The Extremism of the Gingrich Senators and Their Republican Counterparts, 93rd to 111th Congresses (1973–2010).

House and Senate tenures, and Jim Talent (0.305), whose Senate service was only four years—had a lower extremism score than the average Republican senator during this time period. The uniqueness of this lower-right-hand cell in table 3.1, corresponding to the Gingrich Senators, is specific to the Republican party. Those Democrats coming from the House in the age of Gingrich are not nearly as distinct from their fellow partisans as the Gingrich Senators are from other Republicans. The Gingrich Senators have been distinct since Phil Gramm came to the Senate in 1984 (see figure 3.4). The average ideological scores for the other three Republican groups are noticeably lower than those for the Gingrich Senators. Furthermore, the distinction between the other three Republican groups and the Gingrich Senators does not dissipate over time.

C. The Gingrich Senators' Contribution to Polarization

The overall Senate polarization score has increased 0.13 since the 93rd Congress (1973–1974), 0.15 since Gingrich entered the House in the 96th Congress (1979–1980), and 0.11 since Gramm came to the Senate in the 99th Congress (1985–1986). Because the extremism scores of the non–Gingrich Senators (all Democrats, Republicans without House experience, and Republicans with House experience prior to 1978) have been relatively constant within groups and similar across groups, I combine the other seven groups in order to isolate the polarization brought about by the Gingrich Senators. Since the 93rd

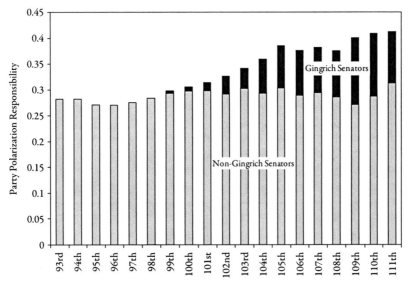

FIGURE 3.5 The Effect of the Gingrich Senators on Senate Polarization, 93rd to 111th Congresses (1973–2010).

Congress, the other seven groups have increased the Senate's polarization by 0.03 (see the grey portion of the bars in figure 3.5). Because Gingrich was not elected to the House until 1978 and because none of his colleagues who entered the House after him won a Senate election until 1984, the Gingrich Senators necessarily had a zero polarization effect on the Senate until the 99th Congress. From Reagan's second term through George W. Bush's second term, the Gingrich Senators' extremism score steadily increased. By the 111th Congress (2009–2010), they contributed 0.10 to the Senate's polarization score. The Gingrich Senators alone can account for 77 percent of the entire Senate polarization under consideration in this analysis and 88 percent of the polarization since the first of their ranks entered the Senate.

To ensure that the averaging of these numbers over time is not creating a finding that would not exist if all of the proper controls were included, I perform a more sophisticated analysis. This analysis, along with all the other statistical analyses throughout this book, are presented in footnotes, though the significance of these findings is described in the main body of the book.[4] The results of the more sophisticated analysis indicate the fact that House experience contributing to extremism is largely a Republican phenomenon. The extremism score—incorporating the effect for time, party, and experience into the analysis—shows that the score for a non-House Republican who served before Gingrich is 0.36 (see table 3.2), and for a similar member who began service after Gingrich it is 0.39. The predicted score for a Republican senator

Table 3.2 The Extremism Score While Controlling for Other Factors for the Gingrich and Gephardt Senators and Their Partisan Counterparts, 93rd to 111th Congresses (1973–2010)

	Republicans			Democrats	
	No House Experience	House Experience		No House Experience	House Experience
Pre-1978	0.36	0.30	Pre-1978	0.36	0.39
Post-1978	0.39	0.54	Post-1978	0.41	0.45
Gingrich Senator Effect		54%	Gephardt Senator Effect		16%

with House experience prior to Gingrich's election is 0.30.[5] The Republican counterparts' average extremism score is 0.35, and the Gingrich Senators' average extremism score is 0.54. As such, a Gingrich Senator's score is 54 percent more conservative than the average of the other three Republican types.[6] When the individual components that comprise the Gingrich Senators are analyzed independently, the Gingrich Senator Effect declines from 78 percent to 54 percent. Although this decline is not trivial, the distinctiveness of the Gingrich Senators remains even after the polarizing tendencies of the Senate are explicitly taken into consideration.

Among Democrats, the predicted extremism score is 0.36 for a non-House Democrat who served before Gingrich's election, 0.41 for a Democrat with a similar background after Gingrich, 0.39 for a Democratic senator with House experience prior to Gingrich's first election, and 0.45 for a former House Democrat elected after Gingrich's election (see right side of table 3.2). While the latter are 16 percent more liberal than the other types of Democrats, their distinctiveness relative to the rest of their caucus is less than one-third of that for the Gingrich Senators. Independent of how the individual senators' extremism scores are analyzed, the increasing party polarization in the Senate since the 1970s lies overwhelmingly at the feet of previous House Republican members who started serving in the House after 1978.

II. The Pack Mentality among the Gingrich Senators

It would be too much to say that the Senate has three parties—Democrats, other Republicans, and the Gingrich Senators—but at no time since the 1960s when Democrats were divided into a conservative Southern wing and

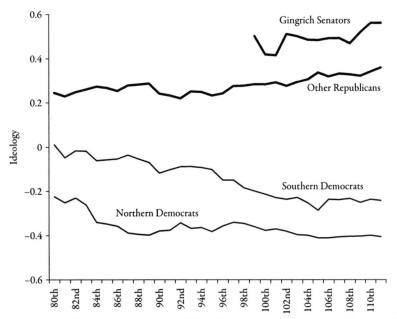

FIGURE 3.6 Ideological Splits in the Political Parties in the Senate, 80th to 111th Congresses (1947–2010).

a progressive Northern wing has such a clear demarcation existed within a single party. I show how the Gingrich Senators' DW-NOMINATE scores are as distinct from other Republicans as the Northern Democrats were from the Southern Democrats in the heyday of the Democratic Party's split in the Senate.

The Conservative Coalition, which was comprised of Republicans and Southern Democrats, dominated the Senate throughout the 1950s and 1960s (Sinclair 1989). Even Democratic presidents who enjoyed huge majorities in Congress were often stymied by the Democratic Party's split into regional wings. In the ten years between 1957 and 1966, the difference in the DW-NOMINATE score between the average Northern Democrat and the average Southern Democrat hovered around 0.30, which was almost the difference between the average Southern Democrat and the average Republican (see figure 3.6). During these congresses, Southern Democrats filled between 23 and 25 of the 26 Southern Senate seats, which accounted for between 33 and 40 percent of the total Senate Democratic Caucus.

By the time that the first Gingrich Senator showed up in the Senate, the Southern Democrats had lost seats and their distinctiveness within the Democratic Party. At the start of Reagan's second term in 1984, only

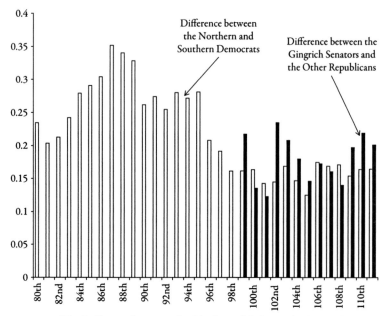

FIGURE 3.7 The Difference between the Ideological Splits in the Senate Parties, 80th to 111th Congresses (1947–2011).

14 Southern Democrats still served in the Senate and they were about half as distinct as they had been 20 years earlier, separated from the Northern Democrats by only 0.16. Since then, the Southern Democrats have only been as distinct in the Democratic Party as the Gingrich Senators have been distinct in the Republican Party in five congresses (see figure 3.7). Furthermore, since the 104th Congress (1995–1996), the number of Gingrich Senators has been greater than the number of Democratic senators from the South. In the 112th Congress, the Gingrich Senators occupied almost four times as many seats as Southern Democrats. The Gingrich Senators in today's Senate are about as distinct in the Republican Party as the Southern Democrats were in the 1980s in their party, and their numbers today are similar to the number of Southern Democrats serving at the end of the 1960s. The Gingrich Senators' distinctiveness today, in their heyday, is only about two-thirds of the distinctiveness of the Southern Democrats in their heyday.

One other crucial difference exists between the Southern Democrats and the Gingrich Senators: the Southern Democrats were in between the Northern Democrats and the Republicans. As such, they frequently had the power and the votes to enact their will with help from either their ideological left or right. Gingrich Senators, on the other hand, make the other Republican senators the crucial group of compromisers in today's Senate. While the other Republicans are distinct from the Gingrich Senators, they are only 0.20 away from them, but 0.60 away from the Southern Democrats and 0.75 away from the average Democrat.

III. House Service in the Senate

At first blush, it seems preposterous that the Gingrich Senator Effect on the Republican Party could be more significant than the Reagan Effect. Teasing out the distinction between these two revolutionary Republican groups is difficult. Because they entered the national stage at about the same time, it is difficult to attribute a shift in a time series of numbers to either one or the other. Evidence from earlier in this chapter has already shed some light on the subject. In table 3.1, figure 3.4, and table 3.2 I show two different groups of Republicans who entered the Senate in the age of Reagan. Those data show that those who went through the House behaved differently than those who did not go through the House. The entering Republican senators without House experience voted similarly to the Republicans in the era before Reagan. It is only the Republicans who entered the Senate after serving in the House that show this increasingly conservative voting pattern.

In this part of the chapter, I loosen up the Gingrich Senators' definition to see if other permutations of it can better explain the voting dynamics among Republicans in the Senate. First, I test to see if 1978 is the crucial year. It is. Second, I test to see if it is the time that the senators enter the Senate or the House that more significantly divides the groups. Surprisingly, it is the House. Third, I test to see if the Gingrich Senator Effect decreases over the course of the Gingrich Senators' careers. Again, surprisingly, it does not; if anything, the effect grows over time.

A. 1978: The Year That Changed Everything

Politicians, political pundits, journalists, and, yes, even political scientists point to particular events as having heightened importance in changing an institution. To all our credit, very few claim that their particular individual event of choice is the *only* reason that an institution changes. Rather, we usually write about events as influencing other events, which, with the luxury of time, we begin to see in a more systematic pattern. In this section, rather than relying on the brief account of party politics in the House in the 1980s or even a thorough reading of the congressional annals to determine what event caused the change, I undertake a systematic analysis to see, precisely, when the House experience of Republicans became a radicalizing influence on their Senate votes.

Since the 93rd Congress (1973–1974), 76 Republican senators have previously served in the House. I have been calling 40 of them "Gingrich Senators." The remaining 36 were elected to the House prior to Gingrich's first successful House election in 1978. The first of these other 36, Carl Curtis (R-Nebraska), began his House service in the 76th Congress (1939–1940); the last, Olympia Snowe (R-Maine), entered the House with Gingrich in the 96th Congress (1979–1980). To underscore the distinctiveness of the Gingrich Senators, their average ideology of 0.51 compares to less than half that (0.24) for Curtis, Snowe, and the other 34 Republicans who were elected to the House prior to Gingrich's tenure.[7]

The demarcation between a Gingrich Senator and the Curtis-Snowe group has been arbitrarily placed at Gingrich's first election to the House. To be sure that the dividing line between the older senators and the newer senators should, in fact, be placed at Gingrich's election in 1978, I analyze all the other potential dividing lines without regard to Gingrich or any other political event. A simple examination of all the other dividing lines shows that they do not perform as well as 1978.

For this analysis, I include only the Republican senators with House experience. Figure 3.8 shows how the ideology for these 70 senators varies by when they were elected to the House. Two patterns become obvious. First, the senators elected earlier did not subscribe to any one particular ideology. Curtis, who was first elected in 1938, had a 0.55 ideology and Hugh Scott (R-Pennsylvania), elected one election later, had a more moderate 0.12. The next two senators (Clifford Case [R-New Jersey] and Jacob Javits [R-New York]) had ideology scores closer to the Democratic average in the Senate than to those of their fellow Republicans.

The second pattern is that the ideology scores seem to become more conservative over time. This trend calls into question the very idea of a distinction between an early group and a more recent group. According to this scatterplot of House entry and Senate ideology, the relationship may best be characterized as becoming increasingly conservative as House entry becomes later. If so, the classification of Gingrich Senators may be misleading, as the senators who entered the House just after Gingrich's election would not look that different from the senators who entered the Senate just before his election. Indeed, a systematic test of this visual inspection reveals that for each subsequent Congress when a future Republican senator enters the House, his (in

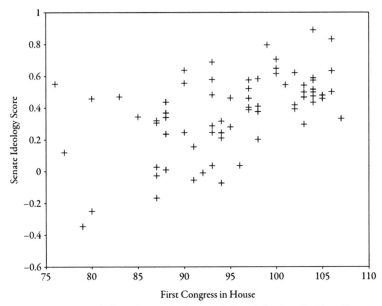

FIGURE 3.8 Senate Ideology Scores for Former House Members by First Congress in House.

all cases other than Snowe) or her ideology is 0.02 greater.[8] According to this analysis, a senator who entered the House in the 100th Congress (1987–1988) is 0.20 more conservative than a senator who entered the House 10 congresses earlier in the 90th Congress (1967–1968). To see if this trend variable can withstand more systematic testing, I include a variable to test for a distinction between an earlier period and a later period. In succession, I in essence draw a vertical line after each election year to see if the senators on the right side of the line are different from the senators on the left side of the line.

Only one of the vertical lines adds appreciably to the model from the simple trend variable—it is the vertical line separating Gingrich's first election to the House in 1978 and Reagan's election to the White House in 1980. The only other indicator variable that comes close to that level of significance is the line dividing Reagan's two terms as president. Not only is the vertical line after the 96th Congress statistically significant, but it renders the time trend variable insignificant. The line dividing entry into the House after the 1978 election is the only vertical line that predicts Senate ideology better than the continuous variable measuring when a future Republican senator enters the House. Furthermore, the model that best predicts Senate ideology is the one that includes the House entry variable and the 96th Congress indicator variable. This analysis strongly demonstrates that among Republican senators, there definitely is an "early" group and a "later" group and that the dividing line between them is the 96th Congress (1979–1980), which was Gingrich's first in the House.

B. Arrival in the House Matters More Than Arrival in the Senate

The aforementioned analysis still makes one assumption about the Gingrich Senators that I test in this section. Up until this point in my book, the Gingrich Senators have been defined by the time period in which they entered the House, not the Senate. This section tests to see if that assumption is appropriate. If Senate behavior can be explained temporally, we might expect that the beginning of a Senate career is more important than when the future senator entered the House.

To see which matters more—arrival in the House or arrival in the Senate—I test the relationship between the Republicans' arrivals into the respective chambers and their ideology scores in the Senate.[9] In other words, what is a better predictor of senators' ideologies: their arrival time into the House or their arrival time into the Senate? Both relationships are strong predictors of Senate ideology, but the relationship between arrivals into the House and Senate ideology is bigger and more statistically significant than their arrivals into the Senate.

In a model that includes both entry dates, the House is not only more significant but also renders the Senate entry date irrelevant. Although there is not a big difference between the predictive powers of Senate and House entry, the statistical results tilt toward House entry, which we would think would be a harder case to prove given that we are trying to predict ideology in the Senate. If arrival into the House competes against arrival into the Senate, it wins when they are tested both independently and jointly.

C. The Gingrich Senator Effect Does Not Fade

One of the reasons that the Gingrich Senators have had such a lasting effect on the U.S. Senate is because their distinctiveness does not appear to diminish over the course of their Senate career. Senate history is replete with examples of senators who came into the chamber as firebrands, hell-bent on reforming the institution, being transformed into "Senate Men"—and presumably "Senate Women"—with time. To see if this argument holds for the Gingrich Senators, I divide all the senators' careers based on the amount of time they have served in the Senate. If Gingrich Senators are like other senators in that they become "Senate Men" as they serve in the Senate, we would expect that

Table 3.3 The Gingrich (Gephardt) Senator Effect within Terms in Senate

Length of Time in Senate	No House Exp. Elected before 1978	House Exp. Elected before 1978	No House Exp. Elected after 1978	Gingrich (Gephardt) Senators	Gingrich (Gephardt) Senator Effect
Republicans					
2 or Less	0.36	0.29	0.35	0.51	0.53
3–6	0.26	0.17	0.35	0.53	1.02
7–12	0.26	0.21	0.33	0.54	1.05
Greater than 12	0.30	0.20	0.34	0.54	0.95
Democrats					
2 or Less	0.30	0.39	0.38	0.43	0.21
3–6	0.23	0.35	0.34	0.42	0.37
7–12	0.25	0.36	0.35	0.44	0.38
Greater than 12	0.34	0.43	0.37	0.44	0.17

the Gingrich Senator Effect is biggest in the senators' first terms and that the effect wanes as the senators' terms accumulate.[10]

The data simply do not bear out this expectation for the Gingrich Senators. In their first congress in the Senate (the first two years that they serve), the Gingrich Senator Effect is 0.53; that is, the Gingrich Senators are 53 percent more polarized than their Republican counterparts (see table 3.3). In the remainder of the senators' first term—their third to sixth years in the Senate—the Gingrich Senator Effect jumps to 1.02. In their second term— the seventh through twelfth years in the Senate—the Gingrich Senator Effect increases again to 1.05. In the years of service after the second term—which only includes nine Gingrich Senators—the effect settles down to 0.95.

While it was plausible that the Gingrich Senators would become "Senate Men" in time, the results indicate that they just don't. They are even more distinctly conservative in their second and third terms than they are in their first two years in the Senate.

IV. Conclusion

The Gingrich Senators have taken their more conservative voting record from the House to the Senate. In fact, almost the entire increase in party polarization in the Senate can be accounted for in the Gingrich Senators' increasingly conservative voting record and in their increasing numbers. No other group has been as responsible for transforming the Individualized Senate into the Partisan Senate as the Gingrich Senators. In fact, the difference between the Gingrich Senators and the other Republicans can be compared to the difference between the Northern and Southern Democrats when they were most at odds with each other.

Furthermore, this chapter reveals several key characteristics about the set of legislators that I have been calling the "Gingrich Senators." The sharpest definition for these transformative senators is that they entered the House (and not the Senate) after 1978. No other variable involving their House experience or when they entered either the House or Senate better encapsulates their distinctive ideology than the simple indicator of coming to the House after Gingrich's first election. The remainder of Part II of this book examines various other causes for the Gingrich Senator Effect. While some of these variables influence senators' ideologies, the Gingrich Senator Effect remains. The transformation of the Republican Conference in the House under the direction of Newt Gingrich was not a one-chamber phenomenon. Those House members elected in and after the Gingrich Era who go on to serve in the Senate are more polarizing than their Republican colleagues.

4

The Constituencies of the
Gingrich Senators

UPON RETURNING HOME from his job as a kitchen appliance salesman in North Carolina one day in 1991, Richard Burr told his wife that he was running for Congress. His wife was shocked not only because he had never run for any political office before but also because he had never shown much of an interest in politics. Despite his inexperience in that first race, he made a strong showing in a losing effort. Two years later, he won the seat when the Democratic incumbent retired rather than facing the strong winds of change that would catapult the Republicans into the House majority for the first time since 1954.

Although he entered the House with a class of members who were known more for their confrontational style than their legislative acumen, Burr quickly proved that he was interested in tackling difficult public policy problems. Early in his first term, he took an interest in reforming the Food and Drug Administration to make its approval process more efficient, especially for drugs that treated life-threatening diseases. The following congress, his language was included in a bill signed into law by President Clinton. This early legislative success characterized a House career that centered on health care legislation.

Although his first run for the House in 1992 was shocking, Burr's 2004 run for the Senate was not; he entered the race in the weeks after winning a fifth House term. The race became easier when the incumbent, Senator John Edwards (D-North Carolina), opted for a presidential bid rather than what was certain to be a tough reelection. After defeating Erskine Bowles, Clinton's former chief of staff, by more than 4 percentage points, Burr became the junior senator from North Carolina. The senior senator, Elizabeth Dole (R-North Carolina), had only been elected two years earlier to the seat left open by the retirement of Senator Jesse Helms (R-North Carolina).

Dole, while certainly more moderate than her predecessor, quickly developed a reputation for being a reliable Republican vote in the Senate. In fact, shortly after the 2004 election, the Republicans named her chair of the National Republican Senatorial Committee. In the 109th Congress (2005–2006), Burr's first in the Senate, he had an extremism score of 0.59. Dole's extremism score, on the other hand, was considerably lower (0.40).

While both Burr and Dole had a reputation for being more pragmatic than extreme, while both were elected by similar percentages in similar campaign contexts, and while both represented the exact same constituency, Burr was almost 50 percent more conservative than Dole. This disparity is typical of the Gingrich Senators. In this chapter, I evaluate the extent to which the Gingrich Senators' service in the House contributes to that more conservative voting record while explicitly considering their constituency. I do so in a number of steps. First, I compare the Gingrich Senators to the senators they succeeded. Second, I examine all of the Gingrich Senators who served in the Senate with their same-state colleagues as a way to control for the partisan tilts of the states they represent. Third, I incorporate constituency-related variables into a more sophisticated statistical model to see if the Gingrich Senators remain distinct even after systematically controlling for their constituencies. In the final analysis, constituency does play a minor role in the Gingrich Senators' more conservative voting record. Even after controlling for their more conservative constituencies, however, the Gingrich Senators remain distinct from their fellow Republican senators.

I. The Gingrich Senators' Predecessors

The Senate has a long tradition of recognizing the "seats" that senators hold. For example, the senior senator from Kentucky always sits in the desk that Henry Clay used when he was a senator; so, too, the senior senator from New Hampshire uses Daniel Webster's desk and the senior senator from Mississippi uses Jefferson Davis's desk. More recently, John Kerry (D-Massachusetts), upon the 2009 death of his friend and colleague from Massachusetts, Ted Kennedy (D-Massachusetts), moved into his desk. The desk tradition is so ingrained that upon leaving the Senate, retiring senators will etch their names in the desks' drawers.[1]

These Senate desk traditions not only make for interesting history but also can be utilized to examine the Gingrich Senators' voting records. Except for deaths, births, and residents who move across state lines, a new senator will represent the same constituency as his or her predecessors. By comparing voting records, we can see how distinct Gingrich Senators are after taking into consideration the constituencies that they represent.

Twenty-one of the 41 Gingrich Senators succeeded Democrats.[2] Not surprisingly, they were more conservative than their predecessors. Not only were they more conservative, but they were more conservative than the Democrats were liberal.[3] Their Democratic predecessors were more extreme than the Gingrich Senators in only three instances.[4] The Edwards-to-Burr switch in 2005 was typical of the Democrat-to-Gingrich-Senator switches. Edwards left the Senate with a 0.38 extremism score and Burr's score was 0.59 in his first Congress in the Senate. On average, the Gingrich Senators were 0.20 more polarizing than the Democrats they replaced. Given that the average extremism score of the Democrats was 0.31, the Gingrich Senators were 65 percent more extreme than the Democrats they replaced.

Most political pundits think that the candidate that can most genuinely appeal to the middle-of-the-road voter has an easier time winning elections. The exceptions that prove the rule are the Gingrich Senators. Four of the six Gingrich Senators who defeated Democratic incumbents were more ideologically extreme than the incumbents they defeated. The election that most flies in the face of the pundits' predictions was when Max Cleland, with an extremism score of 0.28 in his last congress, lost in 2002 to Saxby Chambliss, who had a score of 0.52 in his first congress. The immensely polarizing effect of the Gingrich Senators was particularly felt when they took over from retiring Democrats. On average, the Gingrich Senators (0.54) were twice as extreme as the retiring Democrats (0.27). These data alone cannot necessarily be interpreted as a sign that the Gingrich Senators are more extreme once we control for the senators' constituencies because these moderate-Democrat-to-conservative-Republican transitions may have happened in more conservative states. The average voter in these states may be closer to the Gingrich Senators than the Democrats that they replaced because the voters in that state may be more conservative than the average voter in the country.

Twenty Gingrich Senators took over from Republicans. In all but two cases, their Republican predecessors retired or resigned their seats. In 1996, Sam Brownback defeated Sheila Frahm (R-Kansas) in the Republican primary after Frahm was appointed to Bob Dole's seat upon his resignation during his 1996 presidential campaign. In 2004, John Sununu defeated fellow Gingrich Senator Bob Smith in the New Hampshire Republican primary. This Smith-to-Sununu transition was one of four when a Gingrich Senator replaced another Gingrich Senator.

In several cases, their predecessors had come to define conservatism: John McCain's predecessor was Barry Goldwater (R-Arizona), Craig Thomas's predecessor was Malcolm Wallop (R-Wyoming), and, of course, Sununu's predecessor was Bob Smith. Nonetheless, the 16 Gingrich Senators who took over from Republicans who were not Gingrich Senators were, as a whole, more conservative (0.52) than their predecessors (0.49).[5] While this difference may seem small, the Gingrich Senators were usually taking over from long-entrenched incumbents who typically could vote more freely than junior members. These newly elected Gingrich Senators had to run in open seats that are usually the most competitive of a senator's career, at a time when the motivation to appear moderate is greatest. The biggest change from a retiring senator to a Gingrich Senator was when Rod Grams (0.54) took over for David Durenburger (0.04) in Minnesota in 1995. The four times that a Gingrich Senator took over for another Gingrich Senator have had a minimal effect on Senate polarization.[6] Table 4.1 shows the comparison between the Gingrich Senators and their predecessors.

The predecessor analysis shows that the Gingrich Senators usually remain distinct even after we take into consideration their constituencies, though this factor is not universally strong. While they are much more polarizing than their Democratic predecessors, they were only marginally more conservative than their Republican predecessors. By itself, the predecessor analysis, especially that which is based on the Republican transitions, does not prove the case.

II. The Gingrich Senators' Pairs

The easiest explanation for the more conservative voting record of the Gingrich Senators is that they represent more conservative states. Given that their Republican predecessors were about as conservative, the easiest explanation may be the most accurate. If conservative states elect more conservative senators, and if they also more recently have had a proclivity for electing candidates with experience in the U.S. House, the more conservative voting records of the Gingrich Senators may not have anything to do with their House experience and everything to do with coming from more conservative states.

In the 111th Congress, Maine sent two moderate Republicans to the Senate—Susan Collins, with a 0.06 extremism score, and Olympia Snowe, with a 0.04 score. Wyoming, on the other hand, sent two very conservative Republicans to the Senate—Mike Enzi and John Barrasso, both with 0.63

Table 4.1 The Gingrich Senators and Their Predecessors

State	Congress	Gingrich Senator	Extremism Score	Predecessor	Extremism Score	Change in Extremism Score
Predecessors Are Democrats						
Florida	101	Mack	0.41	Chiles	0.18	0.23
Arizona	104	Kyl	0.65	Deconcini	0.22	0.43
Ohio	104	DeWine	0.20	Metzenbaum	0.59	−0.39
Oklahoma	104	Inhofe	0.71	Boren	0.19	0.52
Pennsylvania	104	Santorum	0.39	Wofford	0.39	0.00
Arkansas	105	Hutchinson	0.47	Pryor	0.38	0.09
Kentucky	106	Bunning	0.62	Ford	0.21	0.41
Nevada	107	Ensign	0.57	Bryan	0.33	0.24
Virginia	107	Allen	0.42	Robb	0.32	0.10
Georgia	108	Chambliss	0.52	Cleland	0.28	0.24
Missouri	108	Talent	0.30	Carnahan	0.32	−0.02
South Carolina	108	Graham	0.50	Hollings	0.29	0.21
Georgia	109	Isakson	0.50	Miller	0.13	0.37
Louisiana	109	Vitter	0.63	Breaux	0.10	0.53
North Carolina	109	Burr	0.59	Edwards	0.38	0.21
South Carolina	109	DeMint	0.83	Hollings	0.30	0.54
South Dakota	109	Thune	0.48	Daschle	0.39	0.09
Illinois	111	Kirk	0.33	Burris	0.54	−0.21
		Average Change in Extremism Score				**0.20**

(Continued)

Table 4.1 (Continued)

State	Congress	Gingrich Senator	Extremism Score	Predecessor	Extremism Score	Change in Extremism Score
Predecessors Are Republicans						
Texas	99	Gramm	0.58	Tower	0.42	0.16
Arizona	100	McCain	0.38	Goldwater	0.68	−0.31
Colorado	102	Brown	0.58	Armstrong	0.61	−0.04
Indiana	102	Coats	0.40	Quayle	0.46	−0.06
New Hampshire	102	Smith	0.80	Humphrey	0.65	0.14
Idaho	102	Craig	0.52	McClure	0.57	−0.05
New Hampshire	103	Gregg	0.46	Rudman	0.22	0.24
Minnesota	104	Grams	0.54	Durenberger	0.04	0.51
Wyoming	104	Thomas	0.55	Wallop	0.78	−0.24
Kansas	105	Roberts	0.39	Kassebaum	0.15	0.24
Kansas	105	Brownback	0.47	Frahm	0.52	−0.05
Idaho	106	Crapo	0.50	Kempthorne	0.50	0.00
Oklahoma	109	Coburn	0.89	Nickles	0.67	0.22
Mississippi	110	Wicker	0.43	Lott	0.51	−0.08
				Average Change in Extremism Score		0.04
Predecessors Are Gingrich Senators						
Colorado	105	Allard	0.62	Brown	0.61	0.02
New Hampshire	108	Sununu	0.42	Smith	0.73	−0.31
				Average Change in Extremism Score		−0.14

extremism scores. The differences in how these state delegations vote in the Senate may be a direct consequence of how their states vote. In the 2008 presidential election, Maine gave Barack Obama 58 percent of the vote to John McCain's 40 percent. Given that Obama got 53 percent of the vote nationwide, Maine had a Democratic slant of 5 percentage points. In Wyoming, McCain received 65 percent to Obama's 33 percent. Wyoming's Republican slant was 20 points. Although both states sent Republican delegations to the Senate, the fact that Wyoming's Republican slant was 25 points greater than Maine's surely influences the kinds of Republicans who win and how those Republicans vote in the Senate.

An examination of what states elect Gingrich Senators offers some evidence for the simple argument that the constituencies form the basis of the Gingrich Senators' conservative voting records. The Gingrich Senators come from states where Republican presidential candidates do on average 4.0 percent better than they do nationwide.[7] In contrast, non-Gingrich Republican senators come from states where Republican presidential candidates do a significantly smaller 1.9 percent better than they do nationwide.[8] The difference between the two—2.1 percent—is, indeed, small, but in a quarter of the states in every presidential election since 1972, the winner in the state had a margin of less than 2 percentage points.

Gephardt Senators, like Gingrich Senators, come from friendlier territory, though not as friendly as that of the Gingrich Senators. Gephardt's former House colleagues come from states that, on average, give Democratic presidential candidates 3.5 percent more votes than their nationwide average. Those Democratic senators since the 96th Congress who did not serve in the House with Gephardt come from states that on average gave Democratic presidential candidates 2.2 percent more votes than their nationwide average.[9]

To see if the difference in the more stridently Republican states from which Gingrich Senators come helps explain their more conservative voting record, I compare the Gingrich Senators to their Republican home-state colleagues in the Senate to see if the Burr-Dole dynamic is systematic across the states with Gingrich Senators. The nice characteristic of this test is that it controls completely for both the conservative nature of the Republican Party within the state and the entire constituency in the Gingrich Senators' states. Furthermore, as opposed to the predecessor analysis, it also controls for the time in which the senators serve, the issues on the agenda, and the votes that they take.

This analysis assumes that both Republican senators from the same state serve the same constituency. While that may be true in a legalistic sense,

Schiller (2000) argues that in such instances, senators will purposefully differentiate themselves. Furthermore, Burden (2007) argues that their differences may result from different personal experiences. These important insights add credibility to the test I offer in this section. If the Gingrich Senators always differentiate themselves in a similar way to their home-state, same-party colleagues, it underlies their common view of representation.

Of the 150 times that a state has sent a Gingrich Senator to the Senate, it has paired him 58 times with a Democrat, 37 times with another Gingrich Senator, and 55 times with another Republican who either did not serve in the House or served in the House prior to Gingrich's election. When Gingrich Senators have been paired with each other, their average ideology score has been 0.53.[10] When Gingrich Senators are paired with a Democratic senator they are not as conservative (0.48) as they are when they are paired with another Gingrich Senator. Their Democratic pairs, though, are considerably more moderate (0.31). In fact, out of the 58 pairs, the Democrat is more extreme in only six instances.

These data for Gingrich Senator/Gingrich Senator and Gingrich Senator/ Democrat pairs do not completely isolate the constituency effect. Gingrich Senators who serve with each other come from more conservative states. So, too, could Gingrich Senators who are paired with a Democrat. As with the Gingrich Senators who took over from Democratic senators, the more moderate voting record of these Democrats could be a result of coming from more conservative states. If so, the Gingrich Senators' voting records, while being more extreme at the national level, could be less extreme in comparison to those of their constituents. For example, South Dakota, where McCain did 6 points better than he did nationwide, sent a mixed delegation to the Senate—Democrat Tim Johnson had a 0.31 extremism score compared to Gingrich Senator John Thune's 0.51. While Thune's score is higher, it could be so because he is a Gingrich Senator or because he comes from a Republican state, whereas John McCain's margin over Barack Obama was 8.4 percentage points. Thune's conservatism is more palatable for South Dakotans than a Democrat's liberalism.

The clearest test to evaluate the Gingrich Senators' extremism in light of their constituency's partisanship is to examine the pairs when Gingrich Senators are serving with another Republican who is not a Gingrich Senator. In these 55 pairs, the Gingrich Senators have an average ideology of 0.50, whereas the average ideology of the non–Gingrich Senator Republicans is 0.37.[11] The average pairing is just a bit closer than the difference between Burr (0.59) and Dole (0.40).

Gingrich Senators were more conservative than their other Republican counterparts in 44 of the 58 cases by Congress (76 percent) and in 13 of the 18 cases by unique pairings (72 percent).[12] The largest gap was 0.54 in New Hampshire during the 102nd Congress (1991–1992) between Gingrich Senator Bob Smith (0.77) and Warren Rudman (0.23), whom no one would ever accuse of being a weak-kneed Republican. The five distinct pairings (and 12 congress pairings) that run counter to the hypothesis are: Craig (Gingrich Senator) and Symms of Idaho (102nd Congress), Thomas (Gingrich Senator) and Enzi of Wyoming (105th–110th Congresses), DeWine (Gingrich Senator) and Voinovich of Ohio (106th–109th Congresses), Talent (Gingrich Senator) and Bond of Missouri (108th–109th Congresses), and Crapo (Gingrich Senator) and Risch of Idaho (111th Congress). Table 4.2 shows the difference between the Gingrich Senators and the other Republicans for the 18 distinct pairs.

Figure 4.1 offers a visual depiction of how the Gingrich Senators' voting scores remain distinct even after controlling for the partisan tilt of their states. An analysis of the 111th Congress (2009–2010) shows that the Gingrich Senators (represented by circles) are more conservative than their other Republican colleagues (represented by plus signs) in Democratic and moderate states as well as in extremely Republican ones. The trend lines in the figure show that this distinction is systematic and quite large.

While the predecessor analysis offers only tepid evidence that the Gingrich Senators remained distinct after considering the Gingrich Senators' states, the pairs analysis offers fairly strong evidence. The following section offers the most systematic test of the Gingrich Senators' distinctiveness after controlling for their states' partisanship.

III. Considering the Constituency in the Sophisticated Model

The two previous analyses show that the Gingrich Senators are more ideologically extreme than their Democratic predecessors and Democratic pairs, more conservative (barely) than their Republican predecessors, and much more conservative than their other Republican pairs. In this section, I test to see if the Gingrich Senator Effect persists under more sophisticated scrutiny. I add a number of constituency-related variables to the base model one at a time before adding all of them in a final analysis of the constituencies' effect.

The dependent variable, like that in table 3.2, is the senators' extremism scores. The analysis in this section uses all the independent variables that were used in the chapter 3 analysis, but builds on it by using additional variables to

Table 4.2 The Gingrich Senators and Their Other Republican Pairs

State	Congresses	Gingrich Senator	Extremism Score	Pair	Extremism Score	Change in Extremism Score
Indiana	101–105	Coats	0.41	Lugar	0.29	0.12
Idaho	102	Craig	0.58	Symms	0.70	-0.12
New Hampshire	102	Smith	0.77	Rudman	0.23	0.53
Idaho	103–105	Craig	0.54	Kempthorne	0.49	0.05
Texas	103–107	Gramm	0.59	Hutchison	0.37	0.22
Colorado	104	Brown	0.54	Campbell	0.16	0.39
Oklahoma	104–108	Inhofe	0.67	Nickles	0.63	0.03
Pennsylvania	104–109		0.37	Specter	0.06	0.32
Wyoming	104	Thomas	0.42	Simpson	0.24	0.19
Colorado	105–108	Allard	0.61	Campbell	0.23	0.37
Wyoming	105–110	Thomas	0.54	Enzi	0.58	-0.04
Kentucky	106–111	Bunning	0.63	McConnell	0.47	0.16
Ohio	106–109	DeWine	0.16	Voinovich	0.26	-0.10
Virginia	107–109	Allen	0.41	Warner	0.25	0.16
Missouri	108–109	Talent	0.31	Bond	0.32	-0.02
North Carolina	109–110	Burr	0.58	Dole	0.41	0.17
Mississippi	110–111	Wicker	0.44	Cochran	0.34	0.10
Idaho	111	Crapo	0.52	Risch	0.54	-0.02
		Average Change in Extremism Score				0.14

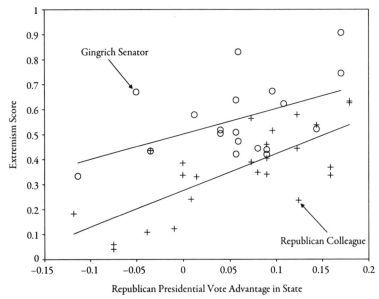

FIGURE 4.1 Comparing the Gingrich Senators to Their Republican Colleagues, 111th Congress (2009–2010).

measure the senators' constituencies. The first new variable is the partisan tilt of the senator's constituency. I estimate the partisanship of the state by using the state's Republican presidential vote advantage (RPVA), which is the number of percentage points the Republican presidential candidate received in the state above or below their two-party national average—sometimes called the "normalized vote"—averaged across the presidential contests by decade.[13] The partisanship of the state has a large effect on senators' voting behavior. Taking a Gingrich Senator in a Democratic state (with a -0.09 RPVA) and placing her in a safe Republican state (with a 0.13 RPVA) increases her extremism by 0.06. These RPVAs of -0.09 and 0.13 represent the 5th and 95th percentiles of the RPVA for Republican senators.[14]

The second constituency variable is the state's region. Scholars have long agreed that the Southern states' transformation in party alignment has had a strong effect on the ideological orientation of both the Democratic and Republican Parties in Congress (see, e.g., Black and Black 2002). It could be that the Gingrich Senator Effect is due to the increase in Republican control of House and Senate seats in the South along with the more conservative ideological orientation of that region's Republicans.[15] Sure enough, being from the South decreases a Democratic senator's extremism score by 0.24, while it increases a Republican's polarization score by 0.13.[16]

Table 4.3 The Extremism Score for the Gingrich and Gephardt Senators and Their Partisan Counterparts Controlling for Constituency's Partisanship, 93rd to 111th Congresses (1973–2010)

	Republicans			Democrats		
	No House Experience	House Experience			No House Experience	House Experience
Pre–1978	0.33	0.28	Pre–1978		0.43	0.47
Post–1978	0.35	0.47	Post–1978		0.44	0.45
Gingrich Senator Effect		47%	Gephardt Senator Effect			1%

A third aspect of the constituencies that might be important in explaining the Gingrich Senator Effect is the size of the state. Rohde (1979) finds that representatives in small states are more likely to seek and secure Senate nominations than representatives in large states. Furthermore, the primary and general-election constituencies in large states are likely to be more heterogeneous than those in small states, creating more opportunities for moderate Republicans. Thus the Gingrich Senator Effect could be due to smaller states being more likely to nominate very conservative Republican representatives as Senate candidates. As it turns out, Gingrich Senators do represent smaller states than Democrats, but their Republican counterparts come from even smaller states than do Gingrich Senators.[17] If a state is one standard deviation smaller than the average state, their senator's DW-NOMINATE score is 0.03 more conservative.[18]

The analysis shows that each of the three constituency measures is statistically significant and reduces the Gingrich Senator Effect. Even when all of the variables are considered simultaneously, each of them retains their statistical significance.[19] The simulation results for the four types of senators in both parties are presented in table 4.3. When the various measures of the constituency are taken into consideration, the Gingrich Senators' polarization score decreases from 0.54 in the base model to 0.47 in the constituency model. The average of the other three Republican senators decreases from 0.35 to 0.32. When the constituency variables are included in the base model, Gingrich Senators are simulated to be 47 percent more conservative than the average of the other three Republican senator groups. In the base model, they were 54 percent more conservative. While the inclusion of the constituency characteristics undeniably reduces the Gingrich Senator Effect, it remains statistically significant and substantively large. Furthermore, table 4.3 offers confirmatory evidence that the Gingrich Senator Effect is not a Reagan Era Effect even after controlling for the senators' constituencies. In the age of Reagan, those Republican senators coming from the House are 34 percent more extreme than those without House experience.

The base model showed that the Gephardt Senators were about one-third as distinct from their Democratic counterparts as the Gingrich Senators were from their Republican counterparts. In the constituency model, the distinctiveness of the Gephardt Senators all but disappears. Their Democratic counterparts have an extremism score of 0.44. The Gephardt Senators are only 0.01 more liberal on the DW-NOMINATE scale at 0.45. The inclusion of the states' partisanship wipes out the distinctiveness of the Gephardt Senators.

IV. Conclusion

The simplest and most plausible explanation for the Gingrich Senator Effect is that the Gingrich Senators come from more conservative states, which in this analysis we define as Republican-voting states, Southern states, and states with fewer people. We find that each of these variables is related to their senators' ideologies. Furthermore, the variables, individually and aggregately, explain away part of the Gingrich Senator Effect.

If the Gingrich Senator Effect shrank from 54 percent in the base model to 47 percent in the constituency model, about 13 percentage points of the distinctiveness of the Gingrich Senators can be explained by the partisan tilt of the states that they represent. This percentage is not inconsequential; neither does it render the remainder of this book irrelevant. Of the total Gingrich Senator Effect, 87 percent of it remains after taking the constituency into consideration. The inclusion of the constituency variables for the Gephardt Senators, on the other hand, makes their distinctiveness among Democrats all but disappear.

5

The Effect of Personal Characteristics and Proximity to Newt Gingrich on the Gingrich Senators

IT COULD BE that this close-knit cadre of House members developed such strong bonds that their political instincts melded, or perhaps Gingrich was such a powerful personality that the rest of the members adapted their instincts to match his. If the power of his personality was so great, it might be true that Gingrich truly did "baptize" his acolytes in the waters of conservatism and confrontational politics. This chapter explores the possibility that the Gingrich Senators truly are *Gingrich* Senators and not just "Republicans who entered the House after 1978 and subsequently served in the Senate."

In this chapter I examine two factors that may explain the distinctiveness of the Gingrich Senators. First, I examine their personal characteristics. A common religion, age, or personal background may have propelled these individuals not only into the House but also into the Senate. If these common characteristics are the underlying cause of their distinctiveness, then their time in the House is only a stage in their development that is eventually transferred to the Senate. Second, I use the story about the Conservative Opportunity Society to motivate the logic that close, personal proximity to Newt Gingrich influences the voting records of the Gingrich Senators. In so doing, I determine the characteristics that best distinguish the Gingrich Senators from their fellow Republican colleagues. In the end, neither personal characteristics nor proximity to Gingrich accounts for much—if anything—of the Gingrich Senators as party polarizers.

I. The Personal Characteristics of the Gingrich Senators

In the 111th Congress (2009–2010), just as in its predecessors, the Gingrich Senators were distinct. While the other Republicans had an average extremism score of 0.29, the Gingrich Senators' average score was 0.51. This ideological distinctiveness in the most recent congress is consistent with the long track record evaluated in chapter 3. The Gingrich Senators were not only distinct ideologically in the 111th Congress but also younger, more likely to practice an evangelical faith, and less likely to be lawyers. On other personal characteristic dimensions, the Gingrich Senators are just like the other Republicans. Both sets were equally likely to serve in the military as well as to pledge a fraternity during their college days. In this half of the chapter, I test to see if these personal characteristics are the root cause of their ideological distinctiveness. The evidence shows that while some of these personal variables may have an effect on their ideology, none of them sufficiently weakens the Gingrich Senator Effect.

To establish the baselines for these demographic analyses, I first present the evidence for the Gingrich Senator Effect for the 111th Congress. The first row of table 5.1 shows how well a model that includes only the constituency variables from chapter 4 predicts Republican senators' ideology scores. I exclude Democrats from these analyses because we aim to uncover only if the demographic variables can help explain the distinction between the Gingrich Senators and the other Republicans.[1] The R^2—a statistic that varies from 0 (no systematic explanation) to 1 (fully explains the variance in the dependent variable)—for this simple model is 0.65. The Gingrich Senators Effect is 57 percent, which means that when the constituency is taken into consideration the Gingrich Senators still have an extremism score that is 57 percent greater than the groups of other Republicans.

A. Age

When Barack Obama took the oath of office in the first couple of weeks of the 111th Congress (2009), only nine Gingrich Senators had celebrated their fiftieth birthday. On the other hand, 17 other Republicans had.[2] When the senators' year of birth is included in the analysis, the R^2 stays at 0.65, though the Gingrich Senators Effect falls to 52 percent.[3]

B. Religion

The Gingrich Senators are more likely to practice an evangelical faith. Whereas just below one-third of the Gingrich Senators (31.6 percent) belonged to an evangelical church, only one-fifth of other Republicans did (and less than 10 percent of Democrats did). The other big religious

Table 5.1 The Gingrich Senator Effect When Controlling
for Personal Characteristics

	No House Exp. Elected before 1978	House Exp. Elected before 1978	No House Exp. Elected after 1978	Gingrich Senators	Gingrich Senator Effect
Constituency	0.30	0.36	0.39	0.55	0.57
Age	0.32	0.37	0.38	0.54	0.52
Religion	0.34	0.35	0.42	0.56	0.53
Veteran	0.32	0.37	0.41	0.57	0.55
Fraternity	0.27	0.32	0.36	0.52	0.63
Occupation	0.24	0.32	0.33	0.46	0.55
Member of "Fellowship"	0.26	0.31	0.37	0.50	0.62
Full Model	0.23	0.31	0.38	0.47	0.54

distinction was among Catholics. Only 3 of the 10 Republican Catholics were Gingrich Senators.[4] Furthermore, the sole Jewish Republican—Arlen Specter—was not a Gingrich Senator, nor would he be a Republican or member of the Senate by the time Obama celebrated his second anniversary in the White House.

The greater preponderance of evangelicals among the Gingrich Senators only marginally decreased the Gingrich Senator Effect to 53 percent, though evangelicals were more conservative than the other religious groups. The R^2 of the model including religion was 0.70.

C. Occupation

The Gingrich Senators had a different route to the Senate. While a bare minority of the Gingrich Senators had a law degree (9 out of 19), the overwhelming number of other Republicans did (16 out of 27).[5] Although all of the Gingrich Senators served in the House, none of them self-reported that their occupation was "politics," in contrast to three other Republicans (Snowe, Collins, and Grassley) and 12 Democrats.[6] Besides the nine lawyers among the Gingrich Senators, there was an association executive, a baseball player, an insurance executive, a marketing consultant, a naval aviator, a newspaper publisher, a physician, a real estate executive, a sales executive, and a veterinarian.

The declared occupation of the Republicans also had an effect on their ideologies as the R^2 increased to 0.67. As with religion, though, their occupation did not reduce the Gingrich Senator Effect, which remained 53 percent.

D. Military Service

Seven of the 19 Gingrich Senators served in the military. Jim Inhofe served two years in the Army. Roger Wicker (28 years) and Johnny Isakson (6 years) served in the Air Force. John McCain had 23 years of service in the Navy, including more than five years as a prisoner of war in Vietnam. Pat Roberts did 4 years in the Marine Corps. Two of the three senators in the 111th Congress who were simultaneously serving in the military were also Gingrich Senators—Lindsey Graham was a colonel in the Air Force and Mark Kirk was a commander in the Navy. The third active member of the military in the Senate was Scott Brown who is a lieutenant colonel in the Army. A similarly proportioned 8 out of 25 other Republicans have military experience.[7]

Military experience also had a small effect on ideology. Those with military experience had about a 0.06 lower extremism score than those without military experience. The R^2 of the model that included military background was 0.67. As with the other variables, it had a negligible effect on the Gingrich Senator variables—the Gingrich Senator Effect was 55 percent.

E. Fraternity

Twelve out of 19 Gingrich Senators were in college fraternities. As with military experience, about the same proportion of other Republicans were also in fraternities.[8] Being in a fraternity increased Republicans' extremism scores by 0.04, though it had a negligible effect on the overall model (R^2 was 0.66) and the influence of being a Gingrich Senator (marginally increasing to 63 percent).

F. The Fellowship

The last personal variable that I test is Republicans' association with the "Fellowship" or "Family," which are names given to a political and religious organization founded by Abraham Vereide in 1935. This group has been the subject of two books by Jeff Sharlet (2008, 2010), who documents the various ways that the group influences politics both explicitly and implicitly. The secretive nature of the Fellowship came under intense scrutiny as three of their members—Senator John Ensign, Congressman Chip Pickering, and South Carolina Governor Mark Sanford—were caught in sex scandals within months of each other in 2009.

The National Prayer Breakfast, held every year on the first Thursday in January, is the Fellowship's primary—perhaps, only—public event. Presidents have regularly been attending this event since it was first held in 1953. The Fellowship does not keep an official list of members, but through various news accounts and personal declarations I have been able to ascertain that 12 senators in the 111th Congress had an association with the group—six of them were Gingrich Senators (Inhofe, Brownback, Ensign, Coburn, Thune, and DeMint).[9]

The Gingrich Senators who were associated with the Fellowship had an average ideology of 0.68, compared to 0.51 for those who did not have an association. None of the personal variables analyzed in this chapter had as big an effect as being associated with the Fellowship, which increased the senators' ideology by 0.15 in the statistical model. The R^2 in this model was 0.75. Although the effect is large, controlling for it only increases the Gingrich Senator Effect, which increases to 63 percent. To be sure, the Fellowship is important in determining Republicans' ideologies, but it does not rival the predictive power of the Gingrich Senator variables.

G. The Full Model

As a final check that the Gingrich Senator variables are not acting as a proxy on the combination of personal characteristics, I perform one final test, which includes all of the personal characteristic variables simultaneously. As the R^2 in the full model jumps to 0.83, several of the personal characteristics remain statistically significant: Catholicism and military service decrease conservatism; Fellowship association increases it. Most importantly for the argument of this book, the Gingrich Senator Effect is largely unchanged. With just the constituency variables, the effect was 57 percent. The inclusion of personal characteristics variables lowers it to 54 percent. While it is true that constituency and personal characteristics are important in understanding the roll-call decisions that Republican senators make, the residual effect of having served in a highly contentious and partisan House persists.

II. Proximity to Gingrich

Chapter 2 analyzed the effect of the Conservative Opportunity Society (COS) on the House of Representatives in the 1980s. Most scholars recognize that these Republican House members were among Gingrich's closest colleagues. Because they did not envision their group as an institutional caucus or a formal group, they never kept attendance records at their meetings and they never developed a formal list of members. The members that were listed in chapter 2 came from a couple of different sources. No one disputes that the members included in this list were critical to the COS; the list may just be incomplete. Many members were probably affiliated with the COS and would attend their meetings on occasion. Of the 10 names that seem to be described as the core members of the COS, at least four are Gingrich Senators: Judd Gregg, Dan Coats, Connie Mack, and Jon Kyl.

No one doubts the enormous impact that Newt Gingrich had on the practice of politics in the post-reform House. To take seriously the proposition that Gingrich's dominance over the House was more personal than institutional, in this section I test a much more personal hypothesis for the Gingrich Senators' distinctiveness. To do so, I examine a number of different Gingrich-specific characteristics to see if any of them can explain the ideology of House members once they reach the Senate. In short, none of these personal ties to Gingrich does a particularly good job of explaining a senator's ideology.

While the precise membership of the Conservative Opportunity Society is not known, I employ a number of other proxies for "closeness to Gingrich." It is unclear if these proxies are an accurate reflection of the members who were "baptized" by Gingrich, but, in total, they can suggest if a personal relationship with him matters when determining Republican senators' ideologies. Furthermore, they begin to assess the characteristics of House experience that may affect Senate ideology.

I perform two different types of analysis in this section. First, I test a series of variables among all Republican senators, serving in the Senate after 1973, who previously served in the House.[10] I include a number of different variables to measure the personal connection between Gingrich and the Gingrich Senators; admittedly, some of these variables may be a stretch, but as long as they are not interfering with the other variables they should just wash away in the analysis. Second, I include the number of terms senators served in the House prior to their Senate service. The more House terms, the more likely they would have been instilled with the House mindset before moving on to the Senate. The next two variables—whether a Republican senator held a position in the House whip organization or on the House Republican campaign committee—indicates the extent to which they might have been involved in the politics and policies of the House prior to their Senate service. Fourth, whether a Republican senator actually served with Gingrich in the

House may influence their Senate service.[11] Finally, I include the definition of what I call a "Gingrich Senator"—whether they began their service in the House after Gingrich's election.

I add these variables, one by one, to see if they can explain the Republican senators' extremism scores. The first two of these variables—number of House terms and serving in the whip organization—did not have a significant effect on extremism.[12] The other three did. Senators who served on the House campaign committee were 0.17 more conservative than those who did not serve. Serving with Gingrich also increased senators' extremism scores by 0.17. Entering the House after Gingrich's first election increased their scores by 0.27. When all five variables are included in the same analysis, serving on the campaign committee still increases a senator's conservatism as does being a Gingrich Senator. Serving with Gingrich, however, loses all significance and even changes signs, which is an indication that coming to a House that already included Gingrich matters much more than actually serving with him.

This analysis includes those senators who served in the House even before Gingrich's election. Including those senators, which the chapter 3 analysis suggests were considerably more moderate, may be masking a real effect specific to Gingrich. To fully explore this hypothesis, the second-level analysis is isolated to the Gingrich Senators only. This analysis includes all of the same variables as those in the previous analysis, except, of course, the Gingrich Senators' indicator variable because the data set is restricted to only the Gingrich Senators.[13] Of these four variables, the only variable that increases a senator's conservatism is serving on the campaign committee, though the increase was roughly half of what it was for all former House Republican members (0.09 compared to 0.17). In this analysis, serving with Gingrich actually decreases a senator's conservatism by 0.14, which is explained by the conservative voting records from the three Gingrich Senators who never served with Gingrich—Isakson (0.50), Vitter (0.63), and DeMint (0.83). All three were elected the year that Gingrich left the House.

Because the analysis is restricted to the Gingrich Senators, I include three other variables that were not tested among all former House Republicans serving in the Senate. First, I include an indicator variable for those four future senators who were named members of the Conservative Opportunity Society. Among all Gingrich Senators, this variable actually decreases a senator's conservatism by 0.05, which is a consequence of the less extreme voting records of the COS members—Kyl (0.65), Coats (0.40), Gregg (0.46), and Mack (0.41)—compared to the other Gingrich Senators.

The last two variables that are tested on the Gingrich Senators only examine the closeness of the future senator with Newt Gingrich as measured by cosponsorship activity.[14] Fowler (2006a, 2006b) shows how cosponsorship activity can reveal networks in Congress. He develops proximity scores that are directional; that is, legislator A's proximity to legislator B is not the same as legislator B's proximity to legislator A. In this sense, it is easiest to think of these scores as legislator A's support for legislator B. Using Fowler's data, we know how much each of the House members who served with Gingrich supported him and were supported by him. We might expect that senators who had close relationships with Gingrich—as measured by his support for their legislation and their support for his legislation—may be more distinctive than those future senators who did not have close relationships with him.[15] When I test these two variables I find that closeness to Gingrich in the House, as measured by cosponsorship activity, did not have a unique effect on a senator's extremism score. In fact, of all the variables tested at this second level, none were as irrelevant as these two variables. When all of the variables are included in the same analysis, little changes in the results. The effect of serving on the campaign committee increases from 0.094 to 0.165, which is about the same magnitude as it was when all former House Republicans were included in the analysis. Furthermore, a future Gingrich Senator's support for Gingrich's legislation in the House causes the Gingrich Senator to have a bit more moderate voting record in the Senate. In addition to being just barely statistically significant, this relationship is substantively small.

III. Conclusion

Some of the personal characteristics and measures of proximity to Gingrich do affect senators' extremism scores, but none of them even modestly weakens the Gingrich Senator Effect. While any individual personal characteristic may propel one member to act in a particular way while another member acts as a result of a different characteristic, I can find no single characteristic or set of characteristics that systematically explains the Gingrich Senators' distinctiveness. Furthermore, it appears from the data analysis that, with regards to proximity to Gingrich, neither the number of the senators' concurrent terms nor their serving in the whip organization nor their connectedness to Gingrich during their House career significantly affects their Senate ideology.

These findings, however, do not speak to the lack of consequence that Gingrich had on the House Republican Conference or the House of Representatives as a whole. His role in the Conservative Opportunity Society and what he did apart from the COS suggest that he left an indelible mark on the House and those members who served in it, especially his Republican colleagues. It is the service in this highly partisan chamber that seems to have affected future senators, not their personal relationships to Gingrich.

6

Getting In and Staying In
the U.S. Senate

THE GINGRICH SENATORS are obviously not the first group of senators who have had a profound effect on the institution. As the conflict over slavery intensified, the Great Triumvirate—John C. Calhoun, Henry Clay, and Daniel Webster—promoted the Senate from the backseat of American politics to the driver's seat. With the Missouri Compromise of 1820 and the Compromise of 1850, the three senators played major roles in the decades leading up to the Civil War though none of them would live beyond 1852, let alone long enough to see the first shots fired on Fort Sumter in 1861 (Peterson 1987). More than a half-century later, Nelson W. Aldrich, William B. Allison, and their allies helped institutionalize the political parties inside the Senate by centralizing their party leadership in the Republican steering committee (Rothman 1966). Their efforts were instrumental in the creation of the floor leader position in the Senate (Gamm and Smith 2002). In the late 1950s and early 1960s a new breed of senator entered the institution, propelling it from the Textbook Senate to the Institutional Senate (Sinclair 1989). The old folkways of the Senate began to break down as the newer members were more forceful in fighting for their liberal causes. They were less willing to bide their time and wait to accrue seniority before playing an important role in the Senate.

The story of the Gingrich Senators is different from the accounts of the Great Triumvirate; Aldrich, Allison, and their allies; and the liberal reforms of 50 years ago. The Gingrich Senators are an organic group whose membership changes and evolves with every election. One Gingrich Senator's retirement or defeat can happen at the same time that two or three new Gingrich Senators are elected. Although the group once had only one member in the chamber, they have had at least 15 members since the 1994 elections. Over the last 15 years, they have comprised between 40 and 50 percent of the Republican Conference in the Senate.

The group's growing numbers and influence are grounded in two basic conditions. First, during the Gingrich Era, Republican House members were more willing to seek a Senate seat than they were before Gingrich entered the House. Second, once in the Senate, Gingrich Senators were more successful at staying in the Senate than their fellow Republicans, especially when taking into consideration their more conservative voting record.

In the last few chapters we found that the senators' constituencies, their personal backgrounds, and their proximity to Gingrich in the House could not fully account for their ideological extremity. In this chapter, we find that the frequency with which they ran and their success in staying in the Senate helps account for the large and lasting effect they have had on the Senate.

I. Getting Elected to the Senate

Former House members usually comprise between 40 and 50 percent of the Senate. Over time that figure has waxed and waned and varied considerably by party. In the six election cycles between 1974 and 1984, for example, only 15 Republican members from the House ran for the Senate, which is an average of 2.5 House members each election. These cycles correspond to the last six cycles prior to the election of the first Gingrich Senator, Phil Gramm. In the 13 election cycles since Gramm's election (1986–2010), 78 Republican House members have run for the Senate, an average of 6 in each cycle. In each election cycle during the Gingrich Senator era, the Republicans have fielded 2.4 times as many House candidates as they did in the six election cycles immediately prior to the Gingrich Senator era. The number of Democrats from the House running for the Senate, on the other hand, has stayed fairly constant. Whereas Democrats used to attract 40 percent more House candidates than Republicans, the Republicans now attract almost 50 percent more (see figure 6.1 for a visual depiction of how the rates of House candidates by party have changed over the last 19 elections). In the 1970s and 1980s, fewer Republicans attempted to make the transition because fewer Republicans served in the House. Interestingly, though, the Democrats—even though they have fewer House members than they did prior to the 1994 election—still run about as many former House members for Senate seats, which suggests it is an issue of supply, not demand. Regardless of the cause, though, the successive waves of Republicans running for the Senate has had an important effect on the Senate's makeup.

The advantage of fielding House candidates in Senate elections is measured in victories on election day. Between 1974 and 2010, 85 percent of the

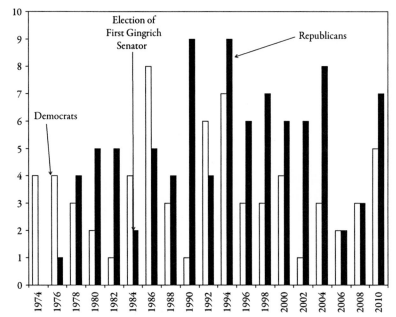

FIGURE 6.1 The Number of Senate Challengers with House Experience, 1974–2010.

senators who ran for reelection were victorious. In comparison, 56 percent of the House members (or former House members) who ran in the general election for a seat in the Senate also won.[1] In contests between Senate incumbents and House challengers, the latter won almost 40 percent of the time.

Candidates who run for the Senate as neither incumbents nor with House experience fare far worse—only 28 percent of them win. Furthermore, less than 12 percent of challengers without House experience defeat sitting senators. These data are consistent with a long line of studies that show that candidates who had previously won electoral office fare better in congressional elections than their political neophyte complements (e.g., Jacobson 2012).

While the number of Republican House members running for the Senate has drastically increased, the electoral dynamics between Senate incumbents with House experience and challengers without House experience have not changed much since the 1970s and are fairly consistent across parties. Republican House members who served prior to Gingrich and those who served with Gingrich each won about three-fifths of their elections. Democrats in the early era did about as well; however, Democrats in the latter era won only two out of five elections. The reduced electoral success of Democrats more recently can be tied directly to the increasing number of would-be Gingrich Senators who have run for the Senate. As Republicans have fielded more House members for Senate contests, all Democratic candidates have suffered including their own House members who are looking for a promotion to the Senate.

To see if these electoral dynamics can withstand a more sophisticated analysis, I evaluate the effect of having House experience in Senate elections while considering other factors. The dependent variable in this analysis is the two-party vote that Republican candidates received in the 656 Senate election races from 1974 to 2010. This variable implicitly considers Democratic candidates as well, because the two numbers—the Republican vote share and the Democratic vote share—always totals one. If a particular factor is helpful for the Republican candidate then it necessarily is harmful to the Democratic candidate.

The primary variables of interest are those characteristics that comprise the definition of would-be Gingrich Senators—being a Republican who was first elected to the House after 1978 and who subsequently *ran* for the Senate. While we are interested in the Gingrich Senator Effect, we cannot restrict the analysis only to the 40 Gingrich Senators because there are other candidates who fit this description except that they lost their Senate race. That is the reason that I use the term "would-be Gingrich Senator." Not every Republican candidate who fulfills the Gingrich Senator criteria was elected to the Senate.

The other possible factors that might affect Republican candidates' performances in Senate elections are the parallel indicator variables for Democratic candidates (coming from the House and first being elected to the House after 1978), because we know that even House Democrats do better than their colleagues without House experience. I also include the Republican Presidential Vote Advantage for each state to account for its partisan tilt. The most important variable to take into consideration in all congressional elections is whether the incumbent—either Democratic or Republican—was seeking reelection.[2]

To measure the effect of House experience properly, we must take into consideration the whole set of variables we included to take account of the would-be Gingrich Senators and the would-be Gephardt Senators. As sets, both the Republican and the Democratic variables have important effects on the two-party vote that the Republican candidates received.[3] Table 6.1 shows the effect for the four groups of candidates in each party. Would-be Gingrich Senators do about 1 percent worse than their fellow Republicans. Because the dependent variable is the two-party vote for Republican candidates, in races that feature a would-be Gephardt Senator Republican

Table 6.1 Predicting the Gingrich Senator Effect on the Two-Party Vote in Elections, 1976–2010

	Republicans			Democrats	
	No House Experience	House Experience		No House Experience	House Experience
Pre-1978	0.40	0.44	Pre-1978	0.40	0.40
Post-1978	0.34	0.39	Post-1978	0.44	0.43
Gingrich Senator Effect		−0.01	Gephardt Senator Effect		0.02

candidates do about 2 percent better than they do in races featuring the other Democrats.

The cursory analysis is consistent with the more sophisticated analysis: the Gingrich Senator Effect cannot be explained by the increased electoral success of former House members in the Gingrich Era. In fact, House members—both Democratic and Republican—did marginally better in Senate elections prior to 1978 than they did after 1978.[4] The data analysis from this section shows that it is the frequency with which would-be Gingrich Senators ran for the Senate, not their improved electoral success, that accounts for their growing membership. More former Republicans running for the Senate, however, is a necessary condition, but not a sufficient one.

II. Trading Moderate Candidates for More Money

The 104th Congress (1995–1996) was grueling for Democrats. Their majority status got swept up in the Republican tsunami that saw Gingrich ascend to the Speaker's chair. Rather than face a competitive election for his fourth term in a chamber that would likely include even more Republicans, Democrat Bill Bradley of New Jersey decided to retire, which opened up a competitive seat in the 1996 elections. Two House members—Democrat Bob Torricelli (with an extremism score of 0.27) and Republican Dick Zimmer (with a score of 0.30)—quickly became their party's preferred candidates to succeed Bradley. In a hard-fought contest, Torricelli ultimately prevailed by 10 points after spending more than $9 million to his opponent's $8 million. Zimmer's House Republican colleague, Jim Ross Lightfoot of Iowa, also lost in 1996, despite having a 0.40 extremism score. He was outraised two-to-one by the incumbent, Tom Harkin, who at the time had one of the highest extremism scores in the Senate.

Four of their House Republican colleagues in 1996, though, were victorious. In Colorado, Wayne Allard (with a 0.60 extremism score) raised about two-thirds of the money raised by his competitor and still won. In Arkansas, Tim Hutchinson (with a 0.41 extremism score) raised $100,000 more in a race where the candidates jointly spent close to $5 million. In Kansas, the Republicans had a clean sweep in votes and money when Sam Brownback (with a 0.54 score) raised twice as much his opponent and Pat Roberts (with a 0.46 score) raised almost four times as much as his opponent. Both won by more than 10 percentage points.

Four of the six House Republicans in 1996 achieved a promotion to the Senate. The four who won were more conservative than the two who lost. At least three of them were able to overcome their more conservative voting record by raising more money than their opponents. The individual data from the 1996 election cycle is consistent across the Gingrich Era. Despite running more conservative candidates, the House Republicans, as a group, did about as well as they had in the 1970s. Prior to the Gingrich Era, the average extremism score of Republicans with House experience who ran for the Senate was 0.22. The Republican House candidates running for the Senate in the Gingrich Era, including the 1996 elections, are more than twice as conservative (0.45 over the entire period and among the six candidates in 1996). The Democratic candidates in the modern era, when they have been less successful, are marginally less extreme (0.28) than they were in the earlier era (0.30).[5]

In addition to transforming the Senate, the Gingrich Senators have also turned Anthony Downs on his head. Downs (1957) famously argued that electoral contests, in their purest form, would see candidates converge to the middle in hopes of capturing the moderates whose votes are necessary for candidates to win elections. He called the person in the middle the "median voter." If our elections are ideological contests, he argued, the candidate that got the median voter would also have the support of all the voters to the median's left or right and would win the election by one vote. In different states, of course, the median voter would occupy a different place on the ideological spectrum. California's median voter, for example, would be more liberal than Oklahoma's median voter. Nonetheless, Downsian analysis presumes that moderate candidates would fare better than extreme candidates in general elections. The trick, in American politics, is for moderate candidates to win primaries, which have become increasingly ideological contests. That is why political pundits frequently talk about candidates running to the extremes in the primaries before running to the middle in the general election.

Would-be Gingrich Senators have won elections despite their conservative voting habits. What they have lost electorally by not being moderate, they have gained in money—the mother's milk in politics. The would-be Gingrich Senators have raised 121 percent more money than their fellow House Republicans from the earlier era. That House Republicans in the Gingrich era raised more money is obvious; all candidates raise more money today than they did in the past. The best comparison might be with the House Democrats. The would-be Gephardt Senators raised 75 percent more than House Democrats in the earlier period. The would-be Gingrich Senators, in comparison, have done almost twice as well.

Two problems complicate this simple result. First, in the analysis, all states are lumped together even though Senate contests are obviously more expensive in California than they are in Wyoming. Second, in the analysis, all the races are lumped together even though some races involve much more money than other races. For example, the competitive contest to fill Barack Obama's Senate seat in 2010, which was won by Gingrich Senator Mark Kirk, brought in more than $23.7 million; Jim DeMint, a fellow Gingrich Senator, and his challenger brought in only $3.7 million for their South Carolina race during the same election year.

A more sophisticated statistical analysis can take account of the increased need for more campaign funds, the different populations of the states, and the individual dynamics of the contests.[6] The results from the more sophisticated analysis, as depicted in table 6.2, are similar to the simple results described above. Would-be Gingrich Senators raise $1.14 million more for their races than do their fellow Republicans, which accounts for about 22 percent more money. In races against would-be Gephardt Senators, on the other hand, Republican candidates raise $120,000 less than they do against other Democrats.

Would-be Gingrich Senators are much more conservative than the pre–Gingrich Republican House candidates trying to move to the Senate and, yet, they won at about the same rate. This analysis suggests that they have compensated—quite literally—for their more conservative voting record by raising more money. These findings are specific to the Republican Party—Democrats during the Gingrich Era are similar to their earlier colleagues trying to transition to the Senate except that they are not as successful.

Table 6.2 Predicting the Gingrich Senator Effect on Campaign Money
Raised (in Millions of Dollars) in Senate Elections, 1984–2010

	Republicans			Democrats	
	No House Experience	House Experience		No House Experience	House Experience
Pre-1978	5.73	4.55	Pre-1978	5.72	6.36
Post-1978	5.39	6.36	Post-1978	7.15	6.29
Gingrich Senator Effect		1.14	Gephardt Senator Effect		-0.12

III. The Would-be Gingrich Senators

This book focuses on the Gingrich Senators. These 40 men, though, came
from a total class of 73 of Gingrich's former colleagues who have run for the
U.S. Senate. Although more than half have become senators, it is not always
on their first try; DeWine, Ensign, Thune, and Toomey all lost races for the
Senate before they eventually won. Of the remaining 33 would-be Gingrich
Senators, 25 of them ran for and lost their Senate elections (including Tom
Campbell, who first lost a primary). The last 8 of Gingrich's Republican col-
leagues ran for and lost in the primary for a Senate seat.

The 40 Gingrich Senators had an average ideology score in the House
that was 0.07 points more conservative than the average House Republican
with whom they were serving. Given that the average extremism score for
Republicans was 0.41, the Gingrich Senators were 17 percent more conservative than an increasingly conservative House Republican Conference.
Gingrich's colleagues who tried but never made it to the Senate were much
more like the average House Republican. The 25 Republicans who lost in the
general election and the 8 who lost in the primary were both about 0.02 points
more moderate than the average of the House Republican Conference.

Much of the ideological distinction between the Gingrich Senators and
the would-be Gingrich Senators can be explained by the House districts that
they represented. Gingrich Senators came from congressional districts where
Republican presidential candidates did about 11 percentage points better than
they did nationwide. The Republicans who lost their Senate seat bids came
from districts that were about half as favorable to Republicans. Furthermore,
the 33 unsuccessful would-be Gingrich Senators ran for the Senate in states
that were more competitive than the states that elected Gingrich Senators.
The would-be Gingrich Senators who became senators did so because they

ran in friendlier territory even though they were more conservative than those who failed.

IV. The Inundation of Gingrich Senators

In the years preceding the Gingrich Era, new Republican senators had ideology scores across the moderate to conservative spectrum (see panel A of figure 6.2). Four of the new senators—Robert Stafford, John Chafee, John Heinz, and Arlen Specter—even ventured into the moderate to liberal range. The average first Congress ideology score for the 46 newly elected Senate

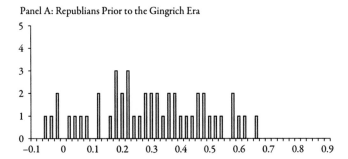

Panel A: Republicans Prior to the Gingrich Era

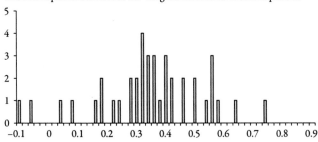

Panel B: Republicans Elected in the Gingrich Era without House Experience

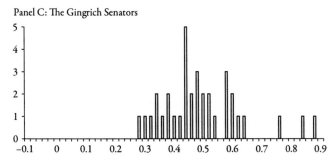

Panel C: The Gingrich Senators

FIGURE 6.2 First Congress Ideology Scores for Selected Groups of Republicans, 93rd to 111th Congresses (1973–2010).

Republicans between 1973 and 1985 was 0.30, which is just above the overall average Republican score of 0.26.

In 1985 the first Gingrich Senator, Phil Gramm, moved from the House to the Senate. He was joined by two other Republican senators from the South—Mitch McConnell (Kentucky) and James Broyhill (North Carolina). In their first congress, Gramm was the ninth-most-conservative Republican with an extremism score of 0.50. Two of those who were more conservative than Gramm have come to define conservatism in the post–civil rights era: Jesse Helms was the most conservative, with a score of 0.68, and Barry Goldwater, who retired in 1986, was the third most-conservative with a 0.66. McConnell (0.31) and Broyhill (0.41) were much closer to the Republican mean of 0.28.

In the following Congress, another Gingrich Senator, John McCain, joined Gramm. McCain, with a 0.32 extremism score, was only the 16th-most-conservative Republican in his first term. With each new congress, a few more Gingrich Senators were elected and most of them had ideology scores closer to Gramm's than McCain's. Other Republicans entered with these new Gingrich Senators though they reflected the ideology of the older Republicans. Panel B shows the distribution of first-Congress ideology scores for non–Gingrich Senators in the Gingrich Era (1985–2010). Although this distribution looks slightly more bell-shaped than panel A, the average (0.35) was not that much different. The distribution of ideology scores that Gingrich Senators earned in their first congress is markedly more conservative (panel C). The average for the Gingrich Senators was 0.50. The second Gingrich Senator, John McCain, had the third-lowest first-congress extremism score—only DeWine (0.27) and Talent (0.31) were lower. The three highest first-congress scores—Coburn (0.91), DeMint (0.83), and Smith (0.77)—were also the three highest for any senator since the early 1970s. In fact, Coburn's score is the highest extremism score of any senator since Glen Taylor (0.99, 79th Congress), a Democrat from Idaho, and the highest polarized score for any Republican senator since David Baird Jr. of New Jersey (0.99, 71st Congress), who was appointed to the seat and served less than one year.

The data from the 104th Congress vividly illustrates the difference between Gingrich Senators and non–Gingrich Senators in their first term. The Republicans took back the Senate, which they had lost six years earlier, with the election of 11 new senators and the switch of one Democratic senator to the Republican Party split equally between Gingrich Senators and non–Gingrich Senators. The new senators had ideology scores that typified the categories to which they belonged. The six new Gingrich Senators had an average ideology score of 0.46 compared to the non–Gingrich Senators' average score of 0.36.[7] After the Republican Revolution in 1994, the scores have diverged even more, though the number of new Gingrich Senators is almost the same as the number of other new Republicans. Since 1997, the 21 new Gingrich Senators have averaged 0.51 while the 20 new non–Gingrich Senators have averaged 0.35.[8]

Since Gramm's election, the Gingrich Senators have been an increasingly bigger proportion of the Republican caucus. Figure 6.3 shows how their numbers and proportion of the Republican Conference have grown over time. In the 112th Congress (2011–2012), they comprise 43 percent of the Republican Conference. Their increasingly conservative voting habits in combination with their increasing numbers reveal the Gingrich Senators' increasing influence. Figure 6.4 combines quantity with ideology. In the most recent congresses, the Gingrich Senators account for well over half of the Republican caucus's conservative nature.

IV. The Longevity of the Gingrich Senators

The data from the previous section suggests that the Gingrich Senators had such an effect on the Senate because so many of them had conservative voting

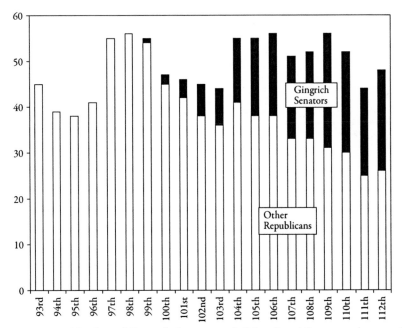

FIGURE 6.3 Number of Gingrich Senators and Other Republicans, 93rd to 112th Congresses (1974–2012).

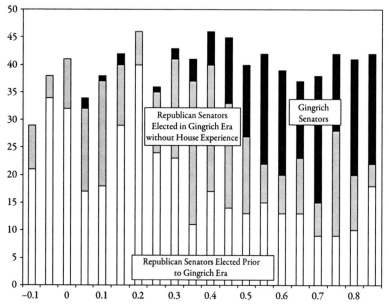

FIGURE 6.4 Ideology of Republican Senator Groupings Aggregated over Time, 93rd to 111th Congresses (1973–2010).

records and came to the Senate in such a short amount of time. While Clay, Aldrich, the liberal reformers from the 1950s and 1960s, and their acolytes had an effect on the Senate, this effect had a shorter life because their numbers never swelled as much as the Gingrich Senators' numbers have nor for as long a period. The Gingrich Senators have enjoyed the thrusts of new members regularly for more than a quarter of a century. Not only did the Gingrich Senators come in droves starting in the mid-1980s, but they have stuck around longer than their fellow Republicans.

Length of Service before Leaving

During the Gingrich Era (1979–2012), 98 Republicans have entered the Senate; the Gingrich Senators accounted for 41 (not 40, since we include Coats twice because he left the Senate and then returned 12 years later). The Gingrich Senators have had more durable careers in the Senate. Of the 98 Republicans, 43 continued to serve into the 111th Congress (2011–2012)—more than half (22) are Gingrich Senators. While 63 percent of the non–Gingrich Senators have left the chamber, only 46 percent of the Gingrich Senators have.[9]

The reasons that these Republicans have left are not dependent upon them having House experience. While 19 non–Gingrich Senators have been defeated, 8 Gingrich Senators have. Fifteen non–Gingrich Senators have voluntarily retired, 10 Gingrich Senators have; and 3 three senators, including Craig Thomas (a Gingrich Senator), died in office. The 36 non–Gingrich Senator Republicans who started and ended their Senate careers after 1978 have served an average of just under 10 years before leaving the chamber. The Gingrich Senators, on average, have served a bit more than 11 years.[10] So, not only are Gingrich Senators less likely to leave the Senate, they also are more likely to serve longer before leaving the chamber.

The Electoral Security of the Gingrich Senators

The combination of these two basic facts about the Gingrich Senators presents a finding that is fundamentally at odds with political science: Gingrich Senators, who are more extreme, have longer Senate careers. Moderate candidates are supposed to be more electorally secure. According to Downs's logic, more extreme candidates should be more easily defeated by moderate challengers of the other party in general elections. And yet, Gingrich Senators, who are more conservative than their fellow Republicans, seem to be more electorally secure.

The Downsian argument appears to work for the Republicans who are not Gingrich Senators. Consider, for a moment, the 50 most conservative Republicans who have served in the Senate since 1973—the 50th, incidentally, was Senate Majority Leader Trent Lott (R-Mississippi). Although 20 of the 50 are Gingrich Senators, only one (Rod Grams) out of the 7 who have lost their reelection efforts was a Gingrich Senator. While the non–Gingrich Senators make up 49 of the 50 most moderate Republicans during this time period, only 5 were defeated—incidentally, the only Gingrich Senator in this range, Mike DeWine, was also defeated.

This cursory analysis could be a bit misleading because we already know that Gingrich Senators are more likely to come from safer Republican territory. To see if the Gingrich Senators are, indeed, more electorally secure, we need to control for other factors that might explain security—most importantly, the partisan tilt of their constituents.[11] As table 6.3 shows, the Gingrich Senators did just slightly better than their fellow Republicans. In comparison, though, to the Republicans who entered the Senate at the same time, the Gingrich Senators do more than 5 percent better in their reelection efforts. This result assumes that the two senators come from states with the same partisan tilt.

Table 6.3 The Two-Party Vote for Republican Incumbent Senators, 1974–2010

	Republicans			Democrats	
	No House Experience	House Experience		No House Experience	House Experience
Pre-1978	0.50	0.50	Pre-1978	0.50	0.47
Post-1978	0.42	0.47	Post-1978	0.55	0.49
Gingrich Senator Effect		0.00	Gephardt Senator Effect		-0.02

In the analysis used to derive table 6.3, a senator's ideology was assumed to have the same effect on Gingrich Senators and non–Gingrich Senators. An interesting phenomenon appears when this assumption is relaxed.[12] It is true that Republican senators pay an electoral price for their extremism, though the price paid by non–Gingrich Senators is much greater than the price paid by Gingrich Senators. If there were moderate Gingrich Senators, they would do about 4 percentage points better than moderate non–Gingrich Senators (see figure 6.5). Non–Gingrich Senators with an extremism score of 0.70 are as likely to win as to lose in their reelection efforts; a Gingrich

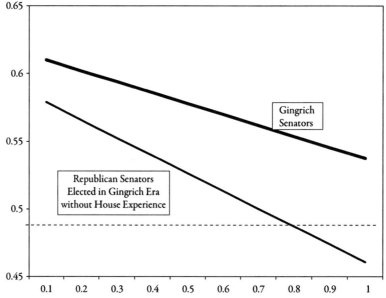

FIGURE 6.5 How the Gingrich Senators Compensate for Their Extremism, 97th to 112th Congresses (1980–2010).

Senator is still projected to get 56.2 percent of the vote. At the most extreme, Gingrich Senators do about 17 percent better than the other Republicans in their reelections. To emphasize the importance of this effect, consider that a Gingrich Senator with a 1.0 extremism score is likely to do as well in his reelection effort as a non–Gingrich Senator with a 0.40 score.

V. Conclusion

Three factors help explain why the Gingrich Senators left an indelible mark on the Senate. First, the Gingrich Senators compensated for their ideological extremism by raising more money in their electoral pursuits. After taking into consideration the other factors that would affect campaign contributions, the Gingrich Senators raised $1.14 million more than their fellow Republicans. Second, Gingrich Senators, despite their more conservative voting records, are more electorally secure than their fellow Republicans. Even when they do retire or lose, they do so later in their careers. Third, the Gingrich Senators entered the Senate in a series of elections that, when combined, resulted in an avalanche. Quite simply, their numbers rose too quickly for the Senate to absorb them and make them "Senate Men." Instead of the Senate changing the Gingrich Senators, the Gingrich Senators changed the Senate. At every stage in the electoral process, their status as Gingrich Senators seems to compensate for their more conservative voting records.

In many respects, these factors combine with the results in chapters 3, 4, and 5 to suggest that the Gingrich Senators have succeeded, to use an idiom, because the dog didn't bark. Both theoretically and empirically, political scientists have shown that ideologically extreme politicians have a harder time winning and keeping their Senate seats. The Gingrich Senators, for the most part, have not fallen victim to these findings. What they lack in political moderation, they have made up for in campaign resources.

PART III

The Gingrich Senators as Partisan Warriors

Part 2 argued that the Gingrich Senators were, indeed, primarily responsible for the increased party polarization in the Senate over the last 30 years. While their constituencies and personal characteristics help to explain a part of their increased extremism, their common experience of serving in a more partisan and confrontational House explains a much larger part. Party polarization, though, is only the first dimension—and I argue, the less important dimension—of how politicians, pundits, and political scientists characterize today's Senate.

In part 3, I explore the second dimension: partisan warrior behavior in the Senate. I show how the Gingrich Senators are not only party polarizers but also partisan warriors. The other Republicans and the Democrats, of course, have not been innocent bystanders. Though the Gingrich Senators have been instrumental in instigating and escalating the war, the other senators and the presidents are now fully engaged. This confrontation is at the root of why Americans—and retiring senators—express such displeasure with the Senate and American politics more generally.

7

Compatriots in the Battle?
The Other Republican Senators

IN THE 1994 midterm elections, Republicans attained majority party status in both the House and the Senate. Few items on the new congressional agenda achieved as much support in the public as the Balanced Budget Amendment. After cruising to passage in the House, all eyes focused on the Senate as it took up the measure in March 1995. What was clear from the proceedings on the floor was that a certain number of Democrats who had supported the amendment in 1994 were planning to switch their votes and back their embattled president, Bill Clinton, and their Senate party leadership, now toiling in the minority. Because the number of Democrats who were planning to switch their votes was in doubt, so too was the final outcome of the amendment.

The Republicans had decided that if they lost the vote, they would blame it on those Democrats who switched their votes from the previous year and accuse them of playing politics with the federal budget. The constitutional amendment ultimately lost by one vote.[1] Every Republican, except Senator Mark Hatfield (R-Oregon), voted for the amendment. Hatfield, who had supported the amendment in 1982, had voted against it in 1986 and 1994 because he thought that "'putting something in the Constitution' [would] not automatically give lawmakers the 'courage' to take the steps needed to balance the budget."[2] Out of loyalty to Majority Leader Bob Dole (R-Kansas), who was angling to take on Clinton in the 1996 presidential election, Hatfield offered to resign his seat so that only 66 votes (out of 99 senators) would be required to send the Balanced Budget Amendment to the states for certain approval. Dole refused Hatfield's offer.

Coming out of the vote, the Republican strategy of blaming the Democrats broke down as newly elected Senator Rick Santorum (R-Pennsylvania), a Gingrich Senator, criticized Hatfield, who had just taken up the chair's gavel of the Appropriations Committee when the Republicans became a majority, for his vote. In an interview with National Public Radio (NPR), Santorum commented:

> And we made promises, and it's against my conscience to allow some-
> one such as Senator Hatfield or other committee chairmen stand in
> the way and, in fact, use their chairmanship to block and thwart our
> activities. That's not why we elected him in that leadership position,
> and if you're not going to be a leader in following through with what
> agenda, I think, has clearly been articulated by the Republicans in both
> the House and the Senate, then as far as I'm concerned you may want
> to find some other position in leadership or do something else.[3]

Santorum and the fifth-ranking Republican in the Senate, Connie Mack (R-Florida), also a Gingrich Senator, began circulating a letter calling for a Republican Conference meeting to depose Hatfield as the Appropriations Committee chair. In an effort to thwart their growing momentum, Dole immediately called the meeting.

Six days after the amendment's defeat, the Senate Republicans met behind closed doors to consider Santorum and Mack's challenge to Hatfield's chair-manship. As the meeting began, it became clear that the insurgents would not have enough support to depose Hatfield even though many Republicans shared their frustration. In the end, Dole named Santorum and his 10 fellow newly elected senators—including 5 other Gingrich Senators—to a task force to make committee leaders more responsive to their party.

In July 1995 the Republican Conference adopted three watered-down pro-visions out of the original eight changes recommended by task force leader Senator Jon Kyl, who was also a Gingrich Senator. First, committee chair positions and party leadership positions (with the exception of party leader and president pro tempore) came with a six-year term limit. Second, com-mittees would take a secret ballot to nominate a committee chair. Third, the entire Republican Conference would take a secret ballot on the committees' nominees.[4]

In the end, Santorum and Mack were not successful in stripping Hatfield of his position, though the dustup signaled that the old Senate ways were coming to an end. Santorum explicitly recognized this transformation in an interview with NPR after the Republican Conference meeting:

> You know, I hear so often about the House's, you know, majority
> rules. Body of the Senate's a place where we're supposed to be more

deliberative; that the founding fathers wanted it that way, that we were supposed to be isolated from the public and not prone to swings in the public mood. Well, if that's the case, then the Senate is, in fact, doing what its traditional role has been. I'm not too sure that's truly what the Senate is supposed to be like today. That may have been what the founding fathers intended, but remember—the founding fathers had the Senate elected by the state legislatures, not by the people. When we changed that in the 19-teens, I think the country made a statement that they want the Senate, in fact, to be a little bit more responsive to the public, and we're not doing that. And I think that's to our detriment.[5]

Hatfield's retirement the following year was another indication—and, perhaps, part cause—of a newly emerging Senate.

In this chapter, I explore how the Gingrich Senators have attempted to recruit their fellow Republican senators to join them in the partisan war against the Democrats. I demonstrate this recruitment effort in a number of different ways. First, I show how the Gingrich Senators exhibit a pack mentality. Second, I show how they have transformed the Republican Conference in the Senate. Third, I show how they have transformed, more broadly, the Republican Party.

I walk a delicate line in making these arguments. If I show that the Gingrich Senators are distinct from the other Republicans, then I weaken my case that they have transformed the Republican Conference. If, on the other hand, I show that they, almost single-handedly, transformed the Republican Conference, then I weaken my case in this book that the Gingrich Senators are distinctive and that they have transformed the Senate. I walk this line by showing that the overwhelming systematic evidence points to the distinctiveness of the Gingrich Senators, at least in the beginning of the transformation. On occasion, they have recruited the other Republicans to join the partisan war. This chapter shows how and to what extent that recruitment has taken place.

I. The Pack Mentality among the Gingrich Senators

In chapter 3 I showed how the Gingrich Senators drove the polarization over the last 30 years. In this section I show in a number of steps how they have initiated, engaged, and escalated the partisan war. First, I show the high degree of support that the Gingrich Senators give their fellow members on their amendments. Second, in utilizing a non-roll-call-related measure, I show that the Gingrich Senators are more likely to cosponsor legislation introduced by other Gingrich Senators than they are to cosponsor legislation introduced by the other Republican senators. Third, I turn to a nonlegislative measure altogether. The Gingrich Senators are more likely to contribute to the other Gingrich Senators than they are to the other Republican senators, especially at the early stages of the campaign.

A. Pack Mentality on Amendment Voting

The Republicans were at a substantial disadvantage in the 111th Congress (2009–2010). Not only was a Democrat, Barack Obama, in the White House, but the Republicans were outnumbered by as many as 70 seats in the House and 20 seats in the Senate. The Democrats had not been as powerful on Capitol Hill since Watergate decimated the Republicans in the mid-1970s. Once Arlen Specter became a Democrat (on April 29, 2009) and Al Franken was declared the winner of a highly contested race in Minnesota (on July 7, 2009), the Democrats enjoyed a filibuster-proof margin until Scott Brown was sworn in to finish Ted Kennedy's term (on February 4, 2010). Such overwhelming opposition meant that the Republicans on Capitol Hill had very little ability to pass their favored legislation. Their only legislative hope was to put the brakes on Obama and the congressional Democrats.

The Republicans in the Senate quickly developed a strategy to slow down the legislative process. In the following chapter, I explain it in more detail, but it goes by the name "Death by Amendment." Because the Senate floor operates by unanimous consent, any senator has the power to bring the Senate to its knees. An explicit strategy of filibustering, which is holding the floor and not relinquishing it, would come across as unseemly especially if it were tried too frequently. A less impolitic strategy has senators introducing many amendments. Because each amendment requires debate and, if the Senate so decides, a roll-call vote, "Death by Amendment" has the same effect as filibustering without some of the more negative qualities.

Endlessly introducing amendments has an additional positive quality for the minority. A shrewdly written amendment can divide the majority party, so that electorally vulnerable senators are forced to cast a vote in favor of their party leadership or in accord with their constituents. If the minority can showcase an unappealing roll-call record to a senator's constituents, and if they do it enough, the minority party may some day become the majority.

In the 111th Congress, the Gingrich Senators, though comprising just 18 percent of the Senate, were responsible for introducing amendments that caused 51.3 percent of the roll-call votes taken on amendments.[6] Although the other Republicans outnumbered the Gingrich Senators, their amendments caused only 19.5 percent of the roll-call votes on amendments. Again, in the following chapter, I outline the "Death by Amendment" strategy in greater detail. In this chapter, I discuss the Gingrich Senators' amending activity only to showcase their pack mentality.

DW-NOMINATE scores characterize members' voting behavior on all nonconsensual roll-call votes. A similar methodology can be used to characterize voting behavior on amendment votes only or, even, on roll-call votes resulting from Gingrich Senators' amendments. These scores can be thought of as ideology scores (or extremism scores if we take their absolute value), as revealed by votes only on a particular subset of votes. If we restrict the analysis to the 210 roll-call votes resulting from the Gingrich Senators' amendments and the 80 votes resulting from the other Republicans' amendments, we can see how much more distinctive the Gingrich Senators vote on their fellow Gingrich Senators' amendments than they do on the other Republicans' amendments. Whereas the Gingrich Senator Effect on the other Republicans' amendments is only 11 percent, it is double that percentage on their own amendments (see table 7.1).[7]

This analysis provides insight into the partisan war and the strategy the Gingrich Senators use to wage it. The results from table 7.1 show that the Gingrich Senators vote more distinctly when voting on amendments offered by one of their own than when voting on amendments offered by other Republicans. The distinction cannot have at its roots the senators' constituents or personal characteristics or even an ideological explanation. Only two factors distinguish the amendments analyzed on the left side of the table from the right side: the amendments' sponsors and their content. Even though the analysis cannot distinguish between the two, it shows that an additional

Table 7.1 Amendment Voting by the Gingrich Senators, 111th Congress (2009–2010)

	On Other Republicans' Amendments			On Gingrich Senators' Amendments	
	No House Experience	House Experience		No House Experience	House Experience
Pre-1978	0.64	0.72	Pre-1978	0.33	0.53
Post-1978	0.68	0.80	Post-1978	0.43	0.66
Gingrich Senator Effect		0.11	Gingrich Senator Effect		0.23

dimension beyond ideology motivates the Gingrich Senators' behavior. It is this additional motivator that undergirds the Gingrich Senators' roles as partisan warriors.

B. The Pack Mentality on Cosponsoring Legislation

The Gingrich Senators exhibit a pack mentality not only on roll-call votes resulting from the amendments that they introduce but also in offering non-roll-call-vote support on legislation. When members of Congress introduce legislation, they frequently invite their colleagues to "cosponsor" the measure as a sign of support to either the sponsor or the piece of legislation. While most cosponsors are added to legislation at the time of or shortly after the legislation is introduced, a member may join as a cosponsor at any point in the legislative process.

Unlike roll-call votes, which can be fraught with legislative procedures and downstream implication, cosponsorship has been thought of as being either the first opportunity for members to take a formal position (Talbert and Potoski 2002) or the truest form of preference revelation in the legislative process (Krehbiel 1995; Kessler and Krehbiel 1996; Woon 2008).[8] Political scientists have used cosponsorship data to glean insight into many things, including the personal relationships among legislators, a proposal's ideological tilt, a bill's likelihood of passing, or a legislator's influence in the chamber (see, e.g., Campbell 1982; Panning 1982; Browne and Ringquist 1985; Schiller 1995).

James Fowler (2006a, 2006b) has analyzed these cosponsor data to understand the networks that operate in the House and Senate. In so doing, he codes every cosponsor on every bill to develop a "connectedness" measure that exists between two legislators. His data set begins in the 100th Congress (1987–1988) and ends in the 108th Congress (2003–2004). I used these scores in chapter 5 to analyze the closeness between the Gingrich Senators and Newt Gingrich when they served together in the House. These connectedness scores can be used to analyze another facet of the Gingrich Senators' behavior in the legislative process. I analyze the Gingrich Senators' networks by examining their cosponsorship on bills introduced by both other Gingrich Senators and the other Republicans.

The Gingrich Senators are not always more likely to support legislation introduced by fellow Gingrich Senators than legislation introduced by other Republican senators. Their support is contingent on whether the Democrats constitute a Senate majority (see table 7.2). In the congresses when the Republicans have had a majority in the Senate (104th, 105th, 106th, and 108th),

Table 7.2 The Amount of Support the Gingrich Senators Give the Gingrich Senators and Other Republicans, 102nd to 108th Congresses (1991–2004).

| | Support from Gingrich Senators to: | | | |
	Gingrich Senators	Other Republicans	Difference	Statistical Significance
102nd	2.85	1.01	1.84	0.054
103rd	1.08	0.78	0.30	0.005
104th	1.04	0.99	0.05	0.208
105th	0.96	0.97	0.00	0.476
106th	1.02	1.14	−0.11	0.236
107th	1.30	1.14	0.16	0.189
108th	1.02	1.07	−0.05	0.194
When Democrats are a Majority (102, 103, and 107)			0.77	
When Republicans are a Majority (104, 105, 106, and 108)			−0.03	

the Gingrich Senators have been more supportive of other Republicans' legislation than that of their fellow Gingrich Senators. In the three congresses (102nd, 103rd, and 107th) when at least five Gingrich Senators have served under a Democratic majority, their connectedness score to fellow Gingrich Senators is 0.77 greater than it is to the other Republican senators. When they are in the majority, they are −0.03 less supportive of their fellow Gingrich Senators than they are of the other Republicans.

When the Republicans are most negatively situated in the Senate, it seems as though the Gingrich Senators' behavior becomes most distinct. When they are part of the majority party, their behavior, at least as measured by their cosponsorship activity, is not that different from the other Republicans.

C. Leadership PAC Mentality

Few appointments to vacant Senate seats have been as controversial as the one created when Senator Barack Obama won the 2008 presidential election. In the now-famous words of the sitting Illinois governor, Rod Blagojevich (D-Illinois), who had the power to name Obama's successor: "This is f – -ing golden."[9] By the end of the story, Blagojevich not only was not the sitting governor but was sitting in federal prison. Although Roland Burris got the appointment, he would prove to be only a caretaker until the voters in Illinois would elect a new senator in the 2010 elections.

On July 20, 2009, Congressman Mark Kirk, a Republican from Highland Park, a suburb of Chicago, announced that he was running for the seat. Although he did not face a serious threat in the Republican primary, his former House colleagues who had moved on to the Senate were strident supporters. In the primary phase of the campaign he raised $37,500 from the Gingrich Senators. That the Gingrich Senators would support one of their own is not unusual, but Kirk had a different House career than most of them. As a leader of the moderate House Republicans' Tuesday Group, he led the outreach movement to the Blue Dogs, a group of moderate Democrats. Even before these more formalized meetings, Kirk had a long record of working across the aisle. Nonetheless, the Gingrich Senators contributed handsomely to his Senate race. By the time of the November election, Kirk had amassed $87,500 from the Gingrich Senators and an additional $137,400 from the other sitting Republican senators. In the end, many different explanations could be offered for why Kirk prevailed by two percentage points. No doubt, the early contributions he received from the Gingrich Senators that in part deterred other qualified candidates from entering the Republican primary, permitting him to save his financial resources for the general election, surely helped.

The source of the Gingrich Senator money to Kirk came in the form of contributions from Leadership PACs, which the Federal Election Commission (FEC) defines as nonconnected PACs established "by a candidate or an individual holding federal office, but is not an authorized committee of the candidate or officeholder and is not affiliated with an authorized committee of a candidate or officeholder."[10] Leadership PACs came into existence as a source for party leaders to contribute campaign resources to the rank-and-file members. As the ranks of members who formed Leadership PACs extended down the leadership ladders in both parties, the purpose of Leadership PACs transformed from one where a party leader helps out members in their party to one where a potential leader demonstrates their party loyalty and fundraising bona fides in hopes of obtaining a leadership position (Theriault 2008).

In the beginning, only party leaders had Leadership PACs but over time, most members developed them to enhance their reputations on Capitol Hill. In the 2010 election cycle, 397 different Leadership PACs doled out more than $41 million.[11] Eighty-seven senators serving in the 111th Congress (2009–2010) had a Leadership PAC; in total, they accounted for almost $14 million in contributions (84 percent of which went to Senate candidates). Although the first senator on the list of members with the highest contributions was only fourteenth (Mitch McConnell), senators accounted for 21 of the next 36 spots, including five Gingrich Senators—Burr (17), Kyl (21), Chambliss (35), Thune (43), and McCain (50).

Neither Newt Gingrich nor the Gingrich Senators were the innovators or earliest users of Leadership PACs. In 1988 Gramm and McCain became the first Gingrich Senators to establish Leadership PACs, though both distributed relatively little money. The number of Gingrich Senator Leadership PACs and the amount that they have contributed has grown (see figure 7.1). In the 2010 election cycle all 19 Gingrich Senators had Leadership PACs and they contributed \$2.8 million (86 percent of which went to candidates in Senate races). The data from the Gingrich Senators is not appreciably different from the other Republicans. In the last three election cycles, the Gingrich Senators contributed 48 percent, 40 percent, and 42 percent of the total Republican senator contributions, respectively, when they comprised 45 percent, 42 percent, and 43 percent of the Republican Conferences.

While the growth of the Gingrich Senators' Leadership PACs has not been out of the ordinary, the contributions that they have made to Senate candidates have been striking. From 1998 to 2010, the Gingrich Senators gave 47 percent of their contributions to either Gingrich Senators or would-be Gingrich Senators. The other Republican senators gave only 3 percent less to

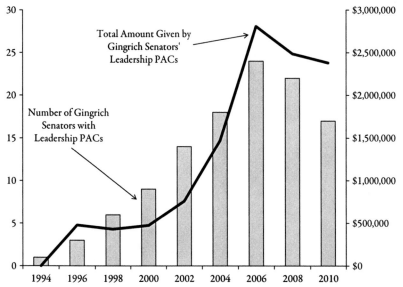

FIGURE 7.1: The Number of Gingrich Senators with Leadership PACs and the Amount They Gave, 1994–2010.

the same set of candidates. Even though this percentage is relatively small, it meant that the Gingrich Senators contributed roughly $400,000 more to Gingrich Senators or would-be Gingrich Senators than if they had divided their money in the same proportion as the other Republican senators.

These aggregate numbers combine contributions made to safe incumbent members as well as those challengers who are either seeking an open seat or challenging an incumbent Democrat (or, in rare instances, challenging an incumbent Republican). The aggregated proportions for these challengers does not differ appreciably from the overall numbers discussed above, but they do hide a more concerted effort among the Gingrich Senators to increase their numbers in particular election cycles (see table 7.3). In the 2000, 2002, and 2004 cycles, the Gingrich Senators gave a disproportionately larger share from their Leadership PACs to would-be Gingrich Senators. In each of those election cycles, they gave about 10 percent more to would-be Gingrich Senators than they did to Republican challengers who did not serve in the House.

Table 7.3 Republican Senator Leadership PAC Contributions to Senate Candidates with House Experience, 1998–2010

Election Year	All Senate Candidates with House Experience			All Senate Challengers with House Experience		
	Other Republicans	Gingrich Senators	Difference	Other Republicans	Gingrich Senators	Difference
1998	$303,581 (29.1%)	$120,187 (29.2%)	0.1%	$172,472 (16.5%)	$73,000 (17.7%)	1.2%
2000	$658,430 (41.7%)	$245,406 (52.1%)	10.4%	$371,510 (23.5%)	$154,000 (32.7%)	9.2%
2002	$976,140 (45.6%)	$416,556 (57.3%)	11.7%	$570,498 (26.7%)	$285,122 (39.2%)	12.6%
2004	$1,366,209 (50.6%)	$857,702 (58.3%)	7.7%	$935,293 (34.6%)	$685,011 (46.5%)	11.9%
2006	$1,386,843 (45.2%)	$1,360,624 (49.9%)	4.7%	$242,100 (7.9%)	$236,750 (8.7%)	0.8%
2008	$1,410,000 (36.3%)	$929,348 (36.9%)	0.7%	$430,500 (11.1%)	$297,000 (11.8%)	0.7%
2010	$1,616,606 (49.4%)	$1,162,999 (48.1%)	−1.3%	$792,106 (24.2%)	$613,500 (25.4%)	1.2%
1998–2010	$7,729,809 (43.6%)	$5,093,322 (47.4%)	3.8%	$3,514,479 (19.8%)	$2,344,383 (21.8%)	2.0%

In the 2006, 2008, and 2010 cycles, though, the Gingrich Senators gave to would-be Gingrich Senators at about the same proportion as the other Republicans in the Senate. Part of the explanation for the 2006 and 2008 cycles is that relatively few would-be Gingrich Senators ran in these elections when Democrats were expected to do—and did—well. Only three would-be Gingrich Senators ran in 2006 (and one lost in the primary) and four ran in 2008 (again, one lost in the primary). All seven would-be Gingrich Senators who made it to the general election in these two cycles lost.

The 2010 cycle's explanation is a bit different regarding both the general electoral climate and the numbers that ran. Nine would-be Gingrich Senators ran in 2010. Two were defeated in the primaries—Todd Tiahrt lost to Gingrich Senator Jerry Moran in Kansas and Mike Castle lost to Christine O'Donnell in Delaware. The seven who made it to the general election all won. Six of these seven received campaign contributions from between 23 and 31 senators' Leadership PACs.[12] In each case, at most three contributors did not contribute the maximum amount under the law for either the primary or general election. Only the following five senators varied from the maximum permitted under the law:

- George LeMieux (R-Florida) only gave $2,400 to each of the six.
- Judd Gregg gave $2,500 to Blunt and the maximum ($5,000) to Coats.
- Lisa Murkowski (R-Alaska) gave $2,500 to Portman and Blunt.
- Pat Roberts gave $2,000 to Moran and the maximum to Blunt, Coats, and Portman.
- Chuck Grassley (R-Iowa) gave $2,000 to Portman, $2,500 to Coats, and the maximum to Blunt and Kirk

Given the consistency of contributions in the 2010 cycle it was difficult to distinguish their giving because almost all senators with meaningful Leadership PACs contributed the maximum that they could to all of the would-be Gingrich Senators as well as the other Republican candidates who were running in competitive races.

While the overall amounts contributed by the Gingrich Senators and the other Republicans to the soon-to-be Gingrich Senators cannot be differentiated, the timing of their contributions can. According to the campaign finance laws in place at the time, each Leadership PAC could contribute $10,000 to each Senate candidate per election—$5,000 for the primary and $5,000 for the general election.[13] During the primary season, the Gingrich Senators gave them almost half of the money (47.7 percent) that they received in the primary from sitting Republican senators (see table 7.4). From the primary to the general election, the Gingrich Senators contributed more than one-third (36.4 percent) of the money that the soon-to-be Gingrich Senators received from the Leadership PACs of sitting senators. The differential between the proportion that the Gingrich Senators gave in the primary and the proportion that they gave in the general election was 11.3 percent.

The differential between the two elections was particularly great for four soon-to-be Gingrich Senators: Boozman, Coats, Kirk, and Moran. These four had the hardest primaries of all seven soon-to-be Gingrich Senators. The lowest differential of the four was 12.4 percent for Kirk, who, again of the four, had the easiest primary. These data strongly suggest that the Gingrich Senators came to the rescue most disproportionately to the would-be Gingrich Senators who were in the toughest primaries.[14]

The data in table 7.4 reveal one other interesting fact about the contributions that Gingrich Senators made from the Leadership PACs in the 2010 election cycle. The Gingrich Senators only contributed $50,000 to two of the seven soon-to-be Gingrich Senators in the general election phase of the campaign. These two—Blunt and Kirk—had two of the three most competitive general election contests. The other soon-to-be Gingrich Senator with a tough general election contest was Pat Toomey, whose relationship to the Gingrich Senators—or at least one Gingrich Senator—was critical not only in his election but also in explaining the entire dynamics of the 111th Congress.

D. Pat Toomey

In 2004, when Pat Toomey challenged Arlen Specter (R-Pennsylvania) in the Republican primary, he came within 28,000 votes of pulling off a major upset. Specter enjoyed a substantial fundraising advantage and the support of most of the key Republicans, including President George W. Bush and Pennsylvania's other senator, Rick Santorum (a Gingrich Senator). Toomey's only notable support was the Club for Growth, who labeled Specter a RINO (a **R**epublican **I**n **N**ame **O**nly).

On March 18, 2009, Specter announced that he would seek a sixth term in the U.S. Senate. He was even more vulnerable in the Republican Party this time around because he had joined with two other Republicans (Susan Collins and Olympia Snowe) in voting for Obama's stimulus package in February. As the calls for his removal from office increased among Pennsylvania Republicans, Specter was defiant about staying in the Republican Party: "To eliminate any doubt, I am a Republican, and I am running for reelection in 2010 as a

Table 7.4 Leadership PAC Contributions to 2010 Class of Gingrich Senators

| | Primary Season | | | General Election | | | | | |
| | Contributions by: | | | Contributions by: | | | | | |
	Gingrich Senators	Other Republicans	Percentage from Gingrich Senators	Gingrich Senators	Other Republicans	Percentage from Gingrich Senators	Differential Between Primary and General Election	Primary Victory Margin	General Election Victory Margin
Blunt	$57,500	$108,500	34.6%	$57,400	$50,820	53.0%	-18.4%	57.8%	14.5%
Boozman	$20,000	$7,500	72.7%	$36,000	$78,890	31.3%	41.4%	35.2%	22.3%
Coats	$37,500	$35,000	51.7%	$34,900	$61,000	36.4%	15.3%	10.3%	15.5%
Kirk	$37,500	$42,500	46.9%	$50,000	$94,900	34.5%	12.4%	37.3%	2.1%
Moran	$15,000	$10,000	60.0%	$26,500	$50,000	34.6%	25.4%	5.2%	45.8%
Portman	$70,000	$103,400	40.4%	$32,500	$39,500	45.1%	-4.8%	100.0%	19.0%
Toomey	$51,000	$55,000	48.1%	$34,000	$49,796	40.6%	7.5%	63.0%	2.0%
Total	$231,000	$253,400	47.7%	$213,900	$374,086	36.4%	11.3%		

Republican on the Republican ticket."[15] Senate Republicans rallied to Specter's cause. By April 1, Specter had already collected $68,500 from Republican senators' Leadership PACs (incidentally, only 25 percent of which came from Gingrich Senators).

To no one's surprise, Toomey announced, on April 15, that he would again challenge Specter in the Republican Primary. On that news, Specter's campaign released a statement arguing that the Republicans would be foolish to support Toomey in the primary because if Toomey were victorious in the primary, the Republicans would surely lose their crucial 41st seat and with it any hopes of stopping Obama and the Democrats' agenda as a united Democratic caucus could invoke cloture without the support of a single Republican.

Eight days after Toomey's announcement, Senator Jim DeMint, who had sat out the 2004 primary, told Specter that Toomey would get not only DeMint's endorsement but also access to his nationwide list of contributors.[16] Three days later, Specter switched parties and the Republicans lost their crucial 41st vote. With Specter's switch, the Democrats had a filibuster-proof margin in the Senate, which would last until Scott Brown's victory the following January.

The timeline from the Specter-Toomey contest suggests that at least one senator—Jim DeMint—was critical not only in helping Toomey win Specter's seat but also equally helpful in handing the Democrats the needed 60th vote to break Republican-led filibusters, many by DeMint himself. While it is difficult to parse all of the financial records to show a distinct pack mentality among the Gingrich Senators, the data suggest that the Gingrich Senators' behavior, again, becomes most distinct when the threat is most real, whether the threat comes in the primary or in the general election.

II. Transforming the Republican Conference

The Gingrich Senators are distinct from the other Republicans serving in the Senate. Broadly, they cast different roll-call votes, they systematically differ in their cosponsorship patterns, and they contribute to electoral campaigns differently and at different times. Some of these distinctions hold up over time. On other matters, the Gingrich Senators have been successful in transforming the Republican Conference. In this section, I outline two of these transformations. First, I show how, over a number of years, the Gingrich Senators have recast the entire debate surrounding the debt ceiling. Second, I show how, over a couple of months, they changed the congressional debate on extending federal unemployment benefits.

A. Raising the Debt Ceiling

From time to time, members of Congress have to take unpalatable votes to maintain the institution. These include raising congressional pay, reforming the congressional pension system, and deciding on the level of staff to help them carry out their duties. Such votes can be used by future opponents as evidence that the members have feathered their own nests. Other times, members have to take unpalatable votes to maintain the economic system of the United States. Raising the debt ceiling is one such vote.

Votes to increase the debt limit of the United States present members with a classic prisoner's dilemma. No member likes to cast a vote in favor of the legislation because it does not spend one penny on enriching domestic programs or protecting the country. It merely raises the amount that the federal government can borrow, making it akin to consumers' limits on their credit cards. A vote in favor of raising the limit does not result in any additional spending—or purchases, if you will. The problem with voting for it is that future opponents have evidence of Congress's financial profligacy and those who enabled it. All members would like to vote against it, but if they all do, the country could go into default, which could have dire economic consequences not only on the United States but also the world financial markets. Solving this prisoner's dilemma has taken various forms.

The House, under the leadership of Representative Dick Gephardt (D-Missouri), came up with, perhaps, the most ingenious solution. In 1979 Speaker Tip O'Neill tasked Gephardt, then a relatively junior member, to manage the debt-ceiling bill for the Democrats. He went from member to member asking them to cast a vote whose only possible effect would be to place their reelection in jeopardy. In consultation with the House Parliamentarian, Gephardt devised a standing rule of the House that upon the adoption of the conference report on the budget, the House was to have "deemed" the debt ceiling raised to accommodate the newly enacted budget. The rule, in actuality, automatically triggers the "engrossment and transmittal to the Senate of a joint resolution changing the debt limit" (Heniff 2008, 1). By tying the debt limit to the budget, Gephardt spared the members the difficult vote of singularly raising the debt limit. The Senate never adopted the Gephardt Rule, so it has always had to explicitly pass debt-limit bills.

As a way to manage the difficult vote in the Senate during the era of the Gephardt Rule in the House, the senators employed a number of different strategies. First, both parties sought political cover by ensuring that the other party had to cast some votes in favor of it. Second, senators who were electorally safer cast the difficult votes to spare their more electorally vulnerable colleagues. Third, senators who were recently reelected—and hence, not facing the voters again for a number of years—voted for the bill to spare the senators who faced the voters more immediately.

As evidence of these multiple strategies, even in 1980, when the Democrats controlled the House, Senate, and White House and in the midst of a competitive presidential race that would ultimately see the Republicans win the White House and a majority in the Senate, the Democrats were able to secure eight Republican votes in the Senate for raising the debt ceiling. The votes cast by the respective party members yields a number that can characterize how divided the parties were on the particular vote. If 100 percent of Democrats and 100 percent of Republicans voted to raise the debt ceiling, the party difference score would be 0. If 100 percent of Democrats voted against 100 percent of the Republicans then the party difference score would be 1. On this particular vote in 1980 when 83 percent of Democrats voted with 21 percent of Republicans to increase the debt ceiling, the party difference score was 0.62. Figure 7.2 shows the party difference scores for the 48 Senate votes since 1980.[17] One-third of these votes (16) were either voice votes or the measure was passed through unanimous consent. Both of these legislative maneuvers suggest that the parties were perfectly cooperating to increase the debt limit because it only takes 11 senators to force a roll-call vote and only one senator to object to a unanimous consent agreement.

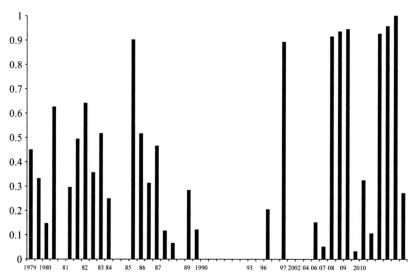

FIGURE 7.2: Party Difference Scores on the 48 Votes to Raise the Debt Limit, 1979–2010.

Only once in the next 14 years did a party contribute less than eight votes in favor of raising the debt ceiling. Less than a month before the 1984 elections, all the Democrats who were present voted against it, forcing Republicans to come up with all of the necessary votes to pass it. Even on this vote, however, the parties may have coordinated their efforts, as the Democrats only mustered 26 "no" votes—the party's other 18 senators did not vote, even though 14 of them cast votes earlier in the day. In the 31 times that the limit was raised from 1979 to 1992, all but once the party difference score was below 0.70.

The debt limit increases in 1989 and 1990 were the last round before the Senate entered a new era of raising the debt limit. With Democratic majorities in the House and Senate and President George H. W. Bush in the White House, the conditions were ripe for bipartisanship. The Senate took eight voice votes, perhaps the epitome of bipartisanship, to raise the debt limit either permanently (once) or temporarily (seven times) in 1989 and 1990. The Senate took a roll-call vote on the ninth increase, which was rolled into the budget reconciliation bill. Thirty-five Democrats joined 19 Republicans to pass the debt-limit increase. Four of the votes against the bipartisan compromise came from the four Gingrich Senators who served during the 101st Congress. Even though they only comprised less than 10 percent of the Republican Conference, they supplied 16 percent of the votes against the compromise.

Beginning in 1993, the bipartisan consensus that had reigned in the Senate on debt-limit votes disappeared. When it was raised as part of a broader budget bill in the first year of the Clinton administration, every Republican voted against it. This scenario of the Democrats tying the debt-limit increase to larger issues and the Republicans, en bloc, voting against it ushered in a new era of debt-limit politics. Since 1993, the debt limit has been raised 8 times under partisan warfare and 9 times through bipartisan compromise. In the 31 times that it was raised in the earlier time period, it was never tied to a matter that was only indirectly related to the debt limit. Since 1993, it has been part of a larger package 6 times.

Two years after the 1993 increase, the debt was reaching its limit. In order for it to be increased again, President Clinton would have to compromise with Republican majorities in the House and Senate. The Republicans, primarily in the House, wanted to use the must-pass legislation to enact much of its agenda that had been stalled by Clinton's opposition and Senate Democrats' threatening filibusters. Speaker Gingrich explained his strategy: "I don't care what the price is. I don't care if we have no executive offices, no bonds for 60 days.... What we are saying to Clinton is: Do not assume that we will flinch, because we won't."[18] When the House-passed bill made its way to the Senate, despite every Democrat voted against it, the Republicans mustered enough votes to pass it. Clinton vetoed the bill. Rather than causing economic malady, the veto did not have drastic consequences because Treasury Secretary Robert Rubin engaged in some tricky bookkeeping practices to keep the debt under the existing limit.

With the 1995 fiasco still in mind, the 1996 and 1997 increases—as well as the one in 2002—reverted back to the old Senate bipartisanship on the debt limit. On each of these votes, though, the Gingrich Senators voted disproportionately against the bipartisan compromise relative to the other Republican Senators. In 2003, 2004, and 2006, with Republicans controlling Congress and the White House, the Democrats overwhelmingly voted against the increases. With the increase in 2007 and the two increases in 2008, when the government was again divided—Bush in the White House and Democratic majorities in Congress—bipartisanship ruled the day. During these debates, though, the old rule of protecting vulnerable senators was sacrificed on the altar of the Gingrich Senators. Although the Gingrich Senators comprised only 45 percent of the Republican Conference, and represented friendlier Republican territory, they cast 65, 54, and 67 percent of the Republican votes against the bipartisan agreements.

As early as the 101st Congress, when only four of them were serving, the Gingrich Senators helped transform the debt-limit ceiling from an issue that garnered bipartisan support into one that became the battleground of the partisan war. The Gingrich Senators were at the forefront of making the debt-limit increases fodder for electoral campaigns. When they were not successful in making the issues partisan, they were sure to line up against the bipartisan agreement in numbers greater than their numbers would suggest. The transformation of this issue from bipartisan to partisan did not happen all at one time. The hand of the Gingrich Senators, though, is present at every step. The transformation of the extension of unemployment benefits happened much more quickly and the role of the Gingrich Senators—or at least one Gingrich Senator—is much more explicit.

B. The 2010 Extension of Federal Unemployment Benefits

In normal economic times, the unemployed have access to 26 weeks of unemployment insurance benefits in a program run by the states and overseen by the Labor Department. During economic downturns, Congress has enacted legislation to extend the time that the unemployed can receive the benefits in a program paid for entirely by the federal government. In the wake of the

9–11 attacks on the United States and the economic turmoil that followed, Congress enacted and President Bush signed such an extension in 2002 and 2003, but as the economy regained its footing, the extension lapsed.

As the economy faltered in 2008, a Republican Congress and a Republican president again extended the unemployment benefit twice. Neither extension was particularly contentious, though a few Republicans voted against the extension because it covered too many people and was too generous. The first extension, which passed in June, had to first survive a point of order from Coburn, which it did on a motion to waive the budget rules, 77–21, before the motion to concur with the House on the extension passed, 92–6. Congress passed the second extension in a lame duck session after the 2008 elections. The key vote in the Senate came on a motion to invoke cloture, which passed 89–6. On each of these three votes, the Gingrich Senators provided a disproportionate number of "no" votes (see table 7.5).

The unemployment benefits were extended again in the 2009 economic stimulus bill that became law in February. The Senate passed the bill 60–38. Due to the many other controversial items in the bill, the Senate spent very little time on the unemployment extension and did not take even a single vote that focused exclusively on it. Congress passed two additional extensions in 2009. In November, the Senate passed a bill, 98–0, that again extended the federal benefit to jobless workers. The following month, they rolled another extension of unemployment benefits into the defense appropriations bill, which passed, 88–10. Again, the Gingrich Senators provided a disproportionate number of "no" votes.

The defense appropriation extension was set to expire on February 28. Senate Majority Leader Reid and Minority Leader McConnell had agreed to a 30-day extension. When Reid sought unanimous consent to codify their agreement on February 25, to everyone's surprise, Senator Jim Bunning, a Gingrich Senator, objected. His objection was particularly meaningful because of its timing. Cloture can only be invoked two days after the motion has been introduced and then only after an additional 30 hours of debate (Davis 2011). Bunning's objection would mean that the unemployment benefit could not be extended until after the February 28 deadline had passed.

Bunning was not opposed to the extension per se, he just did not want the costs of the extension to add to the deficit. While several Republicans complained about the price tag of the extension, no one other than Bunning thought that they should be offset by reductions elsewhere in the budget. In fact, up through the defense appropriation extension, the very idea of even using spending cuts was not part of the conversation surrounding the

Table 7.5 Key Votes in the Extension of the Unemployment Benefit, 2008–2010

Date	Legislative Action	Total		Democrats		Republicans		Other Republicans			Gingrich Senators			
		Yes	No	Yes	No	Yes	No	Yes	No	% Yes	Yes	No	% Yes	Dif.
2008														
June 26	Motion to waive Coburn point of order	77	21	49	1	28	20	22	7	75.9%	6	13	31.6%	44.3%
June 26	Motion to concur in House Amendments	92	6	50	0	42	6	28	1	96.6%	14	5	73.7%	22.9%
Nov. 20	Motion to invoke cloture	89	6	48	0	41	6	24	3	88.9%	17	3	85.0%	3.9%
2009														
Feb. 13	Final passage of Stimulus Bill	60	38	57	0	3	38	3	19	13.6%	0	19	0.0%	13.6%
Nov. 4	Final passage of Unemployment Benefit Extension	98	0	58	0	40	0	21	0	0.0%	19	0	0.0%	0.0%
Dec. 19	Final passage of Defense Appropriations Bill with Unemployment Benefit Extension	88	10	58	1	30	9	18	3	85.7%	12	6	66.7%	19.0%
2010														
March 2	Bunning Amendment	43	53	4	53	39	0	21	0	100.0%	18	0	100.0%	0.0%
March 2	Final passage of Unemployment Benefit Extension	78	19	55	0	21	19	11	11	50.0%	10	8	55.6%	5.6%
June 24	Motion to invoke cloture	58	38	56	2	2	36	2	19	9.5%	0	17	0.0%	9.5%
July 20	Motion to invoke cloture	60	40	58	1	2	39	2	21	8.7%	0	18	0.0%	8.7%
Dec. 15	Final passage of Unemployment Benefit Extension as part of larger Tax Rate Extension Package	81	19	44	14	37	5	20	2	90.9%	17	3	85.0%	5.9%

unemployment extension, which had previously been considered "emergency" appropriations and, hence, off-budget.

Once Bunning announced his objection, both parties tried to both cajole him and, at different times, bludgeon him. Majority Whip Dick Durbin (D-Illinois) implored Republicans to convince Bunning that "this doesn't make anybody look good—the Senate or [the Republican] party and it's hurting a lot of innocent people."[19] At times Bunning was defiant, like when he shouted, "Tough sh-t!" when Senator Jeff Merkley (D-Oregon) pleaded with him to drop his objection.[20] On Friday and over the weekend, Democrats and Republicans tried to bring Bunning back into the fold, but with no success. Reid even offered him the ability to introduce his amendment to pay for the extension with money that had already been allocated in the stimulus. Bunning rejected the offer because he "knew it would not get the amount of votes necessary to pay for it."[21]

On Tuesday morning, Senator Susan Collins (R-Maine) took a turn at trying to persuade Bunning to relent. She was doing so on behalf of herself and "numerous" other Republican senators. She ended her floor speech by saying, "Madam President, I hope that we can act together for the American people, and again I want to emphasize that this issue is so important to Senators on both sides of the aisle."[22] Not only did Bunning still object, but he read a letter complimenting him for taking a principled stand and ridiculing McConnell for not having "the backbone or [the] sense of decency when it comes to keeping [his] promises to the American people."[23]

Later in the day, the pressure on Bunning became too great. After his amendment went down to defeat, 43–53, the unemployment benefit extension passed, 78–19; all the votes opposing final passage were from Republicans, including eight Gingrich Senators.

On June 2, Congress again extended the unemployment benefit. What had been the position of a lone filibusterer in February turned out to be the starting position of the Republican Party three months later. All but four Republicans—none of whom were Gingrich Senators—sided with Coburn who had taken up the Bunning mantle for this round of the unemployment extension. The transformation of the Republican Party over a couple of months was not lost on congressional observers. In the lead on his story of the extension, Perry Bacon of the *Washington Post* wrote:

> In February, when unpredictable Jim Bunning single-handedly stalled extensions of unemployment benefits for several days, his Republican colleagues quickly abandoned him, worried that the GOP would be cast as the party against helping people out of work.

Last month, as jobless benefits were again set to expire, Bunning (Ky.) still objected to funding them in a way that would increase the deficit. But this time, nearly every Republican in the Senate joined him, leading to a month-long impasse in which more than 2 million people briefly lost their benefits. When the extension finally passed last week, only two Republicans backed the $34 billion unemployment measure, compared with 21 who had voted with Democrats in March.[24]

The Congress passed two additional unemployment benefit extensions in 2010—one in July and the other in a lame duck session after the 2010 election, as part of the major year-end tax package that extended the Bush tax cuts for two years. Both debates had the parties reprising their roles from the June extension. What is clear from the debate on the unemployment benefit extension from 2008 to 2010 is the power of one Gingrich Senator in transforming not only the other Gingrich Senators but almost the entire Republican Party.

III. Conclusion

Some distinctions between the Gingrich Senators and the other Republican senators have disappeared as the Gingrich Senators have staked out a position that eventually has been adopted by the entire Republican Conference. Where bipartisanship once ruled the day on raising the debt limit, now these votes have become the most fertile ground for partisan warfare. Furthermore, the position on the extension of the federal unemployment benefit that was once ridiculed within the Republican Conference had within six months become the conference's position.

At times the Gingrich Senators' behavior is distinct from that of the other Republicans. The difference between their voting record and the other Republican senators is more distinct on amendments that they sponsor than it is on the amendments sponsored by the other Republicans. Not only do they vote differently, but they cosponsor differently and they contribute differently and at different times. When the Republicans are in the minority, the distinction between the Gingrich Senators and the other Republicans becomes sharpest. In the animal kingdom as well as in the Senate, when the pack is most threatened, the pack mentality is greatest.

8

The Gingrich Senators as Partisan
Warriors on Roll-Call Votes

PRESIDENT CLINTON'S NOMINEES for U.S. Surgeon General proved to be some of the most controversial of his entire presidency. Shortly after his inauguration, Clinton nominated his state health director in Arkansas, Joycelyn Elders, to be U.S. Surgeon General. Despite a compelling personal story that included being the daughter of a sharecropper and using the GI Bill to attend medical school after serving in the army, she faced questions both on ethical grounds extending from her time on the board of directors at the National Bank of Arkansas and for her controversial public stands on abortion and teenage sex, which led some of her opponents to call her the "Condom Queen."

After a lengthy review process, in July 2003 the Senate Labor and Human Resources Committee voted to recommend her confirmation to the full Senate on a 13–4 vote. Leading the charge against her nomination were Dan Coats and Judd Gregg, the only two Gingrich Senators serving on the committee. Coats worried that her views and style would be "polarizing and divisive," while Gregg based his opposition on her tenure on the bank's board.[1]

Although the committee had spent seven months thoroughly investigating her past, Elders would have to wait until after the summer recess for her nomination to get an airing on the Senate floor. After a contentious floor debate, the Senate voted to confirm her, 65–34. Again, the Gingrich Senators led the opposition. Although 13 of 35 other Republicans voted to confirm Elders, only one of eight Gingrich Senators (Hank Brown) did so.[2]

Coats's admonition proved prophetic. In December 1994, in the wake of the massive Republican victories the previous month, Clinton fired Elders for making controversial comments at a United Nations conference on AIDS about preventing the spread of HIV by promoting masturbation. Clinton's nominee to replace Elders, Henry Foster, was defeated on the Senate floor in June 1995 when the Democrats could not muster enough votes to invoke cloture on his nomination. All 14 Gingrich Senators who were serving in the

104th Congress (1995–1996) voted against cloture twice; 29 of the 40 other Republicans voted with them.[3] When David Satcher was finally confirmed on February 10, 1998, he enjoyed the support of 19 Republicans, only two of whom were Gingrich Senators.[4]

The Gingrich Senators' opposition to Clinton's surgeon general nominees is doubly typical of their role in the Senate: they have been the most strident opponents of Democratic presidential nominations and the biggest supporters of filibusters on the Senate floor. This chapter explores these avenues as well as other roll-call votes to assess the degree to which the Gingrich Senators are partisan warriors. In succeeding sections, I describe how the Gingrich Senators vote on presidential nominations, on issues where the president has a publicly stated position, and on cloture votes. Because voting on the Senate floor consumes a relatively small portion of a senator's day, the following chapter turns to non-roll-call-vote-based measures.

I. Presidential Nominations and the Gingrich Senators

The confirmation battles over Clinton's surgeon general nominees are not atypical, especially as Congress has become more partisan (Binder and Maltzman 2009; Bond, Fleisher, and Krutz 2009). In fact, the entire landscape surrounding presidential nominations has radically changed since the Reagan presidency. First, the number of roll-call votes on the nominations has increased. Whereas senators took only 28 votes on Clinton's nominees during his first two years, they took 75 on Obama's nominees in the same time frame (figure 8.1).

Second, the nominations are subject to much more scrutiny than before. Whereas every one of Reagan's nominations to the appellate court were confirmed in his first two years in office, only 85 of Clinton's, and 62 percent of Obama's, were similarly successful (Binder and Maltzman 2009). George W. Bush, who faced an opposition Senate for most of his first two years, had only a 41 percent success rate (see figure 8.2).

Third, the nominations take longer to get to a vote on the Senate floor. Reagan's judicial appointments took more than two months to get a vote on the Senate floor. Clinton's took more than twice that long and George W. Bush's took twice that again (Binder and Maltzman 2009) (see figure 8.3). The data on nominations to the Cabinet and independent agencies show the same trend (Bond, Fleisher, and Krutz 2009).

These data show that more nominees have faced additional levels of scrutiny before more of them were ultimately rejected by the Senate. While the

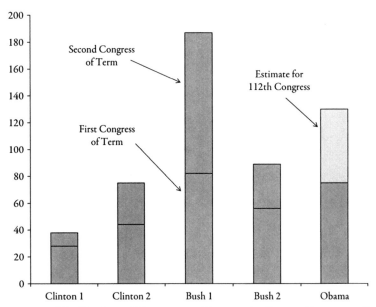

FIGURE 8.1 The Number of Nominations Votes in the Senate, Clinton to Obama (1993–2010).

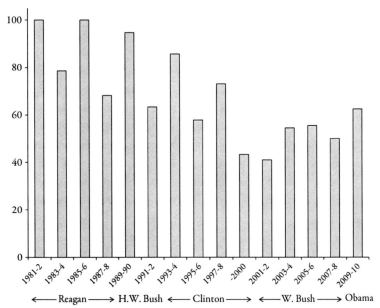

FIGURE 8.2 The Success of Appellate Judicial Nominations, Reagan to Obama (1981–2010).

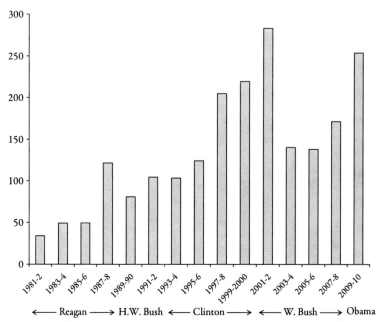

FIGURE 8.3: The Number of Days from Nomination to Vote on Appellate Judicial Nominations, Reagan to Obama (1981–2010).

figures show a general increasing trend on each of these pieces of data, some congresses experience bigger jumps than other congresses. To see if any of these increases introduce a new normal in the battle between senators and presidents over confirmation, I conduct an exhaustive statistical analysis to see if there are any inflection points in the data. In other words, were there any congresses that showed a particularly big increase from the previous congresses, and then did the data stay at this new heightened level for the remainder of the time series? This analysis shows that the number-of-votes trend jumps up in the 105th Congress (1997–1998), the failure rate for Cabinet and judicial appointments jumps up in Clinton's second term (1997–2000), the failure rate for appellate judges jumps up in the 106th Congress (1999–2000), the length of time for Cabinet and judicial appointments jumps up in Clinton's second term (1997–2000), and the length of time for appellate nominees jumps up in the 105th Congress (1997–1998). If the president's nominees now face a rockier road to confirmation, the evidence suggests that the trend changed the most in the late 1990s.

To cast an additional spotlight on these years, I compute senators' support scores on the president's nominees during Clinton's two terms (1993–2000). In his first term, three of the eight Gingrich Senators were in the top 10 (see table 8.1). In his second term, when the Gingrich Senators' numbers increased

Table 8.1 Senators with the Lowest Presidential Support Scores for
Democratic Presidents (Gingrich Senators are in Bold)

Clinton I (1993–1997)			Clinton II (1997–2001)			Obama (2009–2010)		
1	Helms	5.9%	1	**R. Smith**	38.3%	1	**Bunning**	13.0%
2	**R. Smith**	11.8%	2	Faircloth	38.9%	2	**DeMint**	25.0%
3	Abraham	16.7%	3	**Allard**	44.7%	T3	**Vitter**	27.3%
4	**Kyl**	16.7%	4	**Inhofe**	46.7%	T3	**Coburn**	27.3%
5	Thomas	16.7%	5	Helms	48.9%	T5	**Wicker**	28.9%
T6	Kempthorne	20.6%	T6	Enzi	50.1%	T5	**Inhofe**	28.9%
T6	Nickles	20.6%	T6	**Gramm**	50.1%	7	**Roberts**	29.3%
T6	**Craig**	20.6%	8	**Bunning**	51.9%	8	**Ensign**	29.5%
9	Faircloth	21.2%	T9	**Craig**	55.3%	9	Risch	31.8%
T10	Dole	23.5%	T9	**Brownback**	55.3%	10	**Crapo**	32.6%
T10	Lott	23.5%						

to 19, the Gingrich Senators claimed 7 of the top 10 spots. The dominance of the Gingrich Senators at the top of the opposition list persists into the Obama administration, where they claimed 9 of the top 10 spots and two of the next three after that.

To see if these descriptive differences between the Gingrich Senators and the other Republicans can withstand more rigorous analysis, I compute ideology scores based on contested nomination votes in a way similar to how I computed the ideology scores on the Gingrich Senators' amendments in the previous chapter. Because so few Gingrich Senators (7) served in the Senate during George H. W. Bush's presidency, and because there were so few contested votes on nominations (16), the methodology cannot generate reliable ideological summary scores for Bush's term (1989–1992).[5] As such, the data for the more systematic test of how the Gingrich Senators treat nominees comes from Clinton's two terms, Bush's two terms, and the first two years of Obama's first term. In order to provide the most accurate test possible, I aggregate votes by presidential term rather than by congress in computing the confirmation ideology scores.[6]

Not surprisingly, senators' voting behavior on presidential nominations is similar to their voting behavior on all votes. The correlation between DW-NOMINATE and confirmation ideology is more than 0.85 for each presidential term, and in four out of the five terms, the score is more than 0.90.[7] Given both that the correlation is so high for the ideology scores and that the Gingrich Senators' voting record is so distinct on all votes, we should not be surprised if their voting record is also distinct on confirmation votes (see table 8.2 for the confirmation ideology scores not only for the Gingrich Senators but also for the other Republicans and Democrats).

The Gingrich Senators' voting habits on Democratic presidents' nominees remains distinct even after controlling for the constituency variables. After taking into account these variables introduced in chapter 4, the Gingrich Senators' predicted confirmation ideology is 0.75 (see table 8.3).[8] After controlling for the constituency, the Gingrich Senators are 76 percent more polarized on these votes than the other Republican groups. This Gingrich Senator Effect is even bigger than it was on extremism scores.[9]

The tougher stance against the nominations made by Democratic presidents may have an easy explanation. The Gingrich Senators may simply have a higher standard for all presidential nominations, not just those made by Democrats. While this reasoning may be plausible, especially in light of all the various standards that senators use when casting votes on nominations, the systematic record does not bear it out. While the Gingrich Senators voted differently than the rest of the Republican caucus on Bush's nominees, they did so in a more pro-Bush way, though the distinction is relatively small compared to their voting behavior during Democratic administrations.

Table 8.2 Ideology Based on Confirmation Votes in the Senate, Clinton to Obama (1993–2010)

	Years	Democrats	Gingrich Senators	Other Republicans	Difference	Statistical Significance
Clinton I	1993–1997	−0.743	0.666	0.338	0.328	0.025
Clinton II	1997–2001	−0.797	0.482	0.101	0.381	0.001
Bush I	2001–2005	−0.671	0.886	0.793	0.093	0.020
Bush II	2005–2009	−0.283	0.415	0.288	0.128	0.005
Obama	2009–2010	−0.530	0.842	0.641	0.202	0.003
During Democratic Administrations					0.304	
During Democratic Administrations					0.111	

Table 8.3 The Gingrich Senator Effect on Confirmation Ideology, Clinton to Obama (1993–2010)

Panel A: Confirmation Ideology during Democratic Administrations, 1993–2001 and 2009–2010

Republicans			Democrats		
	No House Experience	House Experience		No House Experience	House Experience
Pre-1978	0.26	0.45	Pre-1978	−0.47	−0.45
Post-1978	0.57	0.75	Post-1978	−0.51	−0.44
Gingrich Senator Effect		0.76	Gephardt Senator Effect		−0.08

Panel B: Confirmation Ideology during Republican Administrations, 2001–2009

Republicans			Democrats		
	No House Experience	House Experience		No House Experience	House Experience
Pre-1978	0.45	0.56	Pre-1978	−0.52	−0.51
Post-1978	0.50	0.57	Post-1978	−0.43	−0.52
Gingrich Senator Effect		0.13	Gephardt Senator Effect		0.06

The confirmation ideology of the Gingrich Senators is only 13 percent more polarized, but in Bush's favor (see table 8.2, panel B). Systematically, across the 216 contested confirmation votes since 1993, the Gingrich Senators held Democratic nominees up to a much higher standard than even the rest of their Republican caucus did; and this higher standard does not appear when voting on Republican nominees.

Between Clinton's first two years in office and his last two, a variety of measures indicate that the Senate entered a new era of dealing with presidential nominations. The new era is characterized by more roll-call votes, longer delays in the process, and a higher failure rate. The data over the eight years of the Clinton presidency shows that the Gingrich Senators were the most supportive of subjecting presidential nominations to more scrutiny.

II. Presidential Support Scores and the Gingrich Senators

The Gingrich Senators are not only less supportive of Democratic presidents' nominees but also less supportive of the Democratic presidents' entire legislative agenda. Before diving back into roll-call votes, consider a story from the Obama administration that shows the lack of support—or, perhaps, even respect—that the president gets from the Gingrich Senators, or at least a couple of them.

With the August 2011 unemployment rate holding steady at 9.1 percent, and with his jobs bill and economic recovery program stalled in Congress, President Obama decided to give an address to a joint session of Congress the week after Labor Day. It was to be Obama's first time back in the chamber since the previous January when he gave his State of the Union Address, a speech that was hailed as a triumph of bipartisanship delivered in the wake of the attack on Congresswoman Gabrielle Giffords (D-Arizona) at a constituent meet-and-greet. For the first time, in that January address, the proverbial aisle running down the center of the House chamber did not divide the parties. The week leading up to that address found a Capitol reminiscent of the high school hallways before the prom. Legislators, like their adolescent selves, were seeking a date from the opposite party to attend the speech. Obama captured the bipartisan feel of his immediate audience as he welcomed Speaker John Boehner to the rostrum behind him and many new freshmen who were elected because they had so stridently repudiated him during the 2010 congressional campaigns.

The House chamber would not have the same bipartisan feel for Obama's September address on jobs. The intervening seven months had shown that the parties were as divided as ever. Their disagreement on policy frequently spilled over into personal slights. Obama would be delivering his jobs speech before a joint session of Congress only a day before the second anniversary of Joe Wilson's infamous "You lie!" outburst during Obama's address to Congress on his health care plan. In a game of ratcheting up the harsh partisan tone, Congressman Joe Walsh (R-Illinois) announced that he would not attend the president's speech. In a tweet, he announced: "Instead of being a prop of another one of the President's speeches, next Thursday I will fly home to IL to talk to real job creators."[10]

Although a handful of House members publicized their impending absence, just two senators joined in publicly rebuking Obama and his speech. Jim DeMint, in an interview on ABC News, complained, "I'm so frustrated I don't think I'm going to go … I can't imagine too many Americans wanted to hear another speech with no real plan attached."[11] While DeMint met with Boeing officials during the president's speech, fellow Gingrich Senator David Vitter announced on Fox News that he would be holding a New Orleans Saints football party to kick off the new NFL season. He commented, "As a fanatic, I have my priorities."[12]

DeMint's and Vitter's refusals to attend Obama's speech typified in style the reaction of the Gingrich Senators to Obama's policies in substance. As the record indicates, the policy agreement of the Gingrich Senators with Obama was not that much different from their policy agreement with Clinton. Since the Eisenhower administration, *Congressional Quarterly* has been calculating all the representatives' and senators' "Presidential Support Scores," which includes all the roll-call votes in which an "explicit statement is made by the president or his authorized spokesmen."[13] These scores range from 0, if the member never supported the president on one of these votes, to 100 if they voted with the president on every single vote. Not surprisingly, these votes have become increasingly divided by party in the era of party polarization (see figure 8.4 for the presidential support scores by Democrats, other Republicans, and Gingrich Senators from Reagan to Obama).

Once again, the distinction between the two groups of Republicans is especially stark during Democratic administrations. In fact, in most of the congresses during Republican administrations, the presidential support scores for the two groups are indistinguishable from one another. In each of the five congresses under Democratic presidents, the difference is large and statistically significant.

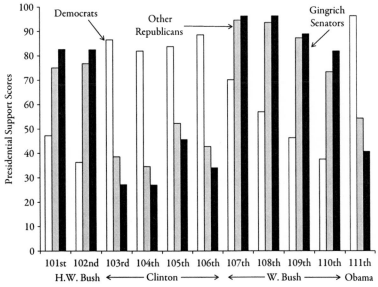

FIGURE 8.4 Presidential Support Scores of Democrats, Gingrich Senators, and Other Republicans, 101st to 111th Congresses.

Table 8.4 Senators with the Lowest Presidential Support Scores for Democratic Presidents (Gingrich Senators are in Bold)

Clinton I			Clinton II			Obama		
103rd Congress (1993–1994)			105th Congress (1997–1998)			111th Congress (2009–2010)		
1	Helms	14.5	1	**Inhofe**	31	1	**DeMint**	29.5
2	**Smith**	15	2	Faircloth	31.5	2	**Coburn**	30
3	Faircloth	17.5	3	Helms	34.5	3	**Bunning**	33.5
4	Nickles	21	4	**Smith**	35	4	**Ensign**	36
5	**Brown**	21	5	Ashcroft	37.5	5	**Inhofe**	37
6	**Craig**	22	6	**Allard**	38	6	**Thune**	37.5
7	Kempthorne	23	7	Nickles	40.5	7	**Vitter**	39.5
8	**Gramm**	26.5	8	Enzi	41	8	Hutchison	40
9	F. Murkowski	28	9	**Craig**	41.5	9	**Roberts**	40
10	Lott	29	10	**Hutchinson**	41.5	10	Barrasso	40.5
104th Congress (1995–1996)			106th Congress (1999–2010)					
1	Faircloth	20.5	1	**Smith**	22			
2	**Gramm**	20.5	2	Helms	24.5			
3	**Kyl**	21.5	3	**Inhofe**	26.5			
4	Helms	22.5	4	**Bunning**	28.5			
5	**Smith**	23.5	5	**Allard**	29			
6	**Inhofe**	25.5	6	Enzi	29.5			
7	**Thomas**	25.5	7	**Hutchinson**	31			
8	**Coats**	26	8	**Gramm**	32			
9	**Craig**	26	9	Sessions	33			
10t	Kempthorne	26.5	10	**Roberts**	33.5			
10t	Ashcroft	26.5						

Table 8.4 lists the 10 senators who were least supportive of Clinton and Obama. The Gingrich Senators are prominent in each of the congresses, and the names across the congresses are fairly constant. The Gingrich Senators were never as opposed as they were during the first two years of the Obama administration. Not only did DeMint skip out on the president's jobs speech, but he was the most systematic opponent to all of Obama's initiatives—more than 7 out of every 10 votes that DeMint cast were in opposition to Obama's publicly stated positions. DeMint had company from other Gingrich Senators

at the top of the list—in fact, the top seven Obama opponents were Gingrich Senators.

The more conservative voting record on presidential items could simply be a reflection of the Gingrich Senators' more conservative constituents. To see if the distinction holds up we again control for the constituency. When these other factors are taken into consideration, the Gingrich Senators are still about 10 percentage points less supportive of Democratic presidents compared to their Republican colleagues (see table 8.5).[14]

Table 8.5 The Gingrich Senator Effect on Presidential Support Scores

Clinton and Obama (1993–2000 and 2009–2010)					
Republicans			**Democrats**		
	No House Experience	House Experience		No House Experience	House Experience
Pre-1978	58.3	57.2	Pre-1978	95.3	95.5
Post-1978	52.9	46.4	Post-1978	95.9	93.1
Gingrich Senator Effect		−0.17	Gephardt Senator Effect		−0.03

The Gingrich Senators have been leading the charge against the president's nominees as well as his public policy agenda in the Senate. That presidents would face additional scrutiny from senators of the opposite party is not new. But, that so many senators would join the efforts of thwarting the president is something that is unprecedented in post–World War II politics. And, that this group of presidential opponents is so easily classified by the time they spent in a highly partisan House is unique. The next section shows that Democratic presidents are not the only Democrats who have had to figure out how to maneuver in an ever-changing political world.

III. Filibustering in the Senate

The Senate deleted the previous question motion in 1806 due to its redundancy and, according to then Vice President Aaron Burr, its lack of use.[15] As a consequence of this simple decision made more than 200 years ago, the Senate permits filibustering and the House does not. Although the rules governing filibusters have changed over the years, the Senate has preserved this unique legislative prerogative. Although the filibuster has increasingly come under fire from the "good government" community, the rules governing its use have not

changed in a serious way since 1975, when the total number of votes required
to invoke cloture went from two-thirds to three-fifths. While the rules may
not have changed, its practice certainly has. In President Clinton's first two
years when he had Democratic majorities in both chambers, the Senate took
31 votes to invoke cloture. In President Obama's two years when he enjoyed
Democratic majorities in both chambers, the Senate took 91 votes (see figure
8.5).[16] While the practice of placing the president's nominees under increased
scrutiny seemed to have changed during the Clinton presidency, the practice
of filibustering seems to have changed in the final days of President George
W. Bush's administration.[17]

The purest form of obstructionism in the Senate that can be most easily
observed and quantified is voting on cloture petitions. It is only through the
filing of a cloture petition and then securing 60 votes to invoke that a determined enacting coalition can thwart a committed minority from filibustering. Koger (2010) shows how the number of filibusters has skyrocketed in the
modern Senate. While it is difficult to figure out who the principal obstructionists are on any given filibuster, how senators vote on all cloture petitions
at least offer insight into who supports the filibusters, even if they are not the
ones primarily responsible for them.

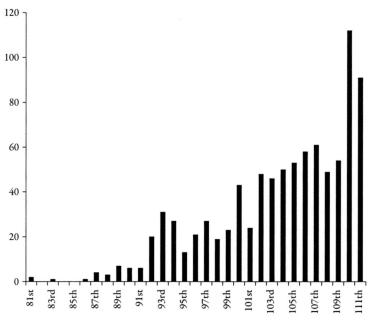

FIGURE 8.5: The Number of Cloture Votes in the Senate, 81st to 111th Congresses
(1949–2010).

Not surprisingly, the majority party is always more likely to support invoking cloture than are members of the minority party. Majority party members typically support cloture more than 95 percent of the time, whereas members of the minority support cloture less than 35 percent of the time. Table 8.6 shows these simple averages for the 103rd to the 111th Congresses, broken down by party and then by Gingrich Senators and other Republican senators. As with the amendment analysis, the voting behavior of the Gingrich Senators has become increasingly distinct from their Republican colleagues. The difference between them in the 110th Congress was only exceeded by their difference in the 111th Congress, when the Gingrich Senators were 43 percent (or 20 percentage points) less supportive of invoking cloture than their Republican colleagues. In the 111th Congress, 9 of the 11 senators least supportive of invoking cloture were Gingrich Senators; the only non–Gingrich Senators to break into the top 12 were Sessions (R-Alabama), who was third, and Cornyn (R-Texas), who was eighth. Only three Gingrich Senators—Gregg (10th), Wicker (18th), and Graham (19th)—were in the 20 Republicans most supportive of invoking cloture.

As with roll calls on the Gingrich Senators' amendments and roll calls on the president's nominations, we can compute W-NOMINATE ideology scores based only on the cloture votes in the Senate. Not surprisingly, the simpler averages that undergird table 8.6 and the ideology scores based

Table 8.6 Support for Cloture Votes in the Senate, 103rd to 111th Congresses (1993–2010)

	Cloture Votes	Democrats	Gingrich Senators	Other Republicans	Difference	Statistical Significance
103rd	32	0.920	0.137	0.219	−0.082	0.174
104th	48	0.189	0.986	0.942	0.044	0.074
105th	39	0.301	0.975	0.945	0.030	0.148
106th	46	0.411	0.970	0.963	0.007	0.585
107th	43	0.961	0.370	0.410	−0.040	0.207
108th	44	0.171	0.960	0.973	−0.013	0.306
109th	40	0.406	0.956	0.950	0.006	0.666
110th	102	0.954	0.373	0.506	−0.133	0.002
111th	88	0.977	0.166	0.338	−0.172	0.001
When Democrats are a Majority (103, 107, 110, and 111					−0.11	
When Republicans are a Majority (104, 105, 106, 108, and 109)					0.01	

Table 8.7 Ideology based on Cloture Votes in the Senate, 103rd to 111th Congresses (1993–2010)

	Cloture Votes	Democrats	Gingrich Senators	Other Republicans	Statistical Difference	Significance
103rd	32	−0.768	0.518	0.359	0.158	0.086
104th	48	−0.840	0.782	0.538	0.245	0.013
105th	39	−0.801	0.632	0.567	0.065	0.179
106th	46	−0.768	0.873	0.821	0.052	0.091
107th	43	−0.704	0.751	0.658	0.093	0.043
108th	44	−0.818	0.385	0.502	−0.118	0.955
109th	40	−0.726	0.256	0.302	−0.046	0.686
110th	102	−0.758	0.699	0.377	0.322	0.000
111th	88	−0.674	0.891	0.685	0.207	0.000
When Democrats are a Majority (103, 107, 110, and 111)					0.20	
When Republicans are a Majority (104, 105, 106, 108, and 109)					0.04	

on cloture votes are highly correlated.[18] The average cloture ideology scores for the Democrats, Gingrich Senators, and other Republicans are reported in table 8.7. In the 111th Congress, the Gingrich Senators' average cloture ideology is 0.89. If every Gingrich Senator voted against invoking cloture on every vote, they would score a 1. If their voting behavior during Obama's first two years in office is any indication, the Gingrich Senators do not have far to go to being complete obstructionists. The last time the Democrats were a majority in the Senate and occupied the White House, only five senators (including just one Gingrich Senator, Gramm) had cloture ideology scores above 0.6. In the 111th Congress, 34 senators, including every single Gingrich Senator, had a cloture ideology score above 0.6.

Because the distinction between Gingrich Senators and the other Republicans is greatest when the Democrats control the chamber, I report the 10 senators most supportive of filibustering only for congresses when the Democrats were a majority in the Senate (see table 8.8). While the Gingrich Senators only accounted for 4 of the top 10 in the 103rd Congress, by the 111th Congress they accounted for 8 of the top 10.

The cloture ideology distinction of the Gingrich Senators persists in a more sophisticated analysis and after controlling for senators' constituencies (see table 8.9, panels A and B, respectively).[19] Taking these factors into consideration, the Gingrich Senators have a cloture ideology of 0.73; this compares to less than 0.6 for the other three Republican groups (see table 8.9, panel B).

Table 8.8 Senators with the Highest Cloture Ideology
(Gingrich Senators are in Bold)

	103rd Congress (1993–1994)			110th Congress (2007–2008)	
1	Helms	0.990	1	**Coburn**	0.970
2	Nickles	0.984	2	**DeMint**	0.966
3	Wallop	0.984	3	**Kyl**	0.961
4	**Gramm**	0.983	4	**Ensign**	0.906
5	Coverdell	0.980	5	**Bunning**	0.901
6	Kempthorne	0.596	6	**Inhofe**	0.899
7	**Craig**	0.596	7	Barrasso	0.877
8	**Mack**	0.596	8	**Vitter**	0.850
9	Simpson	0.590	9	**Allard**	0.800
10	**Smith**	0.590	10	Enzi	0.786
	107th Congress (2001–2002)			111th Congress (2009–2010)	
1	**Gramm**	0.997	1	**Coburn**	0.999
2	Nickles	0.992	2	**Bunning**	0.998
3	**Kyl**	0.963	3	**DeMint**	0.995
4	**Gregg**	0.904	4	Session	0.993
5	F. Murkowski	0.893	5	**Inhofe**	0.992
6	Lott	0.892	6	**Brownback**	0.968
7	**Thomas**	0.886	7	Cornyn	0.961
8	Thurmond	0.849	8	**Roberts**	0.951
9	Enzi	0.838	9	**Ensign**	0.920
10	**Smith**	0.824	10	Kyl	0.920

Since the Democrats became the majority party in the 110th Congress (2007–2008), the Senate has been more consumed with filibusters and cloture votes than they were in the past. In the 111th Congress, 13 percent of the votes on the Senate floor were attempts to break Republican-led filibusters. The Gingrich Senators were the most supportive of filibustering, just as they were in the 110th Congress.

III. Conclusion

The Gingrich Senators, both as individuals and as a group, have caused Democratic presidents and Democratic senators much frustration, at least as can be determined from roll-call votes. Relative to other Republicans, their behavior during the Clinton administration was different. During Obama's

Table 8.9 The Gingrich Senator Effect on Cloture Ideology, 111th Congress (2009–2010)

Panel A: Based on the Cloture Ideology Score

	Republicans			Democrats	
	No House Experience	House Experience		No House Experience	House Experience
Pre-1978	0.77	0.52	Pre-1978	−0.58	−0.68
Post-1978	0.71	0.89	Post-1978	−0.63	−0.76
Gingrich Senator Effect		0.34	Gephardt Senator Effect		0.20

Panel B: Taking into Consideration Constituency Factors

	Republicans			Democrats	
	No House Experience	House Experience		No House Experience	House Experience
Pre-1978	0.59	0.49	Pre-1978	−0.36	−0.54
Post-1978	0.56	0.73	Post-1978	−0.59	−0.62
Gingrich Senator Effect		0.34	Gephardt Senator Effect		0.25

first two years, the difference was stark. So, too, when Democrats have constituted a Senate majority. The Gingrich Senators were much less likely to support the president's nominees or his policies. They were also much less likely to support cloture even as filibusters are becoming a more regular part of senators' daily lives.

Democratic senators, of course, have played the same role for Republican presidents and Republican senators. All senators maintain the prerogative of being a one-person barrier between legislative success and failure. What is different about the Gingrich Senators is that the class of presidential opponents and majority party opponents has never been so clearly defined, especially based on previous legislative experience.

The subsets of roll-call votes in this chapter offer evidence of how the Gingrich Senators are both transforming the Republican Conference and seeking new avenues of confrontation in the Senate. First, during the Clinton presidency, the confirmation ideology difference between the Gingrich Senators and the other Republicans was larger than it was during the Obama administration, suggesting that the distinctiveness of the Gingrich Senators was waning. The Gingrich Senators were more opposed to Obama's nominees than they were to Clinton's, but the difference in scores during the two Democratic presidencies was even greater for the other Republicans. While the Gingrich Senators moved to the end of the continuum, the other Republicans moved faster. Second, the Gingrich Senators have cast more distinctive cloture votes. In the 103rd and 107th Congresses, the difference between the Gingrich Senators and the other Republicans was insignificant. In the 110th and 111th Congresses, the difference is highly statistically significant.

As retiring Senators Olympia Snowe and Evan Bayh complained in announcing their retirement, the Senate simply doesn't operate the way that it ought to, at least, according to them. The chamber is far too partisan and compromise is far too difficult. In this chapter, I document the trend that Snowe and Bayh so aptly described. The Gingrich Senators have been the biggest supporters of the increased confrontation and stalemate that characterizes today's Senate. Once they have convinced the Republican conference on one tactic of the partisan war (e.g., opposing the president's nominees), they implement a new strategy (e.g., filibustering ad nauseum). Roll-call votes, of course, can only tell part of the story. In the following chapter, I continue to document the Gingrich Senators' role as partisan warriors using non-roll-call-vote measures.

9

The Gingrich Senators as Partisan Warriors beyond Roll-Call Votes

TO PROTECT THE people from a corrupt system where members could create plush government jobs for themselves, the U.S. Constitution explicitly prohibits lawmakers from serving in an executive branch position for which they voted either to create or to increase the salary thereof. This restriction, called the "Emolument Clause," has befuddled presidents and their potential appointees for years by erecting barriers for members to serve in the president's Cabinet after they have voted to raise the Cabinet secretaries' pay. The current workaround strategy was first used in 1973 when President Nixon wanted Senator William Saxbe (R-Ohio), who had earlier supported a pay increase for Cabinet officials, to be his attorney general. Nixon asked Congress to pass a law reducing the attorney general's salary to the level it was before the raise that Saxbe supported. The reduced salary would last until the Senate term for which Saxbe was elected ended, at which point Congress would pass another law increasing the attorney general's salary to that of all the other Cabinet officials. This workaround has passed muster by both the courts and Congress ever since.[1]

When Senators Hillary Clinton (D-New York) and Ken Salazar (D-Colorado) took their seats in the Obama Cabinet in 2009, their pay was cut to what the secretaries of state and interior, respectively, made on the day before the terms to which Clinton and Salazar had been elected. As Clinton's Senate term would not have ended until 2013, Salazar would first face the prospect of having his salary raised as a consequence of the second half of what has become known as the "Saxbe Fix" when his term would have ended in 2011. Majority Leader Harry Reid and Minority Leader Mitch McConnell worked out a unanimous consent agreement to pass a bill that would have increased Salazar's pay by $19,600 to $199,700, the same salary that all the other Cabinet secretaries made with the exception of Clinton.

On May 23, 2011, David Vitter, a Gingrich Senator, announced that he was placing a hold on the bill raising Salazar's pay until the Interior Department started "issuing new [deepwater drilling] permits at the same rate as before the Deepwater Horizon oil spill." Vitter argued that it was his "way of keeping the 'boot on the neck' of Interior until they get the job done."[2] Reid, who was blind-sided by the move, criticized Vitter's move: "It is wrong for Sen. Vitter to try to get something in return for moving forward on a matter that the Senate has considered routine for more than a century."[3] He vowed to keep fighting for Salazar's raise.

A day later, Salazar wrote Reid and McConnell a letter asking them to "set aside any effort to address" the inequality in his pay. He feared that he needed to take the issue off the table because of Vitter's actions, which he interpreted as an apparent bribe. A Vitter spokesperson retorted that charging Vitter with bribery would only "make my boss a Louisiana folk hero."[4] Vitter's response was a bit more temperate: "I'm glad the secretary has dropped his push for a pay raise.... Now I hope he starts earning what he already makes and properly issues new permits for much-needed drilling in the Gulf."[5] Salazar, to this day, continues to make nearly $20,000 less than the rest of the Cabinet.[6]

It has become common for senators to put holds on bills to force a presidential administration to take a particular action. It is not even that unusual for a hold to be placed on a bill that has been cleared by both the minority and the majority leaders. It is precisely because bills like this get held up that the leaders circulate their unanimous consent agreements before they offer them on the Senate floor. What is extraordinary about Vitter's actions is the lack of senatorial courtesy with which they were carried out. The actions are even more out of step because they, in effect, punished a former senator who was well respected on both sides of the aisle during his time in the Senate as indicated by the unanimous vote by which he was confirmed as secretary.

This anecdote about the spat between Vitter and Reid/Salazar gives flavor to the stories and analyses presented in this chapter. The relationship between the Gingrich Senators and the Democrats, while perhaps a bit more cordial than this story suggests, is no more productive. In the first part of this chapter, I show how the Gingrich Senators are less likely than the other Republicans to cosponsor bills introduced by Democratic senators, particularly when the Democratic Party is in the majority. In the second section, I outline various strategies the Gingrich Senators have used to make the normal negotiation process between the parties more complicated and difficult. The third section shows how the Gingrich Senators have used the amending process on the Senate floor for nonlegislative purposes. The fourth section shows how the Gingrich Senators are less likely to engage in the social life of the Senate. In examining data from outside the Senate, the fifth section shows how the

Gingrich Senators are the public face of the partisan war. Finally, I show how these partisan warrior tactics have affected the relationship between the Gingrich Senators and their Democratic constituents.

I. Cosponsoring Democratic Senators' Bills

In chapter 7, I used cosponsorship data to show that the Gingrich Senators were much more likely to cosponsor other Gingrich Senators' bills than they were those of other Republicans, especially when the Republicans were a minority in the Senate. This minority/majority distinction also influences the cosponsorship activity of the Gingrich Senators on Democratic senators' bills. From the 100th to the 102nd Congresses (1987–1992), the Gingrich Senators, then just numbering between two and seven senators, were actually more supportive of Democratic bills than were the other Republican senators, though the difference in connectedness scores was not statistically significant (see table 9.1). In the 103rd Congress (1993–1994), when Democrats controlled the White House and both chambers of Congress for the first time since the Carter years in the late 1970s, the Gingrich Senators were much less supportive than the other Republicans of Democrats' bills. In the 104th Congress (1995–1996), when the Republicans won both chambers of Congress, their cosponsorship patterns were not indistinguishable from the other Republicans. In the 105th through 108th Congresses (1997–2004), they

Table 9.1: The Amount of Support Democratic Senators Receive from the Gingrich Senators and Other Republicans

| | Support for Democratic Senators' Bills From: | | | |
	Gingrich Senators	Other Republicans	Difference	Statistical Significance
100th	1.19	1.11	0.08	0.295
101st	1.25	1.17	0.07	0.206
102nd	1.18	1.16	0.02	0.396
103rd	0.81	1.01	-0.20	0.000
104th	0.91	0.89	0.02	0.247
105th	0.87	0.92	-0.04	0.098
106th	0.86	0.99	-0.13	0.000
107th	1.19	1.35	-0.16	0.001
108th	0.97	1.10	-0.13	0.000

revert back to the same pattern that we saw in the 103rd Congress. The difference between the Gingrich Senators and the other Republicans was biggest in the 107th Congress (2001–2002), when the Democrats had majority control for the last 18 months.

These cosponsorship data show that the Gingrich Senators not only vote differently but that they cosponsor Democratic legislation less frequently than the other Republican senators. Having determined that they act differently at the beginning of the legislative process (cosponsorship) and at the end of the legislative process (roll-call votes), I now turn to an analysis of how they operate in the middle of the legislative process.

II. Difficulty in Negotiations

Above and beyond the conservative voting records of the Gingrich Senators, they have made the regular negotiations and compromises required for Congress to perform its duties exceedingly difficult. In this section, I present a number of different strategies that the Gingrich Senators have employed to make the normal legislative process much messier and more complicated—sometimes simply for the purpose of being messy and complex.

A. Moving the Goal Posts during Negotiations, Part 1—McCain in "Don't Ask, Don't Tell"

John McCain's service and dedication to this country has been highly revered by both Democrats and Republicans. Because of the torture that he endured in Vietnam and because of his solid record and concern for the troops during his days in Congress, his voice has always been one of the most respected in the nation on military policy matters. On October 19, 2006, while appearing on *Hardball with Chris Matthews*, McCain discussed his position on the "Don't Ask, Don't Tell" (DADT) policy that forbade gays and lesbians from openly serving in the military. He explained: "The day that the leadership of the military comes to me and says, senator, we ought to change the policy, then I think we ought to consider seriously changing it because those leaders in the military are the ones we give the responsibility to."[7] McCain's position had support both in the military and in the public. A Zogby Poll published two months after McCain's appearance found that only 26 percent of military personnel were in favor of gays serving openly in the military.[8] Although 55 percent of the American public in 2007 backed repealing the law, according to a Harris Poll, a significantly larger proportion of Republicans agreed with McCain's position.[9]

On February 2, 2010 Admiral Mike Mullen, the chairman of the Joint Chiefs of Staff, and Defense Secretary Robert M. Gates, in testimony before the Senate Armed Services Committee—a committee on which McCain sits—testified that they no longer supported the DADT policy. Mullen was more strident in rejecting the current policy: "No matter how I look at the issue, I cannot escape being troubled by the fact that we have in place a policy which forces young men and women to lie about who they are in order to defend their fellow citizens."[10] In lieu of offering his personal opinion, Gates testified that he, as secretary of defense, was trying to find the best possible way of implementing the policy endorsed by the commander-in-chief. To that end, he said that the Defense Department was carrying out a study of military personnel and their opinion on the DADT policy.

McCain expressed his disappointment with Mullen's and Gates's testimonies, arguing that they were trying to change the law through "fiat" rather than through Congress. In an article about the testimony, Dana Milibank of the *Washington Post* wrote about four senators who treated Mullen in such a way as to irritate him, causing him to "purse his lips" and "put his forearms on the table, displaying the admiral stripes on his sleeves," before saying, "This is not about command influence. This is about leadership and I take that very seriously." Those four senators were McCain (a Gingrich Senator), Jeff Sessions, Roger Wicker (a Gingrich Senator), and Saxby Chambliss (a Gingrich Senator). No other Republican senator is even mentioned in the article.[11] A day after the testimony, Colin Powell, a former secretary of state and a former chairman of the Joint Chiefs of Staff, fully endorsed Mullen's testimony.

Once the military brass told him that it was time to repeal the policy, McCain balked. After losing their support for maintaining DADT, he argued against "taking legislative action prior to the completion of a real and thorough review of the law. A complete survey to evaluate the impact of repeal on the men and women serving in our military should be concluded before moving forward."[12] To that end, he solicited letters from other high-ranking military personnel, who wrote that to change the policy before the release of the study would be a "reversal of our commitment to hear their views before moving forward."[13] Nonetheless, the Senate Armed Services Committee approved the bill on May 27, 2010, the same day that it passed the House.

The Democrats in the Senate thought that the easiest way to get the policy repealed was to include it in the defense authorization bill, a move that McCain criticized: "The majority leader is turning legislation on our national defense into a political football."[14] In part to appease McCain and the other military brass who pressed for the policy to remain in place until the study's release, the Democrats postponed the defense bill until after the study could be released, which, incidentally, was also after the November 2010 elections.

On December 1, the study was released. It showed that 70 percent "believed the impact on their units would be positive, mixed, or of no consequence at all."[15] Although the overall thrust of the study showed that changing the policy would not cause much disruption—if any at all—McCain pointed to the 58 percent of Marines and 48 percent of Army combat troops who thought the policy would have a negative effect. Furthermore, McCain argued that the survey did not ask the right questions and, because it was a survey, that it was only the opinion of a sampled 6 percent of the military personnel, not the entire military. He argued that there needed to be more hearings, a more comprehensive study, and more time to examine the issue.[16]

Because the Democrats did not have sufficient votes to invoke cloture on the defense authorization bill, upon the DADT provision removal, both chambers easily passed the slimmed-down version of the bill. As a last-ditch effort, Senators Joe Lieberman (ID-Connecticut) and Susan Collins (R-Maine) introduced a stand-alone bill that repealed DADT. In the last week of the lame duck session, much to McCain's chagrin, the Senate voted to invoke cloture (63–33) and to pass the bill (65–31). The newest of the Gingrich Senators, Mark Kirk, was the only one of the group who voted to invoke cloture, though two other Gingrich Senators—John Ensign and Richard Burr—voted against cloture and then voted for the repeal on final passage.

In 2006 McCain articulated a reasonable position against repealing DADT. When the stipulations for his opposition were finally satisfied, rather than remaining true to his word, he changed his position. Although the military brass said that the repeal's time had finally come, McCain wanted to wait until the military personnel study was released. When the study was released and showed a great deal of ambivalence toward repealing DADT, McCain shifted his position again, saying that the study was poorly conducted and that he needed more time to distill its finer points.[17] Not only did McCain not abide by the earlier level-headed response he gave to Chris Matthews on the policy, but he dug in his heels in firm opposition to the repeal and became its most vociferous opponent.

B. Moving the Goal Posts during Negotiations, Part 1—Kyl in New START

On April 8, 2010, President Barack Obama and President Dmitry Medvedev of the Russian Federation signed the New STrategic Arms Reduction Treaty

(New START), which, upon ratification, would replace the unanimously ratified Strategic Offensive Reductions Treaty that was set to expire in December 2012. The New START would cut the number of strategic nuclear missile launchers in half for both countries, and it would establish a new inspection and verification mechanism.

As with other nuclear weapons policies of the previous 30 years, many eyes, including the president's, turned to Senator Dick Lugar (R-Indiana), who coauthored the 1991 Nunn-Lugar Act, which through spring 2010 had deactivated or destroyed more than 8,300 intercontinental ballistic missiles. Lugar called "arms control issues … the cause of his lifetime."[18] Even from the beginning of the negotiations, however, the eyes of the Gingrich Senators shifted to Jon Kyl, who John Thune described as the "resident expert" on arms control issues and Sam Brownback called "the man," despite the fact that Kyl did not even serve on either the Armed Services or the Foreign Relations Committees. Kyl's rise, according to the über-nonpartisan *CQ Weekly*, is through his "sheer perseverance and the force of his own convictions."[19]

As the details of the impending agreement got worked out in 2009, the Obama administration, with former Foreign Relations Committee Chair Joe Biden serving as point person, established a two-pronged approach as it appeared that they would need the support of both Lugar and Kyl to get the treaty ratified. Both initially expressed some concern about the treaty in a July 2009 letter to the White House. Kyl elaborated on those points in an October speech. He highlighted three funding concerns in particular:[20]

- For the lifetime extension programs for nuclear warheads
- For the stockpile surveillance work through the nuclear weapons complex
- For the new facilities at the Los Alamos National Laboratory and the Y-12 nuclear facilities in Oak Ridge, Tennessee.

In May, the Obama administration outlined a 10-year funding plan that totaled $180 billion. They had initially set the funding at $170 billion, but raised it an additional $10 billion to appease Kyl's concerns.

On September 16, the success of the first prong resulted in a 14–4 vote in the Foreign Relations Committee, where Lugar served as ranking member, to send the treaty to the floor for ratification. Joining Lugar in supporting the treaty at the committee level were the other two highest-ranking Republicans: Johnny Isakson, a Gingrich Senator, and Bob Corker. The four most junior Republicans on the committee (including Gingrich Senators Jim DeMint and Roger Wicker) voted against sending the treaty to the floor.

Kyl's support was not yet secured. In August, he and Corker expressed concern that the amount of money was inadequate. Although the experts in the administration and Lugar thought that the initial proposal had sufficient funds to carry out the treaty, Secretary of Defense Robert Gates, in a November phone call with Kyl, negotiated and then announced that the administration would add an additional $4.1 billion to the bottom line. Corker, who had voted for the treaty in committee, only agreed to support it on the floor with the additional money. At about the same time, five former Republican secretaries of state (Henry Kissinger, George Schultz, Jim Baker, Lawrence Eagleburger, and Colin Powell) announced their support of the treaty.

After these developments, Kyl dropped his funding line of attack and, instead, argued that insufficient time existed in the lame duck session to complete work on the treaty. Kyl maintained that the administration did not do enough work laying the groundwork to pass the treaty, despite that Kyl observed the Geneva round of the talks directly; that Obama's lead negotiator, Rose Gottemoeller, briefed Kyl on Capitol Hill five times during the negotiations; that the State Department's legislative affairs office responded to all of Kyl's requests for more information; that treaty supporters secured a letter from the three directors of nuclear laboratories that they were "very pleased" with the funding levels[21]; and that the Senate held 20 hearings, two all-member briefings, and one all-staff briefing. An administration official declared that it was "difficult to assess motive with him."[22] Outside observers agreed: "There remains ... genuine confusion about exactly what is driving his tough negotiating position."[23]

Kyl never relented. On December 21, he voted against invoking cloture on New START. Nonetheless, the Democrats were able to secure the votes of 11 Republicans, including Lugar and Corker. Of the 17 Gingrich Senators who voted, 16 opposed cloture. Only Isakson, who voted for the treaty in committee, voted to invoke cloture. The other Republicans cast 10 of the 11 votes in favor of cloture. The treaty was ratified the following afternoon. Two of the 17 Gingrich Senators supported it (Isakson and Gregg, who was absent on the cloture vote). The other Republicans split 11–11. In January, Kyl reflected back on the ratification a month earlier: "This was something that could have been done well but was not, and as a result it was less satisfactory from everyone's standpoint. There was not time to do it adequately.... I knew the treaty was not going to be defeated, but I felt I had to have—I had to make the case that it was a very bad way to legislate and that it demeans the Senate to just rubber-stamp an agreement."[24]

C. Intending to Not Make Factual Statements—Kyl and Planned Parenthood

On April 8, 2011, as the government faced a shutdown, the Senate was debating an amendment that would defund Planned Parenthood because it provides abortion services. Federal law, since 1976, had forbidden federal funds from being used for abortion services. Nonetheless, Republicans in the House and Senate argued that by subsidizing other procedures, like mammograms, which were also done at Planned Parenthood, the federal government was implicitly subsidizing abortion services.

Senator Kyl took to the floor to support the amendment. He argued: "Everybody goes to clinics, to hospitals, to doctors, and so on. Some people go to Planned Parenthood. But you don't have to go to Planned Parenthood to get your cholesterol or your blood pressure checked. If you want an abortion, you go to Planned Parenthood, and that's well over 90 percent of what Planned Parenthood does."[25] According to the data that Planned Parenthood must provide the federal government, only about 3 percent of its procedures are abortion-related.

When CNN contacted Kyl's office for comment, his spokesperson said, "His comment was not intended to be a factual statement."[26] The spokesperson later offered the same explanation to ABC News, whereupon it became widely ridiculed including in prime spots on Jon Stewart's *The Daily Show* and *The Colbert Report*. Asked for clarification of the "factual statement" comment, Kyl claimed that he "misspoke" when he made the 90 percent claim. Furthermore, he argued, "[The factual statement] was not [from] me—that was [from] my press person."[27]

D. Dooming Negotiations—The Gang of Six

Even as Congress was trying to avert a government shutdown in April 2011 because it had not yet passed a budget, political and economic experts on Capitol Hill and around the globe feared a much bigger partisan showdown. By July, it was speculated, the federal government would reach its debt ceiling. If Congress did not raise the ceiling, the government was headed not just to a shutdown but to a far more drastic outcome: default on its loans. Under the grey clouds that were gathering on the horizon, Senators Mark Warner (D-Virginia) and Saxby Chambliss (R-Georgia), who shared some ideas with one another on the Senate floor, formed a "Gang of Six," who would search for a bipartisan compromise to the impending crisis. They were joined by Dick Durbin (D-Illinois), Kent Conrad (D-North Dakota), Tom Coburn

(R-Oklahoma), and Mike Crapo (R-Idaho). All three Republican senators participating in the Gang of Six talks were Gingrich Senators.

As the drama of the debt ceiling played out over the spring and summer, the stock of the Gang of Six fell and rose and fell again. When talks between the party leaders and the White House faltered, the eyes of the public and members of Congress switched back to the Gang of Six. In frustration, Coburn quit the group, but then he rejoined it a few months later giving it new life. When Biden convened a panel of party leaders for talks over the summer, and when Obama and Boehner met in the weeks finally leading up to the compromise package, chatter about the Gang of Six reverted to mere background noise.

The issue that irreparably divided the Gang of Six was on the amount of revenue increases that would be part of the final package. At various times, the participants in the compromise efforts seemed to get close, but they could never reach a final compromise. Most talking heads in Washington, D.C., thought that the ground of compromise under discussion in the Gang of Six had more revenue increases than the ground of compromise among the other viable alternatives, which included Biden's working group and the Obama-Boehner talks. While House Republican leaders Boehner and Cantor had been resolute that tax increases could not be part of the package, Chambliss and his fellow Republicans recognized that they had to be part of the solution. Chambliss had argued as such throughout the spring. When word leaked that the Gang of Six was considering tax increases, Grover Norquist, an anti-tax activist, complained that such tax increases would constitute a breaking of the "Taxpayer Protection Pledge" that all three Republicans in the Gang of Six had signed. Chambliss, Coburn, and Crapo raised the hopes for compromise when they rhetorically sparred with Norquist by releasing a letter that such action would not break their pledge, "but rather affirms the oath we have taken to support and defend the Constitution of the United States against all enemies, foreign and domestic, of which our national debt may now be the greatest."[28]

Rather than enacting a final solution to the problem, Congress passed and Obama signed legislation that would form a Joint Select Committee on Deficit Reduction (a.k.a. the "Super Committee"), which was tasked with coming up with $1.5 billion in deficit savings, either through revenue increases or spending cuts, or else they would kick-in an automatic trigger mandating across-the-board cuts, including massive spending cuts in the military. Although few on Capitol Hill were happy that the "can had been kicked down the road," the temporary compromise enjoyed large congressional majorities, including a final passage vote of 74--26 in the Senate. Quixotically, both Chambliss and Coburn opposed the compromise package even though most regarded the compromise package as a much more friendly alternative to conservatives than the rumored compromise that the Gang of Six never released. All three Democrats on the Gang of Six made the difficult decision to support a more conservative alternative than the one on which they were negotiating. The Gingrich Senators cast 10 of the 19 Republican votes against the final compromise.

E. Changing Positions: The Budget Commission

On December 9, 2009, Senators Kent Conrad (D-North Dakota) and Judd Gregg (R-New Hampshire), a Gingrich Senator, introduced S. 2853, a bill to establish the Bipartisan Task Force for Responsible Fiscal Action. The bill had 29 cosponsors, including 12 Democrats, 7 Gingrich Senators (including Gregg), and 10 other Republican senators. Over the next week, 5 more senators signed on as cosponsors (1 Democrat, 2 Gingrich Senators, and 2 other Republicans). The Gingrich Senators comprised 44 percent of the Republican Conference and 43 percent of the cosponsors on this bill. At introduction, President Obama was skeptical of the proposed commission.

On January 20, 2010, President Obama changed his mind and fully endorsed the idea of the commission. Within hours of Obama's announcement, John McCain and Jim Inhofe withdrew as cosponsors of the bill. The next day, Conrad and Gregg formally introduced the language of their bill as an amendment to the debt-limit bill, which was currently being debated on the Senate floor. On the same day, Mike Crapo and Sam Brownback withdrew as cosponsors. On the following day, Kay Bailey Hutchison (R-Texas) and John Ensign withdrew as cosponsors. All of those who withdrew their cosponsorship with the exception of Hutchison were Gingrich Senators. On January 26, Conrad and Gregg were able to get a majority, but not the 60 votes that the bill's unanimous consent agreement required for the underlying bill to be amended. Only 53 senators supported the commission; the only absent senator was Lisa Murkowski (R-Alaska), who remained a cosponsor of the proposal. The Democrats voted 37–23 in favor of the amendment; the Republicans voted 16–23 against the amendment. Those voting "no" included the six Republicans who withdrew as cosponsors of the bill as well as Robert Bennett (R-Utah), who would withdraw as a cosponsor on the bill two days later. The four Gingrich Senators who did not withdraw their names as cosponsors from the bill voted in favor of the amendment.

Various reasons could explain why the seven Republicans voted against the amendment after signing on to the bill. Perhaps the easiest explanations are for Bennett and Hutchison, who were involved in tough primary fights that they would ultimately lose.[29] McCain, too, was involved in a tough primary, but he ultimately prevailed by 24 percentage points. Such obvious rationales do not exist for the remaining four Republicans—all of whom are Gingrich Senators. None of the others faced serious or imminent electoral reprisals. After the bill's defeat in the Senate, Obama created the commission through an executive order.

It is exceedingly difficult to develop systematic data to demonstrate that these complications in negotiations occur more frequently among the Gingrich Senators than among the other Republicans or even the Democrats. These episodes, independently, may not prove the case, but, at a minimum, they are consistent with data that can be generated to test the general proposition that the Democrats have a harder time striking a deal with the Gingrich Senators than they do in striking a deal with the other Republican senators. Compromise is more difficult in the Senate because of the increasing number and increasing conservatism of the Gingrich Senators. These episodes suggest it is even more difficult because of the Gingrich Senators' peculiar negotiating strategies.

III. Amendments for Nonlegislative Purposes

Richard Fenno (1989, 1990, 1991a, 1991b, 1992) studied a number of senators with the basic methodology of observing them as they campaigned, analyzing how their campaigns affected their governing, and then describing how their governing influenced their reelection efforts. As members of Congress became more responsible for their own elections (Cain, Ferejohn, and Fiorina 1987), the governing period became increasingly infiltrated with campaigning, so much so that the phrase, "the permanent campaign" became commonplace in describing American politics (Ornstein and Mann 2000). Rather than returning to their legislative offices in between floor votes, members now head to their party offices outside the Capitol complex to make fundraising calls.

The combination of the permanent campaign and the members' increasing desire to serve in the majority (Rohde and Aldrich 2010) has increasingly caused the electoral campaign to move inside the chamber. Frances Lee (2009) shows how the team mentality and the desire to win elections for both themselves and their fellow partisans have taken up a bigger part of plenary time on the floor. Because the Senate operates under unanimous consent agreements and because it does not have a germaneness rule, the easiest way for senators to get themselves, their fellow partisans, and their opponents on the record is to introduce amendments on the Senate floor. In this section, I explore how the Gingrich Senators have used the amending process on the Senate floor for nonlegislative purposes.

The Number of Amendments

On March 24, 2010, Senator Coburn introduced an amendment that prohibited sex offenders from using the health insurance that was being established in Obama's health care reform package to pay for Viagra. What senator would possibly vote against such an amendment? As it turned out, 55 out of 57 Democrats did.[30] During this particular debate, the Democrats were orchestrating a complex legislative maneuver that could lead to the passage of health care reform without explicitly overcoming a Republican-led filibuster. By passing the measure through the reconciliation process, the Democrats only needed a majority, but they could not change a word in the bill or the entire process might unravel. As such, the Republicans had the Democrats in the difficult position of voting down amendments that might otherwise seem constructive or reasonable.

In addition to voting down the prohibition of paying for sex offenders' Viagra, the Democrats defeated a number of other seemingly uncontroversial amendments during the health care debate, including an amendment by Mike Crapo that would ensure that no individual making less than $200,000 would be subject to a tax increase as a consequence of the legislation, and an amendment by John Ensign to protect the damages in medical malpractice suits resulting from pro bono cases. By voting against each of these amendments, Democrats could be subject to campaign commercials arguing that they voted to give Viagra to sex offenders, to raise taxes on those making less than $200,000, and to subject pro bono health care providers to exorbitant malpractice lawsuits. No Democrat disagreed when Senator Max Baucus (D-Montana) called Coburn's amendment "a crass political stunt aimed at making a 30-second commercial."[31]

The Coburn amendment from the health care debate highlights how amendments can be used to further nonlegislative goals; namely, hurting the Democrats in their next reelection efforts. The more amendments the Republicans offer on the Senate floor, the more likely they can construct a 30-second commercial to hurt the Democrats. Consistent with the Coburn, Crapo, and Ensign amendments during Obamacare, the expectation might be that the Gingrich Senators have devised and are leading this amendment strategy. As it turns out, though, the Gingrich Senators offer, on average, just slightly more amendments than the Democrats. From the 101st through the 111th Congresses (1989–2010), the Gingrich Senators averaged about 48 amendments compared to 43 for the Democrats and 40 for the other Republicans. Aggregating the numbers across all the congresses, however, obscures important congress-to-congress variation (see figure 9.1). The other Republicans offered the most amendments in the 101st, 102nd, and 106th Congresses (1989–1992 and 1999–2000), the Democrats offered the most amendments in the 104th, 105th, 108th, and 109th (1995–1998 and 2003–2006), and the Gingrich Senators offered the most in the 103rd, 107th, 110th, and 111th (1993–1994, 2001–2002, and 2007–2010). Rather than randomly taking turns at offering the most amendments, this alternating pattern lines up perfectly with which party is in the minority except for the 106th, when Republicans were a majority yet still offered more amendments than the Democrats.

As soon as there were more than seven Gingrich Senators, the group offered the most amendments when the Democrats constituted a Senate majority— prior to that, the other Republicans offered the most. The difference between the Gingrich Senators and the other Republican senators was greatest in the

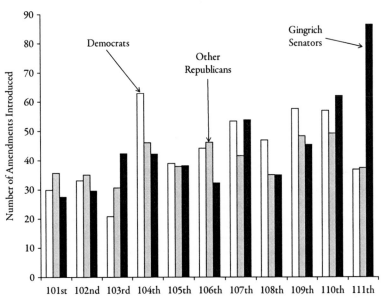

FIGURE 9.1: Amendments Offered by Democrats, Gingrich Senators, and Other Republicans, 101st to 111th Congresses (1991–2010).

111th Congress when the Gingrich Senators, on average, introduced twice as many amendments as either the Democrats or the other Republicans. John McCain introduced the most amendments (492), followed by Coburn (229), Reid (173), DeMint (152), Ensign (122), and Vitter (112). Reid, the Majority Leader, is the only non–Gingrich Senator who offered more than 100 amendments.

The distinction between the Gingrich Senators and the other Republicans holds even under a more sophisticated analysis, which controls for the same independent variables that were used in analyzing the roll-call votes in the second part of the book.[32] The Gingrich Senators introduced 119 percent more amendments than the average of the other three groups of Republicans (see table 9.2, panel A). The Gingrich Senator Effect only grows when constituency factors (133 percent) are taken into consideration (see table 9.2, panel B).[33] Again, the Gingrich Senator Effect on this partisan warrior behavior is even greater than it was on their role as party polarizers.

Amendments, of course, need not be used for nefarious purposes. In the textbook Congress, it would have been absurd to think that all but a few amendments were offered for any reason other than to make the bill better or more in line with the preferences of the senator offering it. After all, it is not likely that Majority Leader Reid was offering amendments to sabotage floor proceedings, especially given that he, along with Minority Leader

Table 9.2 The Gingrich Senator Effect on Amendments Offered, 111th Congress (2009–2010)

	Republicans			Democrats	
	No House Experience	House Experience		No House Experience	House Experience
Panel A: Based on the Number of Amendments Introduced					
Pre-1978	32.13	50.53	Pre-1978	23.05	38.72
Post-1978	35.87	86.42	Post-1978	31.72	49.19
Gingrich Senator Effect		1.19	Gephardt Senator Effect		0.58
Panel B: Taking into Consideration Constituency Factors					
Pre-1978	28.98	53.23	Pre-1978	30.44	45.14
Post-1978	32.09	88.91	Post-1978	33.27	53.02
Gingrich Senator Effect		1.33	Gephardt Senator Effect		0.46

McConnell, was primarily responsible for structuring floor debate.[34] A test of this amendment-as-electioneering strategy is to compare the number of amendments that senators introduce to the number of bills that they introduce. In addition to offering 173 amendments, Reid also introduced 113 bills, putting him in eighth place on the bill introduction list. Providing evidence that this test is appropriate, the correlation between bills introduced and amendments introduced by Democrats in the 111th Congress is 0.58.[35]

The Gingrich Senators, on the other hand, fall from the top of the list for the number of bills that a senator introduces. Vitter, the Gingrich Senator who introduced the most bills, was one slot behind Reid. The only other Gingrich Senators who were in the top 25 were Richard Burr (13th place with 85 bills) and Lindsey Graham (25th place with 69 bills)—McCain, incidentally, was in 69th place with 27 bills. The correlation between bills and amendments among all Republicans is 0.02. Most of the breakdown in the relationship is a consequence of the legislative behavior of Gingrich Senators, whose correlation on the two legislative activities is negative (-0.09).[36]

Roll-Call Votes on Amendments

Teasing out a strategy of electioneering on the Senate floor is difficult. Nonetheless, the number of amendments offered by senators gives us a window into behavior that is consistent with these electioneering purposes, especially when closer examination of the amendments reveals such behavior. Teasing out obstruction on the Senate floor is equally difficult. In an ideal world, we would count the number of holds—or threats of placing holds—that the Gingrich Senators have placed on bills or nominations. Regrettably, because holds are often secret, no reliable count exists. Nonetheless, we can glean insight into obstructionism by examining the number of roll-call votes that are associated with the Gingrich Senators' amendments.

As Coburn's amendment on Viagra showed, offering the amendment is only part of the strategy; getting senators on the record is a new favorite tactic of the Gingrich Senators. Offering amendments is the easiest way that a senator can get his or her colleagues on the record. Offering amendments serves another purpose as well: It delays action in the Senate. Amendments require debate, motions, and points of order, all of which can put otherwise noncontroversial legislation in an endless holding pattern.

As with the number of amendments, the number of roll-call votes associated with the amendments is a new weapon in the Gingrich Senators' arsenal. In the 103rd (1993–1994) and 107th (2001–2002) Congresses, when the Democrats were also a majority, the Gingrich Senators, on average, offered amendments with only slightly more roll-call votes than their Republican colleagues (see figure 9.2). While the minority party has always offered more amendments resulting in more roll-call votes than the majority, the numbers associated with the Gingrich Senators are unprecedented. In the last two congresses, the amendments of six Gingrich Senators have resulted in more than 20 roll-call votes each. In the previous seven Congresses (1993–2006), only 9 Democrats, 2 non–Gingrich Senator Republicans, and 2 Gingrich Senators (McCain and Brown in the 103rd Congress) have surpassed that benchmark.

The number of amendments that the Gingrich Senators have offered has increasingly consumed time on the Senate floor. In the 110th Congress (2007–2008), the Gingrich Senators' amendments resulted in 173 roll-call votes, which is 26 percent of the total number of roll-call votes. The top five roll-call-producing amendment sponsors were all Gingrich Senators: Coburn (34), DeMint (34), Kyl (18), Vitter (17), and Ensign (16). The streak was only interrupted by Senate Majority Leader Harry Reid, whose amendments resulted in 15 roll-call votes.

Once the Democratic majority in the Senate was joined with a Democrat in the White House, the number and proportion of votes caused by the Gingrich Senators' amendments were even greater. In the 111th Congress (2009–2010), the Senate voted 214 times on the Gingrich Senators' amendments—which

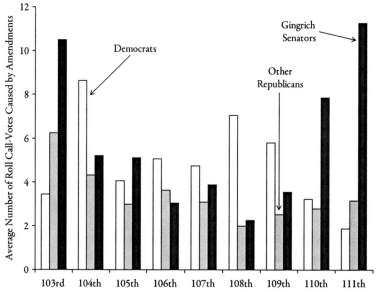

FIGURE 9.2 Number of Roll-Call Votes Caused by Amendments, 103rd to 111th Congresses (1993–2010).

accounted for more than 30 percent of the total number of votes! Forty percent of the Senate votes in the 111th Congress were used to vote either on their amendments or on attempts to end filibusters of which they were the biggest supporters.

Not surprisingly, the Gingrich Senators are at the top of the roll-call amendment sponsor list. Coburn (49), McCain (27), Vitter (23), and Thune (19) were the top four and DeMint (17), Ensign (14), and Kyl (13) were in the top ten. The only other Republican in the top 10 was Sessions (R-Alabama), whose 12 roll-call votes ranked tenth.[37] The other Republicans, who also faced a majority opposition in the Senate and a Democrat in the White House, accounted for 79 roll-call votes on their amendments. The Gingrich Senators were responsible for more than two-and-a-half times as many votes on amendments as were the other Republicans even though the Gingrich Senators were outnumbered 25 to 19 in the 111th Congress.

To be sure that these simple relationships hold up even after considering the senators' constituencies and their electoral performance, we again revisit the more sophisticated model. After controlling for these factors, the Gingrich Senators' record on the frequency with which their amendments are subject to roll-call votes remains distinct. Whereas the Gingrich Senators' amendments result in more than 10 roll-call votes, the average of their Republican counterparts is around 2.5 (see table 9.3, panel A).[38] No category of Democratic senator rises even to 5. As with the number of amendments introduced, these results hold even when controlling for constituency factors (see table 9.3, panel B).[39] The Gingrich Senator Effect, again, is bigger on this partisan warrior behavior than it was on extremism scores. While the trend of obstructionism through amendments and their associated roll-call votes appears to be new, it shows no sign of abating any time soon.

The frequency of roll-call votes, alone, does not prove that the Gingrich Senators are using the amendment process for obstructionism. They may be simply offering all the perfecting amendments to legislation so that the U.S. Code remains internally consistent and the grammarians do not ridicule Senate-passed legislation. But, alas, the Gingrich Senators are far less successful at securing support for their amendments than are even their fellow Republicans. In the 111th Congress, the Gingrich Senators won 11 percent of the roll-call votes on their amendments. While we might expect the minority party to have a difficult time getting their amendments adopted, the Republicans who are not Gingrich Senators do twice as well—they win 22 percent of the roll-call votes on their amendments. The Democrats, on the other hand, win 62 percent of the roll-call votes on their amendments.

Table 9.3 The Gingrich Senator Effect on the Number of Amendment
Roll-Call Votes, 111th Congress (2009–2010)

Republicans			Democrats		
	No House Experience	*House Experience*		*No House Experience*	*House Experience*
Panel A: Based on the Number of Amendments Introduced					
Pre-1978	1.34	2.66	Pre-1978	1.50	4.25
Post-1978	3.67	11.26	Post-1978	1.06	2.59
Gingrich Senator Effect		3.40	Gephardt Senator Effect		0.14
Panel B: Taking into Consideration Constituency Factors					
Pre-1978	0.04	2.47	Pre-1978	2.23	4.60
Post-1978	2.79	10.07	Post-1978	1.05	2.89
Gingrich Senator Effect		4.70	Gephardt Senator Effect		0.10

Not only are the Gingrich Senators less successful in roll-call votes on their amendments, but also, when they failed, they failed miserably. On 22 percent of the unsuccessful roll-call votes associated with their amendments, the Gingrich Senators received less than 35 percent of support from the Senate. This 35 percent standard is less than the number of Republicans serving in the Senate during the 111th Congress, 15 percentage points less than the minimum needed to get their amendment adopted, and 25 percentage points less than the minimum needed to stop a potential filibuster on their particular amendment. Their Republican counterparts do not achieve 35 percent support on only 14 percent of the roll-call votes on their amendments. The Gingrich Senators do almost 50 percent worse in securing support than their Republican colleagues. For whatever reason, the other senators are skeptical of the Gingrich Senators' amendments.

IV. The Face of the Partisan War

Every weekend, while most Americans are sleeping in and going about their normal daily lives, the opinion makers, pundits, politicians, and even political scientists focus their attention on the Sunday morning political talk shows, which includes NBC's *Meet the Press*, ABC's *This Week*, Fox News Sunday, CBS's *Face the Nation*, and CNN's *State of the Union*. With Obama in the White House and the number of Democrats vacillating around a veto-proof margin in the

Senate, these talk shows provide the Republicans with an outlet to voice their concerns over the direction the Democrats are taking the country.

More often than not, the face of the Republicans in the Senate was represented by the Gingrich Senators. Although Senate Minority Leader Mitch McConnell appeared on the shows 18 times in 2010, the Gingrich Senators' total appearances still outnumbered the other Republicans' appearances (46–45). The Gingrich Senators, on average, were on these shows 2.4 times compared to 1.8 times for the other Republicans—if McConnell's appearances are removed from the total for the other Republicans, they only average 1.1 times, which is less than half as much as the Gingrich Senators.[40]

After McConnell, four of the next five Republican senators most likely to make appearances were Gingrich Senators (Graham, Kyl, McCain, and DeMint). The only other Republican to break this string was John Cornyn (R-Texas), who was chair of the National Republican Senatorial Committee. The only Democrats to have more appearances than DeMint were Senate Majority Whip Dick Durbin (D-Illinois) and the chair of the Democratic Senate Campaign Committee Bob Menendez (D-New Jersey). These data suggest that the Gingrich Senators are leading the war not only inside the Senate but also in the media.

V. The Democratic Constituents' View of the Gingrich Senators

The Gingrich Senators pay a price for being partisan warriors. During the entire 109th Congress (2005–2006), Survey USA obtained monthly approval ratings for every senator. They reported not only the overall monthly rating but also the rating based on the respondent's party identification. The 25 Gingrich Senators had a net disapproval rating by their Democratic constituents of 14 percentage points, compared to only 2 percentage points for the other Republicans. John McCain's Democratic net approval of 35 percentage points was the highest among the Gingrich Senators. He ranked third among all Republicans—only Maine's two senators fared better, Snowe with 54 percent and Collins with 48 percent. David Vitter's Democratic net approval of 13 percent (10th place among all Republicans) and Lindsey Graham's net approval of 5 percent (12th place) were the only other Gingrich Senators who had a Democratic net approval.

While the Gingrich Senators were absent from the top of the list, they had more than their share of spots at the bottom of the list. Eighteen of the Gingrich Senators had a Democratic net disapproval compared to only 10 of the other Republicans. Such high negative approval ratings came with an electoral cost. The only non–Gingrich Senator Republicans who lost their subsequent reelection bids—Elizabeth Dole (R-North Carolina), Conrad Burns (R-Montana), and Norm Coleman (R-Minnesota)—all suffered net disapproval greater than 10 percent, as did the five Gingrich Senators who lost their reelection bids (DeWine, Allen, Santorum, Talent, and Sununu). No Gingrich Senator whose Democratic net disapproval was less than 10 percentage points lost their reelection bid, whereas only two other Republicans did: Lincoln Chafee (R-Rhode Island) and Gordon Smith (R-Oregon).

The lower scores for the Gingrich Senators are not a function of their constituencies. Six Gingrich Senators served with other Republicans in the 109th Congress. Every one of the six Gingrich Senators was viewed more negatively than their other Republican same-state colleague. The greatest disparity was in Pennsylvania where Santorum's net disapproval of 34 percent was matched with Specter's approval of 15 percentage points. The second biggest disparity was in Virginia where Allen's negative view of 22 percent was matched with Warner's positive view of 16 percentage points. The lowest disparity was in North Carolina where Burr's negative approval of 14 percent was only 4 percentage points worse than Dole's. The other three disparities— Kentucky (Bunning-McConnell), Ohio (DeWine-Voinovich), and Missouri (Talent-Bond)—were all between 11 and 16 percentage points.

The Gingrich Senators did not compensate for their higher Democratic net disapproval numbers with a bump from their Republican constituents. The Republican constituents gave their Gingrich Senators a net approval of 43 percentage points compared to 49 percentage points for the other Republicans.[41] Even though the approval numbers for their own party constituents are inversely related to the approval numbers for other party constituents at a high level (0.69), the Gingrich Senators did not enjoy as much own-party benefit for their overall lower approval numbers from their Democratic constituents.[42]

VI. Conclusion

The battle lines between the Democrats and the Republicans in the Senate are clearly drawn. Those clear lines are part of the Gingrich Senators' legacy. Not only have they helped define the lines but also they are increasingly taking the lead in developing the battle strategies. The Gingrich Senators are less likely than the other Republican senators to cosponsor bills introduced by Democrats. This pattern is most vivid when the Democrats control the chamber.

Furthermore, the Gingrich Senators have made the unseemly legislative process even more unseemly. Negotiations have increasingly been thwarted as the Gingrich Senators shift positions. Although the evidence for the complications in negotiations was offered only through a series of episodes, it is consistent with more systematic data that show that the Gingrich Senators are the most likely to offer amendments. Additionally, these amendments are taking up an increasing proportion of the Senate's plenary time and are doing systematically worse in attracting support. Again, this distinction between the Gingrich Senators and the other Republicans is most stark when the Democrats constitute a Senate majority.

In 2005 Senator Trent Lott (R-Mississippi) published his memoir, titling it *Herding Cats*, which was a reference to his job as Majority Leader from 1996 to 2001. The visual of senators as cats is compelling because just as it is exceedingly difficult to make a cat sit, beg, or fetch, so it is as hard to make a senator cosponsor, compromise, and vote. The fickle cats that inhabited the Senate during Lott's day have been transformed into tigers who will not only not go along to get along but also explicitly gum up the legislative process using every trick in the book and then using every trick in a new book that they are currently writing. The evidence suggests that the Gingrich Senators harbor more of these tiger tendencies than do the other Republican senators with whom they serve. Furthermore their distinctiveness on this partisan warrior behavior is above and beyond their distinctiveness on conservative voting records. Senate Majority Leader Harry Reid has not yet written his memoir, but "Taming Tigers"—or depending upon the final victor, "Being Devoured by Tigers"—might be an appropriate title.

PART IV

The Future of the Gingrich Senators

For those like retired senators Evan Bayh and Olympia Snowe, the future of the Senate is bleak. With party polarization stagnating Senate action and the partisan war crippling the legislative process, the old Textbook Senate seems more distant than ever before. So, too, the Individualized Senate, where rogue actions of one senator could thwart Senate business. Today those rogue actions are being coordinated into partisan battle plans where stopping the legislative process is only the first step in the quest to win elections. The Gingrich Senators have been at the forefront of these transformations.

Although the American public views the new Partisan Senate with derision, the voters are not punishing these newly implemented tactics. The Gingrich Senators have certainly experienced highs and lows, but those seem most tied to the fate of the Republican Party and not to Senate popularity. In this last part of the book, I show how the tactics of the Gingrich Senators have been emboldened with new compatriots in the battle—the Tea Party Senators. The Partisan Senate is likely to continue until the American people decide that they would rather have an august body where compromise is achieved rather than a battlefield where partisan war is raged.

10

The 2010 Elections, the 112th Congress, the Tea Party Senators, and Gingrich's Presidential Campaign

AS SENATOR JIM DeMint was declaring his intention to make health care reform Obama's "Waterloo" in July 2009, the script for the 2010 congressional midterm was changing—perhaps even because of DeMint's declaration. In July 2009, 61 percent of Americans approved of Obama's presidency, and only 32 percent disapproved.[1] Obama's high numbers were reflected in the predictions that Charlie Cook was making at the time. He projected that the Democrats would retain 58 seats in the 2010 election and that an additional 6 were in the "toss-up" category.[2]

Within six months, the entire political landscape would change. On January 19, 2011, Scott Brown (R-Massachusetts) ended the Democrats' filibuster-proof margin when he won the special election to complete Ted Kennedy's term in the Senate. Brown's victory signaled that Democrats were facing mounting and ominous odds in the 2010 elections. Republicans believed that if they could win in Massachusetts, they could win just about anywhere. The numbers supported their belief. Those approving of Obama exactly equaled those disapproving, and Cook downgraded the Democrat's projection to 51 seats with an additional 12 in the toss-up category.[3]

No politician encapsulates the narrative for the 2010 midterm elections better than Gingrich Senator Jim DeMint. While it is unclear if he led the Tea Party movement or simply got out in front of it after it started, few dispute how crucial he was for its success. In fact, the very definition of what it meant to be a Tea Party candidate according to the *New York Times*, in part, depended upon having his endorsement.[4] This chapter links the Gingrich Senators to the Tea Party Senators and explores their behavior during the first session of the 112th Congress (2011). Before concluding, I briefly explore the links between the Gingrich Senators and Newt Gingrich's presidential run.

I. The 2010 Election

Perhaps no other currently elected official was as closely tied to the Tea Party as Jim DeMint. Former House Majority Leader Dick Armey (R-Texas) and former Governor Sarah Palin (R-Alaska) also played important roles in the Tea Party Movement, but both were out of office in 2010. DeMint, alone, could walk that fine line between being an outsider, which the Tea Party movement valued, while still operating the levers of government power.

Even before his "Waterloo" comment, DeMint had a significant effect on the 2010 election when he endorsed Pat Toomey over sitting Republican Senator Arlen Specter (a situation analyzed in chapter 7). In making his choice of Toomey, DeMint argued, "I would rather have 30 Republicans in the Senate who really believe in principles of limited government, free markets, free people, than to have 60 that don't have a set of beliefs."[5] The Toomey endorsement was only the first of many that would cause the Republican establishment—as best articulated by Senator John Cornyn (R-Texas), who was serving as the chair of the National Republican Senatorial Committee (NRSC)—much heartache. The other endorsements of candidates running against establishment candidates included:

- Marco Rubio, Florida. On June 15, 2009, a week after his Toomey endorsement was publicly announced, DeMint endorsed Rubio, a former Florida House Speaker, over Governor Charlie Crist (R-Florida), who received the NRSC endorsement a month earlier. At the time of DeMint's announcement, Rubio was trailing Crist 54–23 in a Quinnipiac poll.[6] In May 2010, Crist announced that he was dropping out of the Republican primary and would run for the seat as a "non-party-affiliated" candidate. He lost the general election to Rubio by almost 20 percentage points; the Democratic candidate, Congressman Kendrick Meek (D-Florida), finished a distant third with 20 percent of the vote.
- Chuck DeVore, California. On November 4, 2009, almost a year before the 2010 elections, DeMint endorsed DeVore over Carly Fiorina in the Republican primary race to take on Senator Barbara Boxer (D-California). Although Fiorina had not officially earned the NRSC endorsement, she was the candidate of the Republican establishment. In the same month that DeMint endorsed her opponent, Fiorina was the guest of honor at a fundraiser featuring Mitch McConnell (R-Kentucky), Olympia Snowe (R-Maine), and John McCain (R-Arizona), who had named her as one of his chief advisers during his 2008 presidential campaign.[7] DeVore finished

third in the primary with only 19.3 percent of the vote. Fiorina secured 56.4 percent and former Congressman Tom Campbell (R-California) won 21.7 percent. Fiorina lost in the general election to the incumbent.

- Ken Buck, Colorado. On April 14, 2010, DeMint endorsed Ken Buck, the district attorney of Weld County, over former Lieutenant Governor Jane Norton, who was the NRSC's preferred candidate. In March, Norton led Buck 41–13 percent in the polls. In the week after DeMint's endorsement, Buck, for the first time, led the polls, though just by 3 percentage points. Although Buck was outspent by Norton, he won the primary by 4 points but lost the general election to Michael Bennet, who was appointed to the seat after Ken Salazar (D-Colorado) became interior secretary.

- Marlin Stutzman, Indiana. On April 20, 2010, DeMint endorsed a young farmer and businessman, Marlin Stutzman, over former Senator Dan Coats (a Gingrich Senator) and former Congressman John Hostettler (R-Indiana). DeMint's endorsement helped the Stutzman campaign gain traction against Coats, who had the NRSC endorsement. He lost the primary by 10 percentage points to Dan Coats, who easily won the general election. Stutzman would later win a special election to fill the House seat vacancy caused by the resignation of Mark Souder (R-Indiana), who was caught in a sex scandal.

- Rand Paul, Kentucky. On May 5, 2010, DeMint endorsed ophthalmologist Rand Paul over Trey Grayson, the attorney general, who was backed by Kentucky's senior senator, Minority Leader Mitch McConnell, as well as former Vice President Dick Cheney and former New York Mayor Rudy Giuliani. Paul won the primary by more than 20 points and the general election by more than 10 points.

- Mike Lee, Utah. In the week before the Republican convention on May 8, 2010, DeMint made a video endorsing Mike Lee that was to be played only if the incumbent, Senator Bob Bennett, was defeated in early voting. The contents of the video were leaked prior to the vote. Subsequently, Bennett finished third in a preliminary ballot at the convention, knocking him from contention. Although Tim Bridgewater finished first in the final round of voting at the convention, he did not secure the 60 percent of supporters that would have cancelled the primary. Lee reversed the order in the primary by less than 2.5 percentage points and went on to win the general election in a landslide.

- Ovide Lamontagne, New Hampshire. On September 11, 2010, with less than a week to go before the primary, DeMint endorsed Ovide Lamontagne over the establishment candidate, Kelly Ayotte, who was the state's former attorney general. The New Hampshire race was the only Senate race where Sarah Palin and Jim DeMint gave opposing endorsements. Ayotte also had the endorsement of Judd Gregg (whose seat she was seeking), Mitch McConnell, Warren Rudman (R-New Hampshire), and John McCain. Although Lamontagne trailed Ayotte 34 percent to 15 percent in the polls a week before DeMint's endorsement, he ended up losing the race by less than 2,000 votes out of more than 138,000 votes cast. Ayotte went on to win the general election.

- Christine O'Donnell, Delaware. On the same day as he made his Lamontagne endorsement, DeMint also endorsed Christine O'Donnell over Congressman Mike Castle (R-Delaware). Although he made his endorsement only three days before the primary, it may have made the difference as O'Donnell won the primary by less than 4,000 votes. O'Donnell's primary victory compelled Charlie Cook to shift the seat from "Likely Republican" to "Likely Democrat." She was soundly defeated in the general election by Chris Coons (D-Delaware), who was the sitting county executive for New Castle County.

The candidates above are not the only candidates DeMint backed. His endorsements of Ron Johnson (Wisconsin), Dino Rossi (Washington), Tom Coburn (Oklahoma), and John Raese (West Virginia) were not controversial among Republicans. Furthermore, he withheld two endorsements during contested primaries. In Nevada, DeMint found both Sharron Angle and Sue Lowden sufficiently conservative. In Alaska, he respected senatorial courtesy and remained neutral in Joe Miller's challenge to Senator Lisa Murkowski. After the primaries in these two states, he fervently rallied to Miller's and Angle's causes, though both were a losing effort.

DeMint's endorsements, unlike those from almost every other Leadership PAC, came with more than just a check from the Leadership PAC. DeMint not only provided funds directly from his Leadership PAC but also encouraged his followers to contribute to the individual campaigns. While his Leadership PACs gave $135,000, his nationwide network of donors added $6.6 million more through the Senate Conservatives Fund (table 10.1 shows the donations DeMint made in the 2010 Senate races).[8]

While Republicans were overwhelmingly pleased with the results on election night, the record in the Senate for the Tea Party and DeMint was more mixed. While they were pleased with the victories by Johnson (Wisconsin), Lee (Utah), Paul (Kentucky), Rubio (Florida), and Toomey (Pennsylvania), they mourned the losses by Miller (Alaska), Buck (Colordao), O'Donnell

Table 10.1 DeMint Campaign Contributions to Senate Candidates, 2010

Candidate	State	Leadership PACs*	Coordinated through SFC*	State GOP Committees*	Total
General Election Winners					
Marco Rubio	Florida	$10,000	$573,000	$250,000	$833,000
Johnny Isakson	Georgia	$5,000			$5,000
Dan Coats	Indiana	$5,000			$5,000
Jerry Moran	Kansas	$5,000			$5,000
Rand Paul	Kentucky	$5,000	$258,000	$150,000	$413,000
Richard Burr	N. Carolina	$5,000			$5,000
John Thune	N. Dakota	$7,500			$7,500
Rob Portman	Ohio	$5,000			$5,000
Tom Coburn	Okla.		$13,136^		$13,136
Pat Toomey	Penn.	$5,000	$304,000	$150,000	$459,000
Jim DeMint	S. Carolina	$5,000		$350,000	$355,000
Mike Lee	Utah	$10,000	$302,000		$312,000
Ron Johnson	Wisconsin	$5,000	$195,000		$200,000
General Election Losers					
Joe Miller	Alaska	$10,000	$570,000	$100,000	$680,000
Carly Fiorina	California	$2,500			$2,500
Ken Buck	Colorado	$10,000	$871,000	$250,000	$1,131,000
Christine O'Donnell	Delaware	$10,000	$505,000	$250,000	$765,000
Sharron Angle	Nevada	$5,000	$682,000	$156,000	$843,000
Dino Rossi	Wash.	$5,000	$326,000	$100,000	$431,000
John Raese	W. Virginia	$5,000	$70,000		$75,000
Primary Losers					
Chuck DeVore	California	$5,000	$33,776^		$38,776
Marlin Stutzman	Indiana	$5,000	$121,808^		$126,808
Ovide Lamontagne	New Hamp.	$5,000	$1,125^	$100,000	$106,125
Total		$135,000	$4,825,845	$1,856,000	$6,816,845

* Leadership PAC direct contributions from FEC; coordinated through Senate Conservative Fund (SCF) from the SCF website; State GOP Victory Committee contributions from SCF website.

^ Coordinated through SCF from the FEC.

(Delaware), and, especially, Angle (Nevada), who lost to Majority Leader Harry Reid. While the Tea Party was credited with providing the fuel for the overwhelming Republican victories, their overzealousness in the primaries was criticized for keeping the Senate in Democratic hands. Had Norton faced Bennet in Colorado, Castle faced Coons in Delaware, and Lowden faced Reid in Nevada, the pundits reasoned that the Republicans could have picked up an additional three Senate seats.

Jim DeMint, of course, was not the only Gingrich Senator who was involved in the 2010 elections. As chapter 7 showed, the Gingrich Senators gave more than $2.3 million through their Leadership PACs. The other Republicans contributed $3.2 million through their Leadership PACs. While these amounts are quite significant, it does not equal the $6.6 million that DeMint orchestrated. His 2010 contributions, both directly through his Leadership PAC and indirectly through its website, accounted for 73 percent of the Republican total and nearly half of the total Senate Leadership PACs' contributions (including Democrats!). Whether this form of influencing congressional elections will catch on among the other Gingrich Senators or the newly minted Tea Party Senators, only time can tell. At least one Tea Party Senator, Mike Lee, has fashioned his Leadership PAC in the mold of DeMint's.[9]

II. The 112th Congress

In the 2010 elections, the Republicans gained 63 seats in the House and 6 seats in the Senate. While Gingrich Senators Sam Brownback, Jim Bunning, and Judd Gregg were leaving the Senate, six new Republicans with House experience were elected to the Senate; and Dan Coats, who had retired 12 years earlier, was elected again to his old seat. While Gingrich Senators John Boozman, Roy Blunt, Mark Kirk, Jerry Moran, Rob Portman, and Pat Toomey were being welcomed to the Senate, they were not the stars of the show. Republicans and the entire political world were especially eager to see how the Tea Party Senators would adapt to the Senate. Rand Paul, for his iconoclastic beliefs, and Marco Rubio, for his compelling life story, were the two newly elected senators that received the most press. In this section, I describe the behavior of the Gingrich Senators and the Tea Party Senators in the 112th Congress. The Gingrich Senators remained as distinct as ever from the other Republican Senators. The Tea Party Senators learned the lessons of the Gingrich Senators and by the end of their first year had established records on several dimensions that were even more distinct from the other Republicans than were those of the Gingrich Senators.

A. Earmark Ban

The effect of the Tea Party was felt even before the 112th Congress convened on January 3, 2011. Within days of the election, the Republican leaders in the House declared that they would pass a two-year moratorium on earmarks. Jim DeMint and Tom Coburn aimed to get the Senate Republicans to endorse a similar move in the Senate. They faced an uphill battle. Despite an early overture from President Obama, the earmark ban was criticized by Senate Minority Leader Mitch McConnell two days after the election in a speech he made to the Heritage Foundation. He argued, "Every President, Republican or Democrat, would love to have a blank check from Congress to do whatever he chose to do on every single issue.... And we'll be discussing the appropriateness of giving the President that kind of blank check in the coming week." He reasoned, "You can eliminate every congressional earmark and you would save no money. It's really an argument about discretion."[10]

On the day before the Senate Republican Conference met for the first time after the 2010 elections, McConnell backpedaled and supported the earmark ban. On the Senate floor, he offered his explanation:

> Nearly every day that the Senate's been in session for the past 2 years, I have come down to this spot and said that Democrats are ignoring the wishes of the American people. When it comes to earmarks, I will not be guilty of the same thing.
>
> Make no mistake. I know the good that has come from the projects I have helped support throughout my State. I don't apologize for them. But there is simply no doubt that the abuse of this practice has caused Americans to view it as a symbol of the waste and the out-of-control spending that every Republican in Washington is determined to fight. And unless people like me show the American people that we are willing to follow through on small or even symbolic things, we risk losing them on our broader efforts to cut spending and rein in government.
>
> That is why today, I am announcing that I will join the Republican leadership in the House in support of a moratorium on earmarks in the 112th Congress.[11]

The next day, the Republican Conference by voice vote supported the earmark ban.

Two weeks later, in a debate on food safety during a lame duck session of the 111th Congress, Coburn attempted to introduce an amendment that would, in effect, ban earmarks. The procedural motion to bring up the amendment was defeated, 39–56. The Republicans supported the ban, 32–8. The only Gingrich Senator to oppose the ban was Jim Inhofe (Sam Brownback was absent). Seven of the 22 other Republicans who voted also opposed the earmark ban.[12]

Rather than writing an earmark ban into the rules of the Senate, the Appropriations Committee adopted an earmark moratorium that would last for the entirety of the 112th Congress. Not satisfied with an informal and temporary solution, Claire McCaskill (D-Missouri) and Pat Toomey, who was both a Gingrich Senator and a Tea Party Senator, introduced, on February 2, 2012, an amendment to the STOCK Act, which would make the earmark ban permanent. Again, the amendment lost, 40–59. All five Tea Party Senators supported it as did 17 out of 21 Gingrich Senators (Kirk was missing). The other Republicans only marginally supported it, 12–9.[13]

The earmark ban is an incomplete version of the unemployment benefit story from chapter 8. A subset of the Gingrich Senators—this time it was DeMint, Coburn, and Toomey; last time it was Bunning—persuaded a reluctant Mitch McConnell and Republican Conference to fundamentally change the way the Senate operated. Bunning's position became the position not only of the Republican Conference but also of the entire Republican Conference and then became the will of the Senate in 2010. The Gingrich Senators have led the Republican Conference in supporting a permanent earmark ban, but they have yet to convince the Democrats, though a two-year moratorium is in place for the 112th Congress.

B. Roll-Call Voting

The roll-call voting patterns that the Gingrich Senators have established since Phil Gramm entered the Senate in 1985 continued seamlessly in the first session of the 112th Congress (2011). The Democrats had an average extremism score of 0.37.[14] While the other Republicans had a similarly averaged score of 0.38, the Gingrich Senators' polarization score was 38 percent higher at 0.53. This distinction is similar to the differences between the two groups of Republicans over the last few congresses. With the 2010 elections, though, the Gingrich Senators and other Republicans were joined by a third group, the Tea Party Senators. This new group had an extremism score of 0.80, which was slightly less than their primary benefactor, Jim DeMint, at 0.87. The only two senators more extreme than DeMint were Rand Paul (1.00) and Mike Lee (0.99). Figure 10.1 shows the extremism scores for the Senate in 2011.

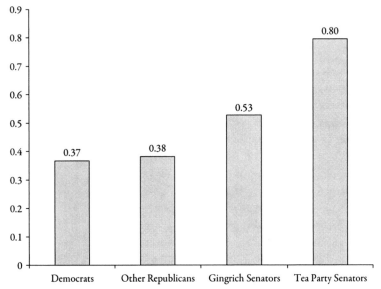

FIGURE 10.1 Extremism Scores Based on Roll-Call Votes in 2011.

While the senators first elected in 2010 act consistently within groups, they exhibit some variation. Table 10.2 ranks these 14 senators according to their polarization score and reports their group membership. While the future of these Tea Party Senators and the Tea Party Senator grouping, more generally, is unclear, the roll-call voting analysis from 2011 suggests that the Gingrich Senators remain as distinct as ever from the other Republicans.

The roll-call votes from the First Session of the 112th Congress suggest that the Gingrich Senators were every bit the party polarizers that they had been in previous congresses. Their direct descendants—at least Jim DeMint's direct descendants—had even larger extremism scores.[15] While the Tea Party Senators were more extreme individually, they had fewer than a quarter of the members of the Gingrich Senators. When the individual polarization scores and the number of members are combined, the total polarizing effect of the Tea Party Senators was only about one-third that of the Gingrich Senators.[16]

C. Amendments, Filibusters, Nominations, and Presidential Support Scores

The Gingrich Senators as party polarizers did not change as a result of the 2010 elections, as least inasmuch as their roll-call voting behavior in 2011 can attest. To see if their role as party warriors changed, I examine a few pieces of evidence that were introduced in the last few chapters.

Table 10.2 Extremism Score of Freshman Senate Republicans, 2011

Rank	Senator	State	Republican Grouping	Polarization Score
1	Rand Paul	Kentucky	Tea Party Senator	1.00
2	Mike Lee	Utah	Tea Party Senator	0.99
3	Ron Johnson	Wisconsin	Tea Party Senator	0.75
4	Pat Toomey	Pennsylvania	Tea Party Senator & Gingrich Senator	0.64
5	Marco Rubio	Florida	Tea Party Senator	0.60
6	Kelly Ayotte	New Hampshire	Other Republican	0.52
7	Dean Heller	Nevada	Gingrich Senator	0.47
8	John Boozman	Arkansas	Gingrich Senator	0.44
9	Dan Coats	Indiana	Gingrich Senator	0.43
10	Rob Portman	Ohio	Gingrich Senator	0.42
11	Jerry Moran	Kansas	Gingrich Senator	0.41
12	John Hoeven	North Dakota	Other Republican	0.32
13	Roy Blunt	Missouri	Gingrich Senator	0.31
14	Mark Kirk	Illinois	Gingrich Senator	0.28
		Tea Party Senator Average		**0.80**
		Gingrich Senator Average		**0.43**
		Other Republican Average		**0.42**

Just as the Tea Party Senators and Gingrich Senators had even higher extremism scores than the other Republicans, so, too, they offered more amendments that resulted in more roll-call votes. Coburn's amendments resulted in the most roll-call votes (13), followed by Paul (10), McCain (6), Dianne Feinstein (D-California, 5), Vitter (4), and DeMint (4). The other four Tea Party Senators offered amendments that resulted in only 3 additional roll-call votes. While the Gingrich Senators were responsible for amendments that resulted in 31 roll-call votes, the other Republicans' amendments only contributed 13 roll-call votes. The Democrats, who still enjoyed a majority albeit smaller than their majority in the 111th Congress, offered amendments that resulted in 30 roll-call votes.

The distinction between the Gingrich Senators and the other Republicans on cloture votes in the Senate shrunk. The Gingrich Senator Effect on cloture votes in 2011 was only 10 percent, as compared to their effect of 34 percent in the 111th Congress. The Tea Party Effect in 2011 was 31 percent. The data on the confirmation votes tells a similar story. While the Gingrich Senator Effect during Clinton's presidency and the first two years of Obama's presidency was

76 percent, it was only 58 percent in 2011. The Tea Party Senator Effect was more than 80 percent.

Because 57 percent of the votes comprising it came from votes on nominations, the presidential support scores in 2011 present a similar trend. While the other Republicans had an average support score of 58 percent, the Gingrich Senators' score was lower (54 percent) and the Tea Party Senators' score was lower still (49 percent). Though these numbers are closer than they were in the 111th Congress, the anchors are still the Gingrich Senators and their descendants. Paul had the lowest score (40.9 percent), followed by DeMint (41.4), Vitter (42.6), Heller (45.1), and Rubio (46.2). Only three other Republicans are among the 15 lowest supporters of President Obama (only Toomey doesn't make the list among the Tea Party Senators).

One way of interpreting these data is that the Gingrich Senators are behaving more like the "other Republicans" as they accrue more experience in the chamber and as they secure more important positions. An alternative view suggests that just as the Gingrich Senators convinced the Republican Conference to play political games with debt-limit votes, to pay for unemployment benefits by reductions elsewhere in the budget, and to ban earmarks, so it is with opposing Democratic efforts to invoke cloture and to defeat Obama's nominations. What at one point in time was a vote based on the substance of a bill or the qualifications of a nominee has become simply another battle in the raging Senate war for majority party control.

The nomination fight for Obama's choice to lead the Consumer Financial Protection Bureau (CFPB) strongly suggests it is the latter. In 2010 Congress passed and Obama signed into law the Dodd-Frank Wall Street Reform Act, which included a provision to establish a CFPB headed by a director. The bill only became law when three Republicans—Scott Brown, Susan Collins, and Olympia Snowe—voted with 57 Democrats to both defeat a filibuster and pass the bill.

In an attempt to mollify the Senate Republicans, Obama passed over nominating Elizabeth Warren, who had been a partisan lightning rod, in favor of nominating Richard Cordray, who had lost his Ohio attorney general reelection bid to Mike DeWine, a Gingrich former Senator, in the 2010 election. No one questioned Cordray's credentials to lead the CFPB. Shortly after Obama announced the nomination, Richard Shelby (R-Alabama), the ranking Republican of the Senate Banking Committee, wrote Obama a letter stating that 44 Republicans would vote to block any nominee to head the CFPB unless Congress made "reasonable changes" to the law to make it more accountable to Congress.[17] On December 8, 2011, the Republicans held true to their promise when a unified conference—but for Brown—upheld a fili-buster to defeat the nomination.[18] Many congressional observers thought that this was the first time a nomination was defeated not because of the nominee's credentials but because of an objection to the underlying law. In a move that escalated the partisan war, Obama made a controversial recess appointment when he installed Cordray into the position on January 4, 2012. Also unprec-edented was that Obama made the recess appointment when it was not clear that the Senate was even in recess.

D. The 2011 Debt-Limit Crisis

While the data tell part of the story of the First Session of the 112th Congress, the partisan war escalated as the stakes grew. The first half of the 2011 debt-ceiling crisis was recounted through the eyes of the "Gang of Six" in chapter 9. When talks broke down in the Gang of Six and also in the talks convened under Biden's leadership, President Obama and Speaker Boehner ultimately drafted a solution that would raise the debt limit in a series of steps and provide for an automatic sequestration of funds unless the "Super Committee" cut $1.5 trillion from the budget over the next 10 years. The House passed the agree-ment 269–161 on August 1, 2011. After the Senate followed suit, 74–26, one day later, Obama signed the agreement into law.

The three Republicans—all of whom were Gingrich Senators—that par-ticipated in the Gang of Six voted against the final agreement (in opposi-tion to their three Democratic counterparts). They were joined in opposition by the five Tea Party Senators and by seven additional Gingrich Senators (the other 12 Gingrich Senators supported the compromise). The other Republicans (16–5) and the Democrats (46–7) overwhelmingly voted for the package.[19]

Each party leader in each chamber named three members to the "Super Committee." Mitch McConnell named Jon Kyl (the Minority Whip), Rob Portman (former director of the Office of Management and Budget for President George W. Bush), and Pat Toomey. All three are Gingrich Senators, with Toomey carrying the mantle for both the Tea Party Senators and the Gingrich Senators. Much like their predecessors, the Super Committee failed.

E. No Reindeer Games for the Gingrich Senators

The first session of the 112th Congress (2011) was difficult for most senators. Democrats were frustrated that the Republicans made legislating exceedingly difficult. The Republicans were frustrated that the Democrats would not consider important legislation passed by the House. The Gingrich Senators and Tea Party Senators were frustrated that Obama was still in the White House, the Democrats were still a majority in the Senate, and the budget deficit continued to rise.

Shortly after Thanksgiving, Senator Al Franken (D-Minnesota), who is Jewish, decided that the Senate needed to ease the mounting tensions. Conspiring with Senator Mike Johanns (R-Nebraska), he sent an email around to his colleagues asking them to participate in a Senate version of Secret Santa. As Franken explained: "I remember one year [as a child] I picked this kid who used to intimidate me on the playground. Turns out after we got to know each other and we became friends. So, I thought Secret Santa would be a good way to cut through the partisan divide here in the Senate. And who knows, maybe it will create some unlikely friendships."[20] Franken and Johanns set the limit at $10 and picked December 13 as the date that they would exchange gifts.

The trick for the Secret Santa to work, though, was for the senators to participate. They did. At least 58—and, perhaps, as many as 61—senators offered their names up for the possibility of increasing comity (and, perhaps, comedy) in the Senate.[21] The participation rate varied by party. While at least 45 percent of the Republicans participated, 70 percent of Democrats did.[22] The differences among the Republican groups were remarkable: 67 percent of other Republican senators participated, 40 percent of the Tea Party Senators, and 23 percent of the Gingrich Senators.[23]

Secret Santa participation cannot be explained by ideology. The other Republicans who participated were slightly more conservative (0.41) than those who did not participate (0.33). For the Tea Party Senators and the Gingrich Senators, the opposite is true, but just barely (0.79 compared to 0.80 for the Tea Party Senators and 0.50 compared to 0.53 for the Gingrich Senators). None of the differences in ideology are close to achieving conventional levels of statistical significance, which suggest that another dynamic was at work.

Not only was one senator unwilling to participate, but he ridiculed the entire enterprise. Pat Toomey, who has the unique distinction of being a Tea Party Senator as well as a Gingrich Senator, scoffed at the gift exchange. When Ginni Thomas, wife of Supreme Court Justice Clarence Thomas, asked him what he would give Majority Leader Harry Reid if he were to have participated, Toomey replied, "I would give him the inspiration to do a budget. I think I would try to inspire him to take responsibility that the majority party in the United States Senate ought to accept, which is to lay out to the American people just what they intend to do with American taxpayer dollars."[24] Perhaps if he had participated, he would have gotten lumps of coal from Senator Joe Manchin (D-West Virginia). Instead, Manchin gave those lumps of coal, which were carved into a donkey and an elephant, to Senator Chuck Schumer (D-New York).[25]

F. Appearances on Sunday Morning Talk Shows

In 2011 the Gingrich Senators continued to make more regular appearances on the Sunday morning talk shows (NBC's *Meet the Press*, ABC's *This Week*, *Fox News Sunday*, CBS's *Face the Nation*, and CNN's *State of the Union*). They made 65 appearances compared to 30 total appearances for the other Republicans. While there were more than five times as many other Republicans in the Senate as there were Tea Party Senators, the latter had about half as many appearances as the former. On average, the Gingrich Senators had 3.0 appearances per senator, compared to 2.8 for the Tea Party Senators and 1.4 for the other Republicans. In 2011 McCain (19) and Graham (18) had more appearances than the elected leader of the Republican Conference, Mitch McConnell.[26]

The 2010 elections only exacerbated the party polarization and partisan war in the Senate.[27] While the other Republicans appeared to behave a bit more like the Gingrich Senators, the introduction of the Tea Party Senators provided reinforcements in the battle. The year 2011 may very well be an inflection point from which the Gingrich Senators went from being distinct in the Republican Conference to taking over the strategy of the conference in an all-out battle with Democrats, not on substantive grounds but on political grounds. While the Gingrich Senators may have led the fight, the Democrats—including Barack Obama—have shown that they will not back down.

III. Newt Gingrich's Run for the Presidency

While the Gingrich Senators disagreed with the Democrats on most major issues in 2011, on one political issue in 2011 and 2012 they had the same opinion: Newt Gingrich would make an awful president. Democrats, of course, opposed him on partisan grounds. The Gingrich Senators; argument was more nuanced. For as thoroughly as they introduced his tactics in the Senate and converted those in the Senate Republican Conference to become fellow partisan warriors, they as thoroughly rejected Gingrich's run for president.

Several Gingrich Senators passively rejected his run by endorsing other candidates. Allard, Blunt, Brown, Burr, Coburn, Gregg, Kirk, Mack, McCain, Portman, Sununu, Talent, and Thune all endorsed Mitt Romney while the nomination battle was still competitive. DeWine, who first endorsed Romney, switched his endorsement to fellow Gingrich Senator Rick Santorum. The only Gingrich Senator to endorse Gingrich was Bob Smith, who, himself, had become a pariah to his party when he ran for president as a candidate of the U.S. Taxpayer Party in 2000. Gingrich did enjoy the support of several of his lieutenants in the House including J. C. Watts (R-Oklahoma), who was a former chair of the House Republican Conference, and Representative Bob Walker (R-Pennsylvania), who helped start the Conservative Opportunity Society with Gingrich in the early 1980s, while several other Republicans in leadership positions during his days in the House remained neutral (such as Dick Armey, Tom DeLay, and John Boehner).

Their rejection of him was not only passive; it was active. During Gingrich's various surges in the campaign, the Gingrich Senators, both those who continued to serve in the Senate and those who had left the Senate, offered the harshest critique of his days in Congress. In December 2011, as Gingrich's numbers were surging, Talent offered this assessment: "[Gingrich is] not a reliable and trusted conservative leader because he's not a reliable or trustworthy leader."[28] At about the same time, Tom Coburn, while he was on *Fox News Sunday*, was a bit more subdued: "The thing is there are all type of leaders. Leaders that instill confidence, leaders that are somewhat abrupt and brisk, leaders that have one standard for the people they are leading and a different standard for themselves. I found his leadership lacking."[29] Burr mimicked their argument: "Newt's biggest deficiency is he lacks discipline."[30]

When Gingrich's numbers were rising after his South Carolina primary victory and as all eyes turned to Florida, Coburn was a bit more pointed: "I can't support [Gingrich] … I don't believe he has the moral rudder that is required to lead this country."[31] McCain's jabs at Gingrich were a bit more humorous: "I think we ought to send Newt Gingrich to the moon and Mitt Romney to the White House."[32] Gingrich had earlier promised to establish a colony on the moon by 2020. Graham piled on: "I've been very disappointed in Newt Gingrich's statements. We've got enough people in politics who are looking to polls and blowing with the wind."[33] While the Gingrich Senators endorsed the spread of Gingrich's politics in the Senate, they certainly did not endorse his run for the White House. Indeed, they used Gingrich's very own tactics against him.

IV. Conclusion

The lesson from the 112th Congress is that the Gingrich Senators have maintained their status as both party polarizers and partisan warriors. In both quests, they have been joined by another battalion of troops, the Tea Party Senators. One Gingrich Senator, Jim DeMint, was crucial in getting the Tea Party Senators elected and acclimated to his style of antiestablishment behavior in the U.S. Senate.

Because of how drastically the Republican Conference in the Senate changed in 2011, Senator Lamar Alexander (R-Tennessee) opted to resign his post as the Republican Conference Chair, the third-ranking Republican in the Senate. Rather than continue in the position for the remainder of his term, he stepped down a full year before the Republicans would shuffle their leadership positions as a result of Minority Whip Jon Kyl's retirement. After making the announcement, Alexander claimed that he felt "liberated." According to a knowledgeable Republican lobbyist, "Alexander was frustrated with some of the new tea-party-inspired Members—especially with their impatience, disdain for deal-making and low regard for Senate tradition and protocol. Even less appealing was trying to wrangle that crowd as the Whip."[34]

In an article published two days before Alexander made his announcement, Burr handicapped the impending whip race between Alexander and Cornyn. His observation was astute not only for how he characterized the race but also for how he depicted the entire Republican Conference in the Senate: "I'd say that the needs we have now and next year are totally different than they were four years ago."[35] Not only were their needs different, but the entire institution of the Senate was, indeed, different because of them.

11

The Future of the U.S. Senate

WHEN GEORGE W. Bush was elected president in 2000, he was the first Republican president to enjoy majorities in both the House and Senate since Eisenhower in the 1950s. Although the Republican majority in the Senate was only as big as Vice President Dick Cheney's tie-breaking vote, the Republicans were able to pass one of the largest tax cuts in the nation's history when 10 Democrats voted with a nearly unified Republican Conference.[1] The Republicans voting on that bill had the highest extremism score of any Republican Conference since the 1920s and, up until that point, the sixth-highest extremism score in the history of the Republican Party.[2] Only 14 Republicans who voted on that tax bill had extremism scores less than 0.30. Of those 14, only one—Susan Collins (R-Maine)—will continue to serve a term as senator in the 113th Congress (2013–2014). Of the other 13, five retired, six lost, and the last two left the Republican Party. Since then, only four Republicans entering the Senate have had an extremism score below 0.30. During the same time period, the number of Democratic senators who have extremism scores under 0.30 has nearly doubled, going from 10 to 18. In 2001 the Senate took 22 cloture votes; ten years later, they took 50 percent more. No one group better explains what the Senate has become than the Gingrich Senators.

When Newt Gingrich was the leader of only a group of backbench Republicans, he claimed, "I have an enormous ambition. I want to shift the entire planet. And I'm doing it."[3] On his way out the door of the House, his rhetoric was almost as exultant: "There were enormous differences between the role of the previous Democratic Speakers and my role. They had been essentially legislative leaders speaking to the press about legislative matters … I, on the other hand was essentially a political leader … seeking to do nothing less than reshape the federal government along with the political culture of the nation."[4] Some may question if he shifted the entire planet, but no one doubts that he had a profound effect on the U.S. House.

In this book, I argue that the effect Gingrich had on the House had, in turn, a profound effect on the U.S. Senate. If not for the Gingrich transformation of the House, it is unlikely the Republican Conference in the Senate would have shifted so dramatically to the right. While his ambition may not be as enormous, the effect that Jim DeMint hoped to have on the Senate was as fundamental. In the days after Obama's election as president, DeMint pushed the Republican Conference to adopt several rule changes that would strike at the seniority system and the power of the Appropriations Committee. In a number of votes, DeMint's changes attracted no more than a handful of supporters. After the vote, Republican Minority Leader Mitch McConnell (R-Kentucky) commented, "Jim, you can't change the Senate."[5] The truth is, DeMint and the other Gingrich Senators had already changed the Senate. DeMint (2001, 23) walked away from his meeting with McConnell not with his tail between his legs, but with fire in the belly: "If the people in the Senate wouldn't change their minds, then I should try to change the people in the Senate." The five new Tea Party Senators elected in 2010 were DeMint's first step toward changing the people in the Senate and the four new Republican senators taking the oath of office in 2012, who all had ties to DeMint, may very well be the second step; it is unclear if he will be as influential from his new perch at the Heritage Foundation or if any of his acolytes will be as successful as he was in such a short amount of time.

I. The Partisan Senate

The Republican Conference in the Senate in 2011–2012 was more conservative than it has been in its entire existence. The anchors of that conservative philosophy were the 22 Gingrich Senators and their direct descendants, the 5 Tea Party Senators. The other 21 Republicans were only as conservative as the Republican Conference had been at the beginning of George W. Bush's administration. The Gingrich Senators and Tea Party Senators, combined, were 50 percent more conservative than the other Republicans.

While the other Republican senators do not cast as many conservative votes as the Gingrich Senators, they have become increasingly engaged in the partisan battlefield that the Senate has become. More cloture votes, more procedural votes, more botched negotiations, and fewer compromises have left the participants in the battle, as well as the political pundits who are scoring the fight, disgusted. Harold Meyerson, a weekly columnist for the *Washington Post*, lamented, "A catastrophic change has overtaken the Senate in recent years. Initially conceived as the body that would cool the passions of the House and consider legislation with a more Olympian perspective, the Senate has become a body that shuns debate, avoids legislative give-and-take, proceeds glacially and produces next to nothing."[6] While Meyerson was most assuredly talking about Mount Olympus, that adjective "Olympian" could as easily apply to Senator Olympia Snowe (R-Maine), who, in the week after she announced her retirement, complained, "I do find it frustrating ... that an atmosphere of polarization and 'my way or the highway' ideologies has become pervasive in campaigns and in our governing institutions."[7] Senator Evan Bayh (D-Indiana), who retired two years before Snowe, warned, "Our political process is stuck at a time when we need to be moving. And that is to great peril of our country."[8] Senator George Voinovich (R-Ohio), after announcing his retirement, was very specific in targeting the cause: "We got too many Jim DeMints and Tom Coburns!"[9]

The Gingrich Senators may not approve of the functioning of the Senate any more than Meyerson, Snowe, Bayh, or Voinovich, but so long as the Democrats control the levers of power in the federal government, a Senate that does not accomplish very much is exactly what the Gingrich Senators want. They have astutely convinced the other Republicans to fall in line. For the Republican Party, a "Do-Nothing" Senate achieves the joint objectives of stalling liberal policy changes and of showcasing the Democratic majority's incompetence. The Democrats were all too eager to play along as it helped President Obama's reelection effort by portraying Congress in the worst possible light.

The partisan battle in the Senate, though, comes at a cost. The fact that problems do not get solved is mere collateral damage in the raging political war. These scorched-earth tactics have caused consternation among the Gingrich Senators' fellow partisans in the House. Representative Kevin McCarthy (R-California), in a rather pointed and blunt interview during the 2012 election season, chastised the Senate Republicans: "They're on the cusp of winning the majority. They want nothing to happen, right? We need to be a majority; we need to get product finished.... The other thing that people don't think about—what we need to achieve lots of times is the opposite of what Republicans in the Senate need to achieve."[10]

II. The Future of the Senate

The short-term future is bleak, at least for those critical of today's more partisan Senate. And because it is bleak, it will become even bleaker. Lamar Alexander (R-Tennessee), the sixth-most-moderate Republican serving in 2012, has already left the Republican leadership team because he was finding it difficult to lead a party and make the necessary compromises to enact policy solutions into law. Senator Olympia Snowe (R-Maine), the second-most-moderate Republican, has already announced her retirement because the short-term prospects for a functioning Senate look remote. It is unclear if departures like Snowe's will result in an increase in the number of true believers or true opponents. What is clear is that it is unlikely that they will be replaced by either moderate Republicans or moderate Democrats.

The partisan war does not only have casualties on the Republican side. Of the 10 most moderate Democrats serving in 2012, two retired, and three more survived hotly contested reelection fights .[11] While it has taken Senate Democrats longer to join the battlefield, and while it may make some of them less willing to serve, what is clear is that the partisan battle is now fully engaged from both sides. Regardless of which side claims a victory in the near future, dysfunction is certain to remain.

One place where the partisan war is not yet raging is in committees. While Senate committees certainly see more contentious fights than they did before, they still on occasion offer the floor bipartisan solutions to public policy problems. On the floor, though, they get trapped in the partisan war and, like Senate moderates, end up as collateral damage. The next battlefront in the war may very well be the committees. When the Republicans were last a majority in the Senate, four Gingrich Senators were full committee chairs: Chambliss (Agriculture), Inhofe (Environment and Public Works), McCain (Indian Affairs), and Craig (Veterans' Affairs). Had the Republicans regained control of the Senate in the 2012 elections, 10 of the 22 Gingrich Senators would be committee chairs and, because they are not in the majority, currently serve as ranking members: Burr (Veteran Affairs), Coats (Joint Economic), Chambliss (Intelligence), Coburn (Homeland Security and Government Affairs), Crapo (Banking, Housing, and Urban Affairs), Inhofe (Armed Services), Isakson (Ethics), Roberts (Rules), Thune (Commerce, Science, and Transportation), and Vitter (Environment and Public Works). As they accrue seniority, their imprint on the Senate committee structure will only grow.

At this point in most books, it is popular for authors to offer a bevy of solutions to the current quagmire if, in fact, they perceive the current situation to be a quagmire. I will refrain from doing so in this book. Plenty of other congressional observers have already engaged in that useful exercise. I will end this book with different messages to my readers based on how they view the transformation to the Partisan Senate. If, like DeMint, you would rather have true believers in the Senate than compromisers, congratulations! The number of true believers who refuse to engage in serious negotiations has never been greater. While the Senate took a lot longer to become trapped in partisan warfare, there can be no doubt that it now mirrors the divide between the Tea Partiers and the Occupiers in the public or the divide between Republican Leader Cantor's troops and Democratic Leader Pelosi's platoons in the House.

If you look at what the Senate has become and shake your head in disgust, there is only one sure strategy for changing it. And, regrettably for you, it requires more than the senators becoming Secret Santas. Thankfully, though, it is a strategy that has already been developed and implemented. And it has already proved to be successful. It is the strategy of Jim DeMint. If you don't think that you can change the votes or the tactics of the current senators, then change the senators. Since Phil Gramm became the first Gingrich Senator 25 years ago, nothing has so invigorated the party polarizers and partisan warriors as the victory of the Tea Party Senators in the 2010 elections. If the Republican voters had opted for Mike Castle in Delaware, Bob Bennett in Utah, or Trey Grayson in Kentucky, or if the voters on election day had opted for Charlie Crist in Florida, Blanche Lincoln in Arkansas, or Joe Sestak in Pennsylvania, they would have sent a very different message. A message that compromise is still a worthy goal. A message that the transformation to the Partisan Senate ought to stop. And, finally, a message that senators can disagree and they can do so with civility.

The voters seemed to have sent the opposite message in 2012, though not, perhaps, in as loud a voice. Extreme Republican Senate candidates went down to defeat across the United States. However flawed Republicans may have thought Mitt Romney was as a presidential candidate, their Senate candidates did immeasurably worse. In the 26 Senate races in which a Republican incumbent was not running, Romney outperformed the Senate candidate in 21. The would-be Gingrich Senators did especially bad. Just one (Jeff Flake in Arizona) out of eight won on election night. As a class, they did 11 percentage points worse than Romney did in their states. Those who received campaign contributions from Jim DeMint did marginally better, winning three out of nine races. His candidates did 7 points worse, on average, than Romney in those nine states.

Indeed, 2012 was especially hard on the would-be Gingrich Senators and those that DeMint supported. Even without all those candidates who lost, the Republican Conference in the 113th Congress (2013–2014) will be even more conservative. Three of the five most moderate Republicans in the 112th Congress did not return to the Capitol on January 3, 2013, when the new Congess was sworn in. To break a filibuster in the 113th Congress, the Democrats will only need five votes—instead of seven as they did in the previous congress. Nonetheless, it will be more difficult for them to find those five votes than it was to get seven in the last congress because of all the moderate Republicans that did not return.

Notes

1 THE PARTISAN SENATE

1. As quoted in "Obama Discusses State of the Economy," *2009 CQ Almanac*, D-7.

2. These polling numbers are from a Gallup Poll conducted on February 23–March 1, 2009. See http://www.gallup.com/poll/116479/barack-obama-presidential-job-approval.aspx, accessed December 16, 2011.

3. The public opinion data came from a Gallup Poll. See http://www.gallup.com/poll/121997/Americans-Healthcare-Reform-Top-Takeaways.aspx, accessed December 16, 2011. The number of Americans without health insurance came from a study by Families USA as reported by CNN (http://articles.cnn.com/2009-03-04/health/uninsured.epidemic.obama_1_families-usa-health-insurance-health-coverage?_s=PM:HEALTH, accessed March 29, 2012).

4. Quoted in Keith Koffler and David M. Drucker, "Obama Aims at GOP Critics," *Roll Call*, July 21, 2009.

5. Quoted in Michael O'Brien, "Voinovich Admits Some GOP Opposition to Health Bill Driven by Politics," *The Hill*, July 22, 2009.

6. As reported by Philip Rucker, "S.C. Senator Is a Voice of Reform Opposition; DeMint a Champion of Conservatives," *Washington Post*, July 28, 2009, A1.

7. Quoted in Karen Tumulty, "Why Grassley Turned on Health-Care Reform," *Time*, September 3, 2009 (http://www.time.com/time/magazine/article/0,9171,1920306,00.html; accessed January 13, 2013).

8. Quoted on C-SPAN; see http://www.c-spanvideo.org/appearance/556943587; accessed December 16, 2011.

9. Quoted in Jason Hancock, "Grassley: Government Shouldn't 'Decide When to Pull the Plug on Grandma,'" *Iowa Independent*, August 12, 2009 (http://iowaindependent.com/18456/grassley-government-shouldnt-decide-when-to-pull-the-plug-on-grandma; accessed December 16, 2011).

10. Quoted in "Sen. Charles E. Grassley," 2009. *CQ's Politics in America 2010: The 111th Congress*, ed. Chuck McCutcheon and Christina L. Lyons. Washington, DC: Congressional Quarterly, Inc, 388.

11. As reported by ThinkProgressive (http://thinkprogress.org/politics/2009/09/05/59499/grassley-secret-fundraiser/; accessed December 16, 2011).

12. As quoted in Norman J. Ornstein, "Obama's Tactic Could Yield Political Results," *Roll Call*, February 8, 2012.

13. Norman Ornstein, "Our Broken Senate," *The American: The Journal of the American Enterprise Institute*, March/April 2008 (http://www.american.com/archive/2008/march-april-magazine-contents/our-broken-senate; accessed January 13, 2013).

14. Quoted in Lynn Sweet, "Sen. Evan Bayh Won't Run Again," *Chicago Sun-Times*, February 15, 2010 (http://blogs.suntimes.com/sweet/2010/02/sen_Evan_bayh_wont_run_again_c.html; accessed January 13, 2013).

15. As quoted in Paul Kane and Chris Cillizza, "Sen. Olympia Snowe Announces Retirement: Can the GOP Hold Her Seat?" *Washington Post*, February 29, 2012 (http://articles.washingtonpost.com/2012-02-29/politics/35444037_1_fewer-senators-partisanship-moderates-from-both-parties; accessed January 13, 2013).

16. For more on these battles between the Senate and President Washington, see http://www.senate.gov/artandhistory/history/minute/The_Senate_Irritates_President_George_Washington.htm; accessed February 24, 2012.

17. Woodrow Wilson, in 1917, was the next president to set foot in the Senate when he was pushing his plan for peace. He would visit the Senate two additional times, giving addresses on women's suffrage and the Versailles Treaty. The only other presidents who visited the Senate were Warren G. Harding (World War I veterans compensation), Herbert Hoover (economic message), Harry S. Truman (United Nations Charter), Richard M. Nixon (Vietnam policy), and Gerald R. Ford (Cost of Living Council). Data supplied by Don Ritchie, Senate historian, in personal communication.

18. See Galloway (1951) or Davidson (1990) for a thorough description of the Legislative Reorganization Act of 1946.

19. See Huitt's (1961) profile on Proxmire for a contrary view.

20. The simplicity of listing these three explanations, of course, does not reflect the development of the polarization literature. First, I have not included a discussion of the electorate polarizing Congress (see Abramowitz 2010 and Hetherington and Weiler 2009 for two good pieces of analysis on this subject). Nothing in this explanation would suggest that the Senate would be more sensitive to it than the House. Second, I do not explicitly consider the different voting agendas in the House and Senate. In the House a mere majority can close down debate; the hurdle for doing so in the Senate is far greater. Because of the use of unanimous consent agreements, the Senate has the potential to cast many more divisive amendment votes, which would increase members' polarization scores. Of course the differences in agenda control could have the opposite effect: the Senate's freer amendment environment could produce a greater number of amendments supported or opposed by only a small minority, which would be less polarizing. Manipulation of the legislative process in both the House and Senate, so it seems, can cut both ways. These considerations are a matter for further research.

21. These extremism scores are based on their DW-NOMINATE scores, which Poole and Rosenthal (1997) derive by analyzing all nonconsensual roll-call votes in the

Senate from the 1st Congress (1789–1790) through the 111th Congress (2009–2010). All senators are arrayed on a continuum from -1 (extreme liberal) to +1 (extreme conservative). While the derivation of the Senate scores are completely independent of the House roll-call votes, ample evidence suggests that the scores can roughly be compared (Theriault 2008).

22. Gephardt was first elected in 1976, two years before Gingrich's election. Three Democrats (Tom Daschle, Bill Nelson, and Richard Shelby) were elected with Gingrich and after Gephardt. The inclusion or exclusion of these members does not affect the "Gephardt Senator" results described through the book.

23. Not nearly as much consensus exists that Gingrich's early nemesis, Speaker Jim Wright from Texas, was not as confrontational as Gingrich. Republicans argue that their confrontation came about because of the partisan fist with which Wright ruled the Senate. The problem with calling this group "Wright Senators" is that Jim Wright was first elected to the House in 1954. As such, "Wright Senators" would unfortunately suggest an earlier time period for the Democrats.

2 NEWT GINGRICH AND THE HOUSE OF REPRESENTATIVES IN THE 1980S

1. Some have attributed this quote to Tip O'Neill. The dean of congressional observers, Norman Ornstein (2008), however, says that he first heard it from Representative Al Swift (D-Washington).

2. Quoted in Bryan Virasami and Glenn Thrush, "Martin Luther King Day Holiday Controversy," *Newsday*, January 17, 2006, 5.

3. In this chapter, I offer only a brief description of how Gingrich transformed politics within the House of Representatives. Several books explore this with much more depth: Rae (1989), a political science account, and Balz and Brownstein (1996), a journalistic account, are two of the best books on the general subject.

4. Quoted in Diane Granat, "Splits in Style, Substance: Deep Divisions Loom Behind House GOP's Apparent Unity," CQ *Weekly*, March 23, 1985, 535.

5. See T. R. Reid, "Minority Objector; Conscientiously Plays Foes with House Rules," *Washington Post*, March 21, 1984, A3.

6. See "Diggs Censure," 1981. *Congress and the Nation*, vol. 5, Washington, DC: Congressional Quarterly, Inc, 5:922.

7. Quoted in Dan Balz and Charles R. Babcock, "Gingrich, Allies Made Waves and Impression: Conservative Rebels Harassed the House," *Washington Post*, December 20, 1994, A1.

8. Quoted in T. R. Reid, "Speaker O'Neill and Republicans Clash Fiercely in House Debate," *Washington Post*, May 16, 1984, A1.

9. Traditionally, the representative giving the address would send a letter marked to the attention of the member prior to the address so that the accuser could defend him- or herself. Gingrich sent the letters through the interoffice mail on the day of the speech. Many of the Democrats did not even receive the letters in time. See

Haynes Johnson, "Small Band of Republican Zealots Evokes Tactic from the Past," *Washington Post*, May 20, 1984, A2.

10. Quoted in Balz and Babcock, "Gingrich, Allies Made Waves and Impression," A1.

11. See Reid, "Speaker O'Neill and Republicans Clash Fiercely," A1.

12. ABC News Iowa Debate, Dec. 11, 2011 (see http://abcnews.go.com/Politics/full-transcript-abc-news-iowa-republican-debate/story?id=15134849&page=30#.T28_YVHeuyM; accessed March 25, 2012). The answer is slightly modified to remove Santorum's verbal tics.

13. Quoted in Balz and Babcock, "Gingrich, Allies Made Waves and Impression," A1.

14. See *Congress and the Nation*, 7:883–84.

15. As reported in Helen Dewar and Tom Kenworthy, "Conservative Republicans Assail Budget Pact; Democrats Skeptical," *Washington Post*, October 1, 1990, A8.

16. As reported in John E. Yang and Steven Mufson, "Months of Contentious Talks Lead Budget Negotiators to 'Big Fix,'" *Washington Post*, October 2, 1990, A9.

17. As quoted in Helen Dewar and Tom Kenworthy, "Budget Optimism in Senate Isn't Echoed by House GOP," *Washington Post*, October 2, 1990, A1.

18. As quoted in George Hager, "Defiant House Rebukes Leaders; New Round of Fights Begins," *CQ Weekly*, October 6, 1990, 3183–88.

19. Quoted in Kenneth Cooper, "Gingrich: Cooperation, Yes. Compromise, No," *Washington Post*, November 12, 1994.

20. The quote is taken from a personal interview with Randall Strahan (2007, 142).

21. To find the break in the time series, I regress a time trend, an indicator variable for the congresses after the break (to account for an intercept shift), and the interaction of the two (to account for a shift in slope) on the average DW-NOMINATE scores for each congressional class of Republicans from the 80th Congress to the 111th Congress (1947–2010). The model that performed best was the one using the 96th Congress as the break (see the R^2). The F-values can be used to make the same judgment, though the F-values for the first two congresses cannot be compared to the remaining congresses because they have different numbers of independent variables (see table 2.A).

22. Regrettably, a definitive list of members who were in the COS does not exist. In a private email exchange with me, Walter Oleszek, a congressional expert at the Congressional Research Service, included the following members as most certainly being in the COS: Jon Kyl (R-Arizona), Duncan Hunter (R-California), Dan Lungren (R-California), Connie Mack (R-Florida), Newt Gingrich (R-Georgia), Dan Coats (R-Indiana), Vin Weber (R-Minnesota), Judd Gregg (R-New Hampshire), Joseph DioGuardi (R-New York), Barbara Vucanovich (R-Nevada), and Robert Walker (R-Pennsylvania).

23. As these internal races are conducted by secret ballot, a definitive list of Gingrich supporters is impossible to determine and verify. Using records from Gingrich's legislative archive, Douglas Harris (2006) has been able to put together a list of Gingrich supporters, at least from Gingrich's perspective.

Table 2.A Testing for the Proper Disjuncture in
House Republican Ideology

Different Congresses as Dividing Lines	Congress–Specific Dividing Line	Time	Interaction Term	Constant	R^2	F–value
80th Congress		0.014**		0.152**	0.815	132.12
		(0.00)		(0.02)		
81st Congress	−0.108	0.014**		0.248**	0.827	69.30
	(0.07)	(0.00)		(0.06)		
82nd Congress	−0.068	0.061	−0.046	0.187	0.862	58.26
	(0.13)	(0.08)	(0.08)	(0.13)		
83rd Congress	−0.145*	0.019	−0.003	0.243**	0.887	72.92
	(0.08)	(0.04)	(0.04)	(0.08)		
84th Congress	−0.189**	0.004	0.013	0.269**	0.905	89.13
	(0.06)	(0.02)	(0.02)	(0.06)		
85th Congress	−0.211**	0.007	0.012	0.263**	0.939	144.48
	(0.04)	(0.01)	(0.01)	(0.04)		
86th Congress	−0.250**	−0.003	0.022**	0.285**	0.946	164.65
	(0.04)	(0.01)	(0.01)	(0.03)		
87th Congress	−0.275**	−0.008	0.027**	0.299**	0.949	174.43
	(0.04)	(0.01)	(0.01)	(0.03)		
88th Congress	−0.291**	−0.006	0.027**	0.294**	0.959	218.76
	(0.03)	(0.00)	(0.00)	(0.02)		
89th Congress	−0.304**	−0.008	0.029**	0.300**	0.960	223.14
	(0.03)	(0.00)	(0.00)	(0.02)		
90th Congress	−0.310**	−0.008	0.029**	0.299**	0.961	227.97
	(0.03)	(0.00)	(0.00)	(0.02)		
91st Congress	−0.310**	−0.007	0.028**	0.297**	0.961	227.60
	(0.03)	(0.00)	(0.00)	(0.02)		
92nd Congress	−0.324**	−0.003	0.025**	0.279**	0.959	220.59
	(0.03)	(0.00)	(0.00)	(0.02)		
93rd Congress	−0.332**	−0.002	0.025**	0.274**	0.960	222.24
	(0.04)	(0.00)	(0.00)	(0.02)		
94th Congress	−0.331**	−0.002	0.024**	0.271**	0.960	220.89
	(0.04)	(0.00)	(0.00)	(0.02)		
95th Congress	−0.308**	−0.002	0.024**	0.272**	0.963	239.85
	(0.04)	(0.00)	(0.00)	(0.02)		
96th Congress	−0.272**	−0.001	0.022**	0.270**	0.967	272.20
	(0.04)	(0.00)	(0.00)	(0.01)		
97th Congress	−0.265**	0.001	0.020**	0.257**	0.953	189.32
	(0.05)	(0.00)	(0.00)	(0.02)		
98th Congress	−0.239**	0.002	0.018**	0.249**	0.947	165.23
	(0.06)	(0.00)	(0.00)	(0.02)		
99th Congress	−0.214**	0.004**	0.016**	0.239**	0.937	138.80

(*Continued*)

Table 2.A (Continued)

Different Congresses as Dividing Lines	Congress–Specific Dividing Line	Time	Interaction Term	Constant	R^2	F–value
	(0.08)	(0.00)	(0.00)	(0.02)		
100th Congress	−0.200**	0.005**	0.014**	0.229**	0.923	112.04
	(0.10)	(0.00)	(0.00)	(0.02)		
101st Congress	−0.136	0.006**	0.012**	0.223**	0.921	108.17
	(0.11)	(0.00)	(0.00)	(0.02)		
102nd Congress	−0.172	0.008**	0.012**	0.209**	0.895	79.67
	(0.15)	(0.00)	(0.01)	(0.02)		
103rd Congress	−0.141	0.009**	0.010	0.202**	0.886	72.63
	(0.19)	(0.00)	(0.01)	(0.02)		
104th Congress	−0.087	0.009**	0.007	0.195**	0.878	67.28
	(0.23)	(0.00)	(0.01)	(0.02)		
105th Congress	−0.097	0.010**	0.007	0.187**	0.864	59.33
	(0.31)	(0.00)	(0.01)	(0.02)		
106th Congress	−0.044	0.011**	0.005	0.181**	0.856	55.38
	(0.41)	(0.00)	(0.01)	(0.02)		
107th Congress	−0.069	0.012**	0.005	0.174**	0.845	50.78
	(0.57)	(0.00)	(0.02)	(0.02)		
108th Congress	−0.104	0.012**	0.006	0.169**	0.836	47.73
	(0.84)	(0.00)	(0.03)	(0.02)		
109th Congress	−0.221	0.013**	0.009	0.164**	0.830	45.44
	(1.37)	(0.00)	(0.04)	(0.02)		
110th Congress	0.965	0.013**	−0.028	0.161**	0.828	44.99
	(2.80)	(0.00)	(0.09)	(0.02)		

N = 32 for all regressions; *Statistically Significant at 0.05; **Statistically Significant at 0.01.

24. The data were obtained from the FEC and include not only GOPAC (1994) but also Gingrich's Conservative Opportunity Society PAC (1986, 1988, and 1990), Monday Morning PAC (1996 and 1998), and Vin Weber's New Majority Leadership PAC (1990 and 1992). In total, they gave to 146 different Republican House members.

3 THE GINGRICH SENATORS AS PARTY POLARIZERS

1. All the senators were quoted in *CQ Weekly*, December 13, 2003, 3069–70.
2. Harry Byrd Jr. (IN-Virginia) left the Democratic Party in 1970, but he continued to caucus with the Democrats until he left the Senate in 1983. Although the average DW-NOMINATE score for the Democrats in the 96th Congress (1979–1980) was -0.29, Byrd's score was 0.23. Incidentally, Javits's score was -0.25 and Mathias's score was -0.15.

3. Two other Republican senators served in the House as Democrats: Richard Shelby (R-Alabama), elected to the House in 1978, the same year as Gingrich, and Ben Nighthorse Campbell (R-Colorado), elected to the House in 1986. Neither of these senators are considered Gingrich Senators because they never served in the House as a Republican. As the analysis later in the book will show, it is this specific experience that forged the behavior of Gingrich's former colleagues when they made it to the Senate. While Phil Gramm was elected to the House the same year as Gingrich (1978) and, hence, should not be considered a Gingrich Senator, he was first elected to the House as a Republican in 1983.

4. To confirm the uniqueness of the Gingrich Senators and to set the stage for an explanation of their effect, I create a baseline multivariate regression model. The dependent variable in this analysis is the senators' DW-NOMINATE scores. I include nine independent variables, though most of them are to develop the triple interaction necessary for isolating the Gingrich Senator Effect, which is comprised of the three indicator variables: senators that entered Congress (either the House or the Senate) after the 96th Congress (1978–1979), Republicans, and former House members. To get a true read on the triple interaction, I also include the three double interactions. As a control variable to account for the increasing polarization in the Senate, I include a time trend and an interaction between Republican senators and the time trend, and to account for the panel nature of the dataset, I include senator random effects. The overall regression performs well (see table 3.A). The R^2 is 0.793, and six of the nine independent variables are statistically significant.

5. These scores are computed by predicting the senators' extremism scores by simulating all of the scores for all the senators based on the regression results presented in table 3.A.

6. These estimates are determined by changing the values in the indicator variables as well as the double and triple interactions. As such, they incorporate the total effect of the interaction terms as well as the primary and secondary effects.

7. The differences between these averages are statistically significant ($p = 0.0000$).

8. The results are presented in the first row of table 3.B. The dependent variable is the average ideology score for a senator who previously served in the House. The six Gingrich Senators elected to the Senate in the 112th Congress (2011–2012) are not included because they do not yet have Senate ideology scores. The regression underlying the table includes only the Congress in which a future senator enters the House (and in all rows after the first, the indicator variable testing for a difference between an earlier period and a later period is defined by the year in column A). The table shows that only one indicator variable is statistically significant—the one that separates those elected before Gingrich from those elected after Gingrich.

9. I first test the relationship or arrival independently. As table 3.C shows, the difference between senators' first Congress in the House (column A) and their first Congress in the Senate (column B) is fairly marginal. The coefficient for entry to

**Table 3.A The Baseline Model for Determining the Effect of
Gingrich Senators on DW-NOMINATE**

Independent Variables	Coefficient (Standard Error)
Time Trend	−0.005**
	(0.0003)
Republican	0.535**
	(0.04)
Former House Member	−0.051*
	(0.04)
Post–96th Congress	−0.037
	(0.04)
Time Trend * Republican	0.011**
	(0.001)
Republican * Former House Member	−0.011
	(0.06)
Republican * Post–96th Congress	0.064
	(0.06)
Former House Member *	−0.009
Post–96th Congress	(0.07)
Republican * Former House Member *	0.220**
Post–96th Congress (Gingrich Senators)	(0.09)
Constant	−0.265**
	(0.02)
Member Random Effects	Yes
N	1821
R² Within	0.216
R² Between	0.787
R² Overall	0.793

*Statistically Significant at 0.10; **Statistically Significant at 0.05.

the House is bigger, more statistically significant, and a better predictor of Senate ideology than is a senator's entry into the Senate. In the model that forces the two entry dates to compete against one another, entry to the House is again a better fit for Senate ideology (see column C).

10. Because the DW-NOMINATE algorithm restricts all members to moving linearly between congresses, those members who were elected in less partisan eras may be anchored to those less partisan eras, making them appear to be more moderate in more partisan eras. As such, these data are inappropriate to use to see if the Gingrich Senators' distinctiveness changes throughout their career. To test this proposition, I use extremism scores based on DW-NOMINATE scores that remove the linearity restriction. These scores are computed to permit members to change

Table 3.B Testing for the Correct Dividing Line in Predicting Senate Ideology

Different Congresses as Dividing Lines	First Congress in House	Congress-Specific Dividing Line	Constant	R^2
No Congress Dividing Line	0.018**		-1.339**	0.304
	(1.34)		(0.32)	
76th Congress	0.021**	−0.575**	−1.027**	0.372
	(0.003)	(0.21)	(0.33)	
77th Congress	0.021**	−0.363*	−1.300**	0.353
	(0.004)	(0.16)	(0.31)	
79th Congress	0.019**	−0.069	−1.360**	0.307
	(0.004)	(0.14)	(0.32)	
80th Congress	0.021**	−0.575	−1.027**	0.372
	(0.003)	(0.21)	(0.33)	
83rd Congress	0.021**	−0.400	−1.521**	0.319
	(0.004)	(0.12)	(0.35)	
85th Congress	0.022**	−0.168	−1.599**	0.328
	(0.004)	(0.11)	(0.36)	
87th Congress	0.017**	0.020	−1.290**	0.305
	(0.005)	(0.10)	(0.41)	
88th Congress	0.018**	−0.010	−1.372**	0.304
	(0.005)	(0.10)	(0.46)	
90th Congress	0.024**	−0.126	−1.822**	0.322
	(0.006)	(0.09)	(0.48)	
91st Congress	0.019**	−0.025	−1.438**	0.305
	(0.006)	(0.10)	(0.50)	
92nd Congress	0.016*	0.041	−1.170**	0.306
	(0.006)	(0.10)	(0.51)	
93rd Congress	0.019*	−0.013	−1.397**	0.304
	(0.006)	(0.09)	(0.52)	
94th Congress	0.011	0.124	−0.766	0.323
	(0.006)	(0.09)	(0.53)	
95th Congress	0.011	0.125	0.759	0.324
	(0.006)	(0.09)	(0.53)	
96th Congress	0.008	0.188*	−0.467	0.349
	(0.006)	(0.09)	(0.51)	
97th Congress	0.012*	0.125	−0.784	0.325
	(0.006)	(0.09)	(0.50)	
98th Congress	0.011*	0.144	−0.730	0.334
	(0.005)	(0.08)	(0.47)	
100th Congress	0.018**	−0.004	−1.353**	0.304
	(0.005)	(0.08)	(0.45)	
101st Congress	0.018**	−0.013	−1.390**	0.304

(Continued)

Table 3.B (Continued)

Different Congresses as Dividing Lines	First Congress in House	Congress-Specific Dividing Line	Constant	R^2
	(0.005)	(0.08)	(0.44)	
103rd Congress	0.017**	0.041	−1.235**	0.307
	(0.004)	(0.08)	(0.38)	
104th Congress	0.018**	0.017	−1.320**	0.304
	(0.004)	(0.11)	(0.34)	
105th Congress	0.017**	0.093	−1.271**	0.309
	(0.004)	(0.13)	(0.33)	

N = 70 for all regressions; *Statistically Significant at 0.05; **Statistically Significant at 0.01.

Table 3.C Testing if First House Matters More than First Senate

Independent Variables	House Only	Senate Only	Both
First Congress in House	0.0181**		0.0204*
	(0.003)		(0.01)
First Congress in Senate		0.0177**	−0.0026
		(0.004)	(0.01)
Constant	−1.339**	−1.375*	−1.313**
	(0.32)	(0.35)	(0.35)
R^2	0.304	0.276	0.305

N = 70 for all regressions; *Statistically Significant at 0.1; **Statistically Significant at 0.01.

Table 3.D Measuring the Gingrich Senator Effect within Terms in Senate

	(A)	(B)	(C)	(D)	(E)
			Years in Senate		
Independent Variables	Base Model	2 or Less	3–6	7–12	Greater than 12
Time Trend	−0.005**	0.001	0.008*	0.002	−0.007
	(0.0003)	(0.005)	(0.005)	(0.004)	(0.001)
Republican	0.535**	0.645**	0.637**	0.575**	0.515**
	(0.04)	(0.05)	(0.05)	(0.06)	(0.05)
Time Trend * Republican	−0.051*	0.001	−0.013	−0.006	0.011**
	(0.04)	(0.007)	(0.007)	(0.006)	(0.002)
Former House Member	−0.037	−0.080	−0.120**	−0.095*	−0.036
	(0.04)	−(0.05)	−(0.05)	−(0.05)	−(0.05)

Table 3.D (Continued)

Independent Variables	(A) Base Model	(B) 2 or Less	(C) 3–6	(D) 7–12	(E) Greater than 12
			Years in Senate		
Post–96th Congress	0.011**	−0.092	−0.129	−0.105	−0.088
	(0.001)	(0.07)	(0.06)	(0.06)	(0.06)
Republican * Former House Member	−0.011	−0.012	−0.027	−0.043	0.064
	(0.06)	−(0.08)	−(0.07)	−(0.08)	−(0.07)
Republican * Post–96th Congress	0.064	0.078	0.213**	0.171*	0.130
	(0.06)	(0.09)	(0.09)	(0.09)	(0.10)
Former House Member *	−0.009	0.042	0.051	0.011	0.020
Post–96th Congress	(0.07)	(0.07)	(0.08)	(0.09)	(0.11)
Republican * Former House Member *	0.220**	0.191*	0.222**	0.258**	0.283*
Post–96th Congress (Gingrich Senators)	(0.09)	(0.10)	(0.10)	(0.12)	(0.16)
Constant	−0.265**	−0.305	−0.317	−0.272	−0.258
	(0.02)	(0.04)	(0.04)	(0.04)	(0.03)
Member Random Effects	Yes	No	Yes	Yes	Yes
N	1821	218	418	454	735
R^2 Within	0.216		0.088	0.022	0.080
R^2 Between	0.787		0.796	0.775	0.757
R^2 Overall	0.793	0.841	0.791	0.761	0.763

*Statistically Significant at 0.10; **Statistically Significant at 0.05.

maximally between congresses (see Nokken and Poole 2004 for more information on these scores). Keith Poole has not yet generated these scores including the 111th Congress (2009–2010), so the data analysis is performed only through the 110th Congress (2007–2008). For ease of interpretation, I include the base model results (from table 3.A) in column A of table 3.D. Column B has the results for the senators in their first two years in the Senate. The succeeding columns show the results for the remainder of their first term (column C), their second term (column D), and the remainder of their careers (column E). Care should be used in interpreting the results because of all the interaction terms. The Gingrich Senator Effect numbers include not only the triple interaction Gingrich Senators variable, but also the primary and secondary effects.

4 THE CONSTITUENCIES OF THE GINGRICH SENATORS

1. For more interesting tidbits about senators' desks, see the Senate Historian's webpage: http://www.senate.gov/artandhistory/art/special/Desks/history.cfm,, accessed January 13, 2013.

2. The reason that the number is 41 instead of 40 is because Coats has succeeded two different senators—Dan Quayle in the 101st Congress (1989–1990) and Evan Bayh in the 112th Congress (2011–2012).

3. For this analysis, the seven Gingrich Senators who began their Senate career in 2011 are deleted from the analysis (including Coats's second round) because they do not yet have polarization scores in the Senate.

4. The four cases where the addition of a Gingrich Senator had a less polarizing effect on the Senate are when Santorum took over for Harris Wofford in 1995, DeWine took over for Howard Metzenbaum in 1995, Talent took over for Jean Carnahan in 2003, and Kirk took over for Roland Burris in the 111th Congress (2010).

5. Two transitions cannot be analyzed because Blunt, who replaced Bond (R-Missouri), and Portman, who replaced Voinovich (R-Ohio), do not yet have polarization scores since they are serving in their first Senate.

6. Only two of the four Gingrich-Senator-to-Gingrich-Senator transitions can be analyzed, because two of the Gingrich Senators—Heller and Moran—are currently serving in their first term.

7. The Republican Presidential Vote Advantage (RPVA), which is used throughout this book to assess the partisanship of the states, is based on the decade's average of the state's voting patterns so as to smooth out the individual effect of any given election year. In each instance that I use the RPVA, I always check to see if using the data from the most previous presidential election would alter the results. It never does.

8. The difference between these two numbers is statistically significant ($p = 0.0005$).

9. The difference between these two numbers is on the cusp of statistical significance ($p = 0.067$).

10. While the Gingrich Senators have served with other Gingrich Senators on 37 separate occasions, most of the pairs come from a few different states: New Hampshire (Gregg-Smith and Gregg-Sununu), Arizona (McCain-Kyl), Kansas (Roberts-Brownback), Idaho (Craig-Crapo), Georgia (Chambliss-Isakson), Oklahoma (Coburn-Inhofe), and South Carolina (DeMint-Graham). States that would send two Gingrich Senators to the Senate, not surprisingly, are generally pretty conservative states.

11. The difference between these two numbers is statistically significant ($p = 0.0000$).

12. The fourth-largest gap was between Rick Santorum and Arlen Specter before the former lost his second bid for reelection and the latter switched to the Democratic Party. This pairing is particularly interesting because Barry Burden (2007) uses it in his excellent book, *The Personal Roots of Representation*, to highlight the fact that sometimes personal experiences have an effect on the way members of Congress legislate and vote. While Santorum and Specter were both Republicans from Pennsylvania and lawyers before entering politics, they had different personal experiences that could explain their gap in voting that exceeded 0.32 on the polarization score scale. One of the factors that Burden does not consider is Santorum's experience in the House.

13. I average the elections across the decade to smooth out the effect of state- and region-specific outcomes. Using the straight normalized vote (without averaging across the decade) does not change the results at all.

14. For ease of comparison, the chapter 1 results are presented again in column A of table 4.A. In addition to being statistically significant, the RPVA's inclusion reduces the coefficient on the Gingrich Senators from 0.220 to 0.209 (see column B of table 4.A). Care should be taken in evaluating the substantive effect of this reduction because the effect of the Gingrich Senators variable's triple interaction depends not only on its coefficient but also on the coefficient for the three main effects and the three secondary effects. Because of the main, secondary, and tertiary effects with the construction of the Gingrich Senators variable, the best marker for evaluating the Gingrich Senators Effect is not the triple interaction variable; rather, it is the simulated results presented in the main text of this book. Only these simulated results take account of the triple interaction and all of its subsidiary effects.

15. I follow the common practice of including the 11 former Confederate states, plus Kentucky and Oklahoma, in the "South" indicator variable. The inclusion of the latter two states seems particularly appropriate here because of the high proportion of white voters in their electorates and the related conservatism of their congressional delegation. Column C of table 4.A presents the data related to this possibility. The impact of region is captured by an indicator variable for the South and an interaction variable between Republican and South so that the effect of region can be differentiated by party. The results show that, as with partisanship, these constituency indicators are both important determinants of the extremism score.

16. The 0.13 comes from the South indicator variable (0.24) and the South-Republican interaction term (-0.10). The inclusion of region reduces the Gingrich Senators' triple interaction coefficient from 0.220 in the base model to 0.171. Again, care should be used when drawing conclusions from this one coefficient.

17. Democrats represent states that contain, on average, 4.95 million people. The Gingrich Senators' states have 4.87 million and their Republican counterparts come from states with 4.16 million constituents. The only relationship that is statistically significant is that between party and state population ($p > |t| = 0.0034$). The population of the Gingrich Senators' states is not statistically significantly different from either their Republican counterparts or the Democrats.

Table 4.A The Effect of the Gingrich Senators and Constituency Characteristics on Extremism Scores

Independent Variables	Base Model	Constituency Controls			
		Partisanship	Region	Population	All
Time Trend	−0.005**	−0.005**	−0.005**	−0.005**	−0.005**
	(0.0003)	(0.0004)	(0.0003)	(0.0003)	(0.0004)
Republican	0.536**	0.532**	0.584**	0.534**	0.577**
	(0.04)	(0.03)	(0.04)	(0.04)	(0.03)
Time Trend *	0.010**	0.010**	0.010**	0.010**	**
Republican	(0.001)	(0.001)	(0.001)	(0.001)	(0.001)
Former House Member	−0.051*	−0.049*	−0.038	−0.051*	−0.035
	(0.04)	(0.03)	(0.03)	(0.04)	(0.03)
Post−96th Congress	−0.038	−0.037	−0.016	−0.030	−0.007
	(0.04)	(0.03)	(0.03)	(0.04)	(0.03)
Republican * Former	−0.011	−0.011*	−0.020	−0.008	−0.017
House Member	(0.06)	(0.05)	(0.05)	(0.06)	(0.05)
Republican * Post 96th	0.065	0.066	0.032	0.066	0.034
Congress	(0.06)	(0.05)	(0.05)	(0.06)	(0.05)
Former * House	−0.009	−0.003	0.018	−0.008	0.024
Member					
Post−96th Congress	(0.07)	(0.06)	(0.06)	(0.06)	(0.05)
Republican * Former	0.220**	0.209**	0.171**	0.206**	0.144**
House Member *					
Post−96th Congress	(0.09)	(0.08)	(0.08)	(0.09)	(0.07)
(Gingrich Senators)					
Republican Presidential		0.250**			0.253**
Vote Advantage		(0.04)			(0.04)
(RPVA)					
South			0.235**		0.234**
			(0.03)		(0.03)
Republican * South			−0.104**		−0.096**
			(0.04)		(0.04)
State Population				−0.027**	−0.029**
				(0.01)	(0.01)
Constant	−0.265	−0.265**	−0.340**	−0.266**	−0.340**
	(0.02)	(0.02)	(0.02)	(0.02)	(0.02)
Member Random Effects	Yes	Yes	Yes	Yes	Yes
N	1825	1825	1825	1825	1825
R^2 Within	0.213	0.213	0.213	0.218	0.226
R^2 Between	0.787	0.787	0.829	0.789	0.844
R^2 Overall	0.793	0.793	0.834	0.796	0.851

*Statistically Significant at 0.10; **Statistically Significant at 0.05.

18. To see if these bivariate relationships affect the multivariate testing of a senator's extremism score, we include a variable for the state's population. The population variable is standardized by congress so that the natural population increases do not track with more polarized congresses. The results in column D of table 4.A confirm that this constituency measure also has a significant impact. As with the other two variables, the inclusion of state size reduces the coefficient on the Gingrich Senators.

19. Column E of table 4.A adds all of the constituency variables to the base model. They reduce the Gingrich Senators' coefficient by almost one-third. Again, care needs to be used when interpreting this reduction because it also depends upon the magnitude of the coefficients on the main and secondary effects.

5 THE EFFECT OF PERSONAL CHARACTERISTICS AND PROXIMITY TO NEWT GINGRICH ON THE GINGRICH SENATORS

1. The individual variable results would be exactly the same if I included the Democrats and fully interacted them with their party.

2. The Democrats were about the same age as the other Republicans.

3. See table 5.A for the full set of regression results for all of the personal characteristic variables. Care should be exercised in evaluating these regression results. First, only 44 observations are being analyzed, and with the number of variables (16 in the full model) and the interplay of the variables comprising the Gingrich Senators, the data are being tortured much more than they were in chapters 3 and 4.

4. The Democrats had the same proportion of Catholics as the other Republicans (28 percent).

5. The Democrats had just one more lawyer than nonlawyers in their ranks during the 111th Congress.

6. Two Gingrich Senators (Coats and Mack), who were not serving in the 111th Congress, do claim politics as an occupation.

7. While one-third of both groups of Republicans had military experience, only 22 percent of Democrats did.

8. While almost two-thirds of both groups of Republicans were in fraternities, fewer than two-fifths of Democrats were.

9. Democrats Bill Nelson (D-Florida) and Mark Pryor (D-Arkansas), as well as other Republicans Chuck Grassley (R-Iowa), Dick Lugar (R-Indiana), Jeff Sessions (R-Alabama), and Mike Enzi (R-Wyoming), were also associated with the group. Most of these names came from Sharlet's books.

10. For this analysis, Curtis, Scott, Case, Cotton, Javits, and Hruska are all deleted from the analysis because they served in the House prior to the 83rd Congress (1953–1954), which is the last congress for which I do not have data for who served in House leadership positions. In order to keep the analysis focused on the same set of

Table 5.A The Effect of Personal Characteristics on Extremism for Republicans, 111th Congress (2009–2010)

Independent Variables	Constituency Model	Personal Characteristic Controls						All
		Age	Religion	Veteran	Fraternity	Occupation	"Fellowship"	
Former House Member	0.054	0.053	0.012	0.048	0.050	0.082	0.051	0.075
	(0.11)	(0.11)	(0.11)	(0.10)	(0.11)	(0.12)	(0.09)	(0.10)
Post–96th Congress	0.084	0.065	0.079	0.085	0.088	0.089	0.110*	0.152**
	(0.08)	(0.08)	(0.08)	(0.08)	(0.08)	(0.08)	(0.07)	(0.08)
Gingrich Senators (Former House Member * Post–96th Congress)	0.108	0.108	0.133	0.112	0.108	0.050	0.085	0.016
	(0.11)	(0.11)	(0.11)	(0.11)	(0.11)	(0.13)	(0.09)	(0.11)
Republican Presidential Vote Advantage (RPVA)	1.156***	1.221***	1.280***	1.122***	1.140***	0.953***	1.088***	0.772**
	(0.30)	(0.31)	(0.32)	(0.29)	(0.30)	(0.33)	(0.26)	(0.34)
South	0.103**	0.097**	0.073	0.112**	0.105**	0.113**	0.102**	0.123***
	(0.05)	(0.05)	(0.05)	(0.05)	(0.05)	(0.05)	(0.04)	(0.05)
State Population	-0.012	-0.008	-0.004	-0.017	-0.017	-0.020	0.001	-0.025
	(0.03)	(0.03)	(0.03)	(0.03)	(0.03)	(0.03)	(0.03)	(0.03)
Age		0.002						-0.001
		(0.00)						(0.00)
Catholic			-0.093					-0.104
			(0.06)					(0.06)
Jewish			-0.174					-0.114
			(0.13)					(0.12)
Mormon			-0.149					-0.049
			(0.09)					(0.09)
Protestant			-0.024					-0.023
			(0.05)					(0.04)
Veteran				-0.059				-0.116
				(0.04)				(0.04)
Fraternity					0.041			0.011
					(0.04)			(0.04)

Table 5.A (Continued)

Independent Variables	Constituency Model	Personal Characteristic Controls						
		Age	Religion	Veteran	Fraternity	Occupation	"Fellowship"	All
Lawyer						-0.076		-0.024
						(0.04)		(0.04)
Politician						-0.117		-0.140
						(0.12)		(0.11)
Member of "The Family"							0.149***	0.135***
							(0.04)	(0.04)
Constant	0.192**	-2.778	0.257***	0.210***	0.164**	0.256***	0.152**	2.121***
	(0.07)	(4.31)	(0.09)	(0.07)	(0.08)	(0.08)	(0.06)	(4.05)
R^2	0.647	0.652	0.702	0.670	0.658	0.679	0.746	0.832

N = 44; *Statistically Significant at 0.10; **Statistically Significant at 0.05.

senators, even when I have their data for other dependent variables, I do not include them in the analysis.

11. Nine future Republican senators who served with Gingrich began their House careers before him: James Broyhill (North Carolina) in 1968; James Abdnor (South Dakota), Mark Andrews (North Dakota) Trent Lott (Mississippi), and Steve Symms (Idaho) in 1972; Chuck Grassley (Iowa) and Jim Jeffords (Vermont) in 1974; and Dan Quayle (Indiana) and Paul Trible (Virginia) in 1976. Olympia Snowe (Maine) was first elected to the House in the same election as Gingrich.

12. I added each of these variables one by one before entering them all in the same regression. I tried many other slight variations on these indicator variables such as the number of terms that they served in a party leadership position, whether the party leadership position was held while Gingrich was still in the House, and whether serving in both a whip organization and a campaign committee had an interactive effect. None of these variables came even close to being statistically significant.

13. As with the regression results from all the former House Republicans serving in the Senate, I tried multiple variations of the variables to increase their predictive power. In the end, these variations did not have a significant effect on the results.

14. Because Isakson, Vitter, and DeMint never served with Gingrich in the House, they are excluded in the analysis; and because Andrews, Broyhill, Abdnor, Lott, Symms Grassley, Jeffords, Quayle, Trible, and Snowe did serve with him in the House, they are included in the analysis.

15. Fowler (2006a, 2006b) calculates closeness scores for each pair of legislators for each congress in each direction. The transformation of these pairwise by congress to over-

Table 5.B Proximity to Gingrich and Its Effect on Republicans' Extremism Scores

Independent Variables	(A)	(B)	(C)	(D)	(E)	(F)
Terms in the House	−0.015					−0.020*
	(0.01)					(0.01)
Whip Position		0.041				0.002
		(0.06)				(0.06)
Party Position			0.172**			0.146**
			(0.05)			(0.07)
Served with Gingrich				0.169**		−0.047
				(0.06)		(0.07)
Gingrich Senator					0.274**	0.231**
					(0.05)	(0.06)
Constant	0.450**	0.382**	0.301**	0.287**	0.251**	0.299**
	(0.06)	(0.03)	(0.04)	(0.05)	(0.03)	(0.06)
R^2	0.019	0.007	0.140	0.126	0.357	0.412
N = 63						

*Statistically Significant at 0.10; **Statistically Significant at 0.05.

Table 5.C Proximity to Gingrich and Its Effect on the Gingrich Senators' Extremism Scores

Independent Variables	(A)	(B)	(C)	(D)	(E)	(F)	(G)	(H)
Terms in the House	−0.006							−0.027
	(0.02)							(0.02)
Whip Position		−0.038						−0.040
		(0.05)						(0.07)
Party Position			0.094*					0.165**
			(0.06)					(0.07)
Served with Gingrich				−0.144*				−0.037
				(0.09)				−(0.09)
Conservative Opportunity Society					−0.05			0.098
					(0.08)			−(0.08)
Support for Gingrich						−0.008		−0.047*
						(0.04)		(0.03)
Support from Gingrich							−3E−04	−0.027
							(0.06)	(0.05)
Constant	0.547**	0.539**	0.456**	0.655**	0.531**	0.459**	0.456**	0.572**
	0.061	(0.03)	(0.05)	(0.08)	(0.03)	(0.03)	(0.03)	(0.11)

Table 5.C (Continued)

Independent Variables	(A)	(B)	(C)	(D)	(E)	(F)	(G)	(H)
R^2	0.005	0.017	0.085	0.083	0.013	0.001	0.000	0.312
N = 33								

*Statistically Significant at 0.10; **Statistically Significant at 0.05.

all closeness involved two steps. First, I determine the standardized closeness score for each congress that the future senators served with Gingrich. I standardize the scores so that unusual cosponsorship activity in any one congress does not swamp the results from the other congresses. Second, I average the congress-by-congress closeness scores across the entire career that each future senator served with Gingrich.

6 GETTING IN AND STAYING IN THE U.S. SENATE

1. The data for this sentence and the rest of the analysis in this section examines only general election contests. As such, the 13 senators who failed to get their parties' nomination are excluded from the incumbent reelection percentage as are the House candidates who do not survive their parties' primaries.

2. I also include 18 election-year indicator variables to take account of wave election years. The model performs well with an R^2 of 0.546. Table 6.A shows the regression output, though the individual variables should be interpreted very carefully because of all the interaction terms and their constitutive components.

3. Some of the principal components of these terms do not achieve conventional levels of statistical significance, but both sets of variables are jointly significant.

4. The simulated results in table 6.1 are for Republican candidates. As such, according to this simulation, Republican candidates got 40 percent of the vote against former House members prior to 1978 and 43 percent—3 percentage points better—against former House members during the Gingrich Era.

5. The difference in the Republican polarization score is highly statistically significant (p = 0.0000), whereas the Democratic difference is not (p = 0.3749).

6. In the more sophisticated analysis, the dependent variable is the amount of money the Republican candidate raised, according to the Federal Election Commission, adjusted to 2010 dollars to take account of inflation. The data set includes the 485 individual Senate races from 1984 through 2010. The independent variables include the indicator and interaction variables for the would-be Gingrich and Gephardt Senators as well as a series of control variables including the amount of inflation-adjusted money the Democratic candidate raised (which helps act as a proxy for race competitiveness), the state population (logged to take account of

Table 6.A Predicting the Republican Two-Party Vote in Senate Elections, 1976–2010

Independent Variables	Coefficient (Standard Error)	Independent Variables	Coefficient
Republican Presidential Vote Advantage	0.560*** (0.07)	1986 Election	0.072** (0.03)
Republican Incumbent	0.069*** (0.01)	1988 Election	0.091*** (0.03)
Democratic Candidate with House Experience	−0.008 (0.01)	1990 Election	0.098*** (0.03)
Democratic Candidate Running after 1976	0.038** (0.02)	1992 Election	0.100*** (0.03)
Would–be Gephardt Senator	−0.008 (0.02)	1994 Election	0.149*** (0.03)
Democratic Incumbent	−0.084 (0.01)	1996 Election	0.103*** (0.03)
Republican Candidate with House Experience	0.032* (0.02)	1998 Election	0.121*** (0.03)
Republican Candidate Running after 1976	−0.067 (0.02)	2000 Election	0.104*** (0.03)
Would–be Gingrich Senator	0.018 (0.02)	2002 Election	0.153*** (0.03)
1976 Election	0.043* (0.03)	2004 Election	0.122*** (0.03)
1978 Election	0.064** (0.03)	2006 Election	0.088*** (0.03)
1980 Election	0.118*** (0.03)	2008 Election	0.074*** (0.03)
1982 Election	0.058* (0.03)	2010 Election	0.164*** (0.03)
1984 Election	0.109*** (0.03)	Constant	0.413*** (0.02)
N		656	
R^2		0.565	

*Statistically Significant at 0.10; **Statistically Significant at 0.05

the increasing costs, at a decreasing rate, in more populated states), the partisan tilt of the state, indicator variables if the race involved an incumbent Democrat or Republican, and fixed effects for the election years. The model performs well. As shown in table 6.B, the adjusted R^2 is 0.452. The triple interaction variable as well as the set of variables used to construct it are statistically significant.

Table 6.B Predicting Campaign Fundraising for
Republican Candidates, 1984–2010

Independent Variables	Coefficient (Standard Error)	Independent Variables	Coefficient
Democratic Candidate	0.426***	1990 Election	0.078
Amount Raised	(0.04)		(1.27)
State Population*	1.682***	1992 Election	−0.503
	(0.27)		(1.31)
Republican Presidential	−5.072	1994 Election	1.653***
Vote Advantage	(3.87)		(1.32)
Democratic Incumbent	−3.338	1996 Election	−1.130***
	(0.76)		(1.34)
Democratic Candidate	0.636	1998 Election	−0.226***
with House Experience	(1.00)		(1.37)
Democratic Candidate	1.424	2000 Election	−1.545***
Running after 1976	(1.02)		(1.36)
Would–be Gephardt Senator	−1.498	2002 Election	−0.396***
	(1.29)		(1.36)
Republican Incumbent	1.325*	2004 Election	−0.353***
	(0.74)		(1.38)
Republican Candidate	−1.178	2006 Election	0.482***
with House Experience	(1.09)		(1.39)
Republican Candidate	−0.343	2008 Election	−0.473***
Running after 1976	(1.00)		(1.36)
Would–be Gingrich Senator	2.148*	2010 Election	1.896***
	(1.29)		(1.36)
1986 Election	1.091	Constant	1.747***
	(1.32)		(1.52)
1988 Election	−0.459		
	(1.31)		
N		485	
R^2		0.452	

The dependent variable is the amount that the Republican candidates raised in their Senate races.

*State Population is the log of state population to take account of the increasing costs of Senate campaigns, though at a decreasing rate, in more populous states.

*Statistically Significant at 0.10; **Statistically Significant at 0.05.

7. The difference does not reach traditional standards of statistical significance ($p = 0.304$).

8. The difference is statistically significance ($p = 0.000$).

9. The difference in the proportions is statistically significant at the 90 percent confidence level ($p = 0.084$).

Table 6.C Predicting the Two-Party Vote for Republican Incumbents, 1974–2010

Independent Variables	Coefficient (Standard Error)	Independent Variables	Coefficient
Ideology	−0.152	1988 Election	0.044
	(0.04)		(0.08)
Republican Presidential	0.785***	1990 Election	0.120***
Vote Advantage	(0.12)		(0.08)
Democratic Candidate	−0.024	1992 Election	0.081***
with House Experience	(0.06)		(0.08)
Democratic Candidate	0.053	1994 Election	0.116***
Running after 1976	(0.07)		(0.08)
Would–be Gephardt Senator	−0.035	1996 Election	0.072***
	(0.07)		(0.08)
Republican Candidate	0.005	1998 Election	0.145***
with House Experience	(0.02)		(0.08)
Republican Candidate	−0.077	2000 Election	0.135***
Running after 1976	(0.02)		(0.08)
Gingrich Senator	0.050*	2002 Election	0.200***
	(0.03)		(0.08)
1976 Election	0.025	2004 Election	0.157***
	(0.05)		(0.08)
1978 Election	0.083*	2006 Election	0.081***
	(0.04)		(0.08)
1980 Election	0.042	2008 Election	0.08019***
	(0.08)		0.07672
1982 Election	−0.012	2010 Election	0.142189***
	(0.08)		0.07913
1984 Election	0.119	Constant	0.528823***
	(0.07)		0.033638
1986 Election	0.066		
	(0.07)		
N		242	
R²		0.420	

*Statistically Significant at 0.10; **Statistically Significant at 0.05.

10. The difference in the proportions is not statistically significant at the 95 percent confidence level (p = 0.548).

11. In the more sophisticated analysis, I try to explain the two-party percentage that Republican incumbents receive in their reelection efforts. I include variables that

Table 6.D   Predicting the Two-Party Vote for Republican Incumbents Permitting Ideology to Vary, 1974–2010

Independent Variables			
Ideology	−0.184	1984 Election	0.116***
	(0.06)		(0.07)
Republican Presidential	0.788***	1986 Election	0.065***
Vote Advantage	(0.12)		(0.07)
Democratic Candidate	−0.022	1988 Election	0.040***
with House Experience	(0.06)		(0.08)
Democratic Candidate	0.056	1990 Election	0.117***
Running after 1976	(0.07)		(0.08)
Would-be Gephardt Senator	−0.030	1992 Election	0.080***
	(0.07)		(0.08)
Republican Candidate	−0.005	1994 Election	0.113***
with House Experience	(0.03)		(0.08)
Republican Candidate	−0.095	1996 Election	0.066***
Running after 1976	(0.04)		(0.08)
Gingrich Senator	0.031	1998 Election	0.143***
	(0.07)		(0.08)
Republican Candidate with	0.030	2000 Election	0.133***
House Experience * Ideology	(0.09)		(0.08)
Republican Candidate Running	0.053	2002 Election	0.196***
after 1976 * Ideology	(0.10)		(0.08)
Gingrich Senator * Ideology	0.020	2004 Election	0.155***
	(0.16)		(0.08)
1976 Election	0.027	2006 Election	0.081***
	(0.05)		(0.08)
1978 Election	0.081*	2008 Election	0.076***
	(0.04)		(0.08)
1980 Election	0.042	2010 Election	0.134***
	(0.08)		(0.08)
1982 Election	−0.016	Constant	0.538***
	(0.08)		(0.04)
N	242		
R^2	0.423		

*Statistically Significant at 0.10; **Statistically Significant at 0.05.

measure their ideology, the partisan tilt of their state, and the indicator variables that make up the would-be Gephardt Senators (the "would-be" is required because some of the Democratic challengers succeed and others lose) and Gingrich Senators (the "would-be" is not required because the analysis is restricted to incumbents, they are already Gingrich Senators if they have the characteristics). I also include fixed effects for election year to account for the various wave elections that have happened throughout the time period. The model performs well—see the results in table 6.C.

12. In this analysis, the data is restricted to only the elections from 1980–2010. As such, we can use a simple indicator variable if the Republican incumbent is a Gingrich Senator. We interact this indicator variable with the ideology score to see if the effect varies by ideology. The results of the model are presented in Table 6.D.

7 COMPATRIOTS IN THE BATTLE? THE OTHER REPUBLICAN SENATORS

1. In order to preserve his prerogative to reconsider the vote later in the Congress, Majority Leader Dole switched his vote to "nay" when it became clear that the Senate had defeated—at least temporarily—the Balanced Budget Amendment.

2. Julianna Gruenwald, "Hatfield: A Majority of One," *CQ Weekly Online*, March 11, 1995; (http://library.cqpress.com.ezproxy.lib.utexas.edu/cqweekly/WR407342; accessed October 6, 2010).

3. "Santorum—GOP Leadership Must Push Onward," *Morning Edition*, NPR, March 15, 1995.

4. Adam Clymer, "Senate Sets Term Limits for Committee Posts," *New York Times*, July 20, 1995, 11.

5. "Santorum—GOP Leadership Must Push Onward."

6. As the amendments were responsible for 58.9 percent of all roll-call votes, the Gingrich Senators' amendments caused 30.1 percent of the all the roll calls taken in the 111th Congress.

7. Both models perform exceedingly well with R^2 above 0.9, though much of this explanatory power comes from the inclusion of party in the model. The W-NOMINATE scores, based solely on the amendments, show a deep party division. On the other Republicans' amendments, the parties are 77 percent polarized; on the Gingrich Senators' amendments, they are 70 percent polarized. The full model results are in table 7.A. The Gingrich Senator Effect must be evaluated by considering not only the triple interaction but also the primary and secondary effects. The set of variables comprising the Gingrich Senators is statistically significant.

8. The cosponsoring literature has two other branches. First, a number of studies examine the influence that the number of cosponsors has on successful lawmaking (Browne 1985; Fenno 1989; Light 1992; Wilson and Young1997; Koger 2003; Krutz 2005). Several scholars have studied cosponsorship within specific policy areas to understand the process more thoroughly. See Rocca and Highton's (2005) study on abortion policy, Gilmour and Rothstein's (1994) and Theriault's (2005) studies on term limits, and Schickler, McGhee, and Sides's (2003) study on House reform as examples.

9. Quoted in Scott Paulson, "Blagojevich Sentenced 14 Years: Illinois to Have 2 Former Governors behind Bars," *Examiner*, December 7, 2011 (http://www.

Table 7.A Amendment Voting in the 111th Congress (2009–2010)

	Other Republican Amendments	Gingrich Senators Amendments
Republican	1.268***	0.909***
Former House Member	(0.09)	(0.15)
Post–96th Congress	−0.046	−0.127
	(0.07)	(0.10)
	0.029	−0.020
	(0.07)	(0.11)
Republican * Former House Member	0.131	0.328**
Republican * Post–96th Congress	(0.09)	(0.14)
	0.016	0.122
	(0.09)	(0.14)
Former House Member * Post–96th Congress	−0.002	0.057
	(0.07)	(0.11)
Republican * Former House Member * Post–96th Congress (Gingrich Senators)	0.035	−0.029
	(0.10)	(0.15)
Republican Presidential Vote Advantage (RPVA)	1.421***	1.615***
	(0.20)	(0.31)
South	0.047	0.080
	(0.06)	(0.09)
Republican * South	−0.002	0.058
	(0.07)	(0.11)
State Population	−0.008	0.004
	(0.01)	(0.02)
Constant	−0.629	−0.581
	(0.07)	(0.11)
R^2	0.978	0.933

N = 103; *Statistically Significant at 0.10; **Statistically Significant at 0.05.

examiner.com/conservative-in-national/illinois-to-have-2-former-governors-behind-bars-blagojevich-gets-14-years; accessed December 13, 2011).

10. http://www.fec.gov/data/Leadership.do?format=html; accessed December 6, 2011.

11. http://www.opensecrets.org/pacs/industry.php?txt=Q03&cycle=2010; accessed December 8, 2011.

12. The one would-be Gingrich Senator who does not fit into this category is Jerry Moran, who after defeating Todd Tiahrt in a contentious primary faced only nominal opposition in the general election. The other six would-be Gingrich Senators faced more serious opposition.

13. Leadership PACs could have contributed an additional $5,000 for each runoff election, though none of the soon-to-be Gingrich Senators had a runoff.

Table 7.B Key Changes in the Debt Limit in the United States, 1979–2011

Date	New Limit	Total		Democrats		Republicans		Other Republicans			Gingrich Senators			Dif.
		Yes	No	Yes	No	Yes	No	Yes	No	% Yes	Yes	No	% Yes	
4/2/1979	*	62	33	48	10	14	23	14	23	0.378				
9/29/1979	879.0	49	29	34	10	15	19	15	19	0.441				
5/30/1980	879.0	47	10	26	3	21	7	21	7	0.750				
6/28/1980	925.0	54	39	46	9	8	30	8	30	0.211				
12/19/1980	935.1	Voice Vote												
2/7/1981	*	73	18	27	15	46	3	46	3	0.939				
9/30/1981	*	64	34	18	28	46	6	46	6	0.885				
6/28/1982	*	49	41	8	33	41	8	41	8	0.837				
9/30/1982	*	50	41	14	26	36	15	36	15	0.706				
5/26/1983	1389.0	51	41	12	31	39	10	39	10	0.796				
11/21/1983	1490.0	58	40	20	24	38	16	38	16	0.704				
5/25/1984	1520.0	Voice Vote												
7/6/1984	1573.0	Voice Vote												
10/13/1984	1823.8	37	30	0	26	37	4	37	8	0.822				
11/14/1985	1903.8	51	37	13	29	38	8	37	8	0.822	1	0	1.000	0.178
12/12/1985	2078.7	61	31	22	22	39	9	38	9	0.809	1	0	1.000	0.191
8/21/1986	*	36	35	10	26	26	9	26	9	0.743	0	0		
10/21/1986	*	61	25	28	15	33	10	32	10	0.762	1	0	1.000	0.238
5/15/1987	*	58	36	33	18	25	18	24	17	0.585	1	1	0.500	0.085
7/30/1987	*	Voice Vote												
8/10/1987	*	51	39	33	14	18	25	18	23	0.439	0	2	0.000	0.439
9/29/1987	2800.0	64	34	31	21	33	13	31	13	0.705	2	0	1.000	0.295

8/7/1989	*	Voice Vote												
11/8/1989	3122.7	Voice Vote												
8/9/1990	*	Voice Vote												
10/2/1990	*	Voice Vote												
10/9/1990	*	Voice Vote												
10/19/1990	*	Voice Vote												
10/25/1990	*	Voice Vote												
10/28/1990	*	Voice Vote												
11/5/1990	4145.0	54	45	35	20	19	25	19	21	0.475	0	4	0.000	0.475
4/6/1993	*	Voice Vote												
8/10/1993	4900.0	51	50	50	6	0	44	Partisan Vote						
2/8/1996	*	Voice Vote												
3/12/1996	*	Voice Vote												
3/29/1996	5500.0	Voice Vote												
8/5/1997	5950.0	85	15	42	3	43	12	32	6	0.842	11	6	0.647	0.195
6/28/2002	6400.0	68	29	37	14	31	15	21	8	0.724	10	7	0.588	0.136
5/27/2003	7384.0	53	44	3	43	50	1	Partisan Vote						
11/19/2004	8184.0	52	44	2	43	50	1	Partisan Vote						
3/20/2006	8965.0	52	48	0	45	52	3	Partisan Vote						
9/29/2007	9815.0	53	42	26	22	27	20	22	7	0.759	5	13	0.278	0.481
7/30/2008	10615.0	72	13	45	0	27	13	18	6	0.750	9	7	0.563	0.188
10/3/2008	11315.0	74	25	40	10	34	15	23	5	0.821	11	10	0.524	0.298
2/17/2009	12104.0	60	38	57	0	3	38	Partisan Vote						
12/28/2009	12394.0	60	39	59	1	1	38	Partisan Vote						
2/12/2010	14294.0	60	39	60	0	0	39	Partisan Vote						
8/2/2011	14694.0	74	26	46	7	28	19	16	9	0.640	12	10	0.545	0.095

* Indicates a temporary increase in the debt limit.

14. No sitting senator gave any of the primary opponents of these seven soon-to-be Gingrich Senators any campaign contributions from their Leadership PACs except Mitch McConnell, the Republican Leader, and Chuck Grassley—neither of whom are Gingrich Senators—who gave $5,000 and $2,500, respectively, to Gilbert Baker, a state senator, who challenged Boozman in the primary.

15. Quoted in Thomas Fitzgerald, "Specter Staying on Republican Ticket," *Philadelphia Inquirer*, March 19, 2009 (http://web.ebscohost.com.ezproxy.lib.utexas.edu/ehost/detail?vid=6&hid=24&sid=1e195885-03c1-4094-b98d-895142a3bc43%40sessionmgr11&bdata=JnNpdGU9ZWhvc3QtbGl2ZQ%3d%3d#db=nfh&AN=2W62W61931869838; accessed on January 12, 2013).

16. The Leadership PAC data from the 2004 election are as telling as the data presented in table 7.4. During the primary season, Specter collected $92,500 from senators' Leadership PACs—only 13.7 percent came from the Gingrich Senators. Toomey did not receive any contributions from senators' Leadership PACs. During the general election, Specter raised an additional $82,000 from Republican senators' Leadership PACs, and 45.7 percent came from the Gingrich Senators. The Gingrich Senators' proportion differential between the primary and the general election was -32.0. So long as a would-be Gingrich Senators was in the primary, most Gingrich Senators, like Jim DeMint, stayed on the sidelines. After Toomey was defeated, however, Specter received relatively more support from the Gingrich Senators, though none from DeMint.

17. All of the debt-limit votes and their characteristics are outlined in table 7.B

18. Quoted in "Debt Limit 'Weapon' Lacks Force," *CQ Almanac 1995*, 51st ed. (Washington, DC: Congressional Quarterly), 2–63–2–65.

19. Quoted in Manu Raju, "Jim Bunning's Lone Stand," Politico, February 26, 2010 (http://www.politico.com/news/stories/0210/33603.html; accessed December 13, 2011).

20. Reported in Raju, "Jim Bunning's Lone Stand."

21. Quoted in Ezra Klein, "Jim Bunning's Campaign to End the Filibuster," *Washington Post*, February 26, 2010 (http://voices.washingtonpost.com/ezra-klein/2010/02/jim_bunnings_campaign_to_End_t.html; accessed December 13, 2011).

22. Quoted in Emily Pierce, "Collins Tries to Stop Bunning Filibuster," *Roll Call*, February 26, 2010 (http://www.rollcall.com/news/-43712-1.html; accessed on January 12, 2013).

23. Ibid.

24. Perry Bacon Jr., "GOP Lawmakers Optimistic about 'No' Votes," *Washington Post*, July 26, 2010, A2.

8 THE GINGRICH SENATORS AS PARTISAN WARRIORS ON ROLL-CALL VOTES

1. For the Coats quote, see Ceci Connolly, "Health: Panel Recommends Elders, Approves Three Bills," *CQ Weekly*, July 31, 1993, 2068. For Gregg's opposition, see Nancy Mathis,

"Panel Approves Elders/Nominee Awaits Full Senate Vote," *Houston Chronicle*, July 31, 1993, 8. An extensive search of the other two no votes—Strom Thurmond and Orrin Hatch—did not reveal any public statement, comment, or quote.

2. The difference in voting between the Gingrich Senators and the other Republicans is statistically significant ($p = 0.042$).

3. The difference in voting between the Gingrich Senators and the other Republicans is statistically significant ($p = 0.000$).

4. The difference in voting between the Gingrich Senators and the other Republicans is statistically significant ($p = 0.000$).

5. The problems with generating the scores are even worse than this text suggests. In the 101st Congress (1989–1990), when the Senate took 10 contested votes, only 4 Gingrich Senators served. In the 102nd Congress (1991–1992), with 6 contested votes, 7 Gingrich Senators served. Quite simply, too few votes exist to generate confirmation ideology scores.

6. Separating these votes by congress could lead to unreliable estimates as the number of votes in some congresses is too few (again, see figure 8.1).

7. In each case, the correlation between the ideology scores is statistically significant ($p = 0.0000$).

8. The regressions used to arrive at these simulated scores are parallel to the table 4.A regressions, with only minor modifications. First, instead of using a random effects model and a time trend variable, the regression results below used a fixed effects model based on presidential term. See table 8.A for the full results for the ideology based on confirmation votes during Democratic presidential administrations (column A) and Republican presidential administrations (column B). While the triple interaction is insignificant, the set of variables comprising it are statistically significant. The simulated effect, as presented in table 8.2, shows a significant consequence to being a Gingrich Senator, especially during Democratic presidential administrations.

9. While it may be alluring to see if the effect can withstand multivariate testing that includes a measure of ideology, such a test would be inappropriate for two reasons. First, theoretically, it would confound the two dimensions that I outline in the first chapter. Including ideology in an equation of partisan warrior behavior is no more appropriate than including measures of warrior behavior in a model of ideological extremism. Surely these behaviors are mutually reinforcing. Untangling the results seems like a fool's errand. Suffice it to say the Gingrich Senator Effect on these votes is even larger than on extremism scores. Second, empirically, it is unseemly to use a summary measure of voting on both sides of a regression equation. Using ideology derived from roll-call votes to predict ideology as measured by roll-call votes is not prudent.

10. As reported by Felicia Sonmez, "Some Republican Lawmakers Plan to Skip Obama's Jobs Speech," *Washington Post*, September 7, 2011 (http://www.washingtonpost.com/blogs/2chambers/post/some-republican-lawmakers-plan-to-skip-obamas-jobs-speech/2011/09/07/gIQAPKmV9J_blog.html; accessed December 18, 2011).

Table 8.A Confirmation Ideology, Clinton to Obama (1993–2010)

Independent Variables	(A) Democratic Presidents	(B) Republican Presidents
Republican	0.681***	1.031***
	(0.08)	(0.14)
Former House Member	0.018	0.008
	(0.07)	(0.12)
Post–96th Congress	−0.038	0.091
	(0.06)	(0.11)
Republican * Former House Member	0.179	0.092
	(0.12)	(0.19)
Republican * Post–96th Congress	0.354***	−0.042
	(0.09)	(0.15)
Former House Member * Post–96th Congress	0.054	−0.096
	(0.10)	(0.14)
Republican * Former House Member * Post–96th Congress (Gingrich Senators)	−0.071	0.061
	(0.14)	(0.21)
Republican Presidential Vote Advantage (RPVA)	1.058***	0.485
	(0.25)	(0.35)
South	0.054	0.194**
	(0.06)	(0.09)
Republican * South	0.208***	−0.239
	(0.08)	(0.11)
State Population	−0.020	−0.025
	(0.02)	(0.02)
Term = Clinton1	−0.194	
	(0.03)	
Term = Clinton2	−0.347	
	(0.03)	
Term = Bush1		0.069
		(0.04)
Constant	−0.484	−0.566
	(0.06)	(0.10)
Member Random Effects	Yes	Yes
N	290	198
R^2 Within	0.475	0.012
R^2 Between	0.884	0.870
R^2 Overall	0.866	0.769

***Statistically Significant at 0.001; **Statistically Significant at 0.01; *Statistically Significant at 0.05.

Table 8.B Predicting Presidential Support Ideology, Clinton and Obama

Independent Variables	Coefficient (Standard Error)
Republican	−35.674
	(2.05)
Former House Member	0.159
	(1.86)
Post–96th Congress	0.615
	(1.61)
Republican * Former House Member	−1.297
	(2.91)
Republican * Post–96th Congress	−5.998
	(2.32)
Former House Member * Post–96th Congress	−3.018
	(2.46)
Republican * Former House Member * Post–96th Congress (Gingrich Senators)	−2.385
	(3.63)
Republican Presidential Vote Advantage (RPVA)	−35.654
	(6.32)
South	−2.031
	(1.55)
Republican * South	−5.633
	(2.01)
State Population	0.468
	(0.48)
103rd Congress	−12.420
	(1.02)
104th Congress	−16.914
	(1.00)
105th Congress	−6.136
	(0.97)
106th Congress	−9.518
	(0.96)
Constant	95.765**
	(1.60)
Member Random Effects	Yes
N	500
R^2 Within	0.430
R^2 Between	0.948
R^2 Overall	0.917

**Statistically Significant at 0.01; *Statistically Significant at 0.05.

Table 8.C Cloture Ideology, 111th Congress (2009–2010)

Independent Variables	(A)	(B)
Republican	1.345***	0.974***
	(0.17)	(0.17)
Former House Member	−0.103	−0.180
	(0.13)	(0.11)
Post–96th Congress	−0.052	−0.224
	(0.13)	(0.11)
Republican * Former House Member	−0.143	0.086
	(0.19)	(0.17)
Republican * Post–96th Congress	−0.004	0.196
	(0.18)	(0.16)
Former House Member *	−0.020	0.152
Post–96th Congress	(0.14)	(0.12)
Republican * Former House Member *	0.447**	0.110
Post–96th Congress (Gingrich Senators)	(0.20)	(0.18)
Republican Presidential Vote Advantage		1.710***
(RPVA)		(0.38)
South		0.169
		(0.11)
Republican * South		−0.079
		(0.13)
State Population		−0.025
		(0.03)
Constant	−0.579	−0.397
	(0.12)	(0.11)
N	101	101
R²	0.873	0.912

***Statistically Significant at 0.001; **Statistically Significant at 0.01; *Statistically Significant at 0.05.

11. As reported by Jonathan Karl, "DeMint Says He'll Likely Skip Obama's Econ Speech," ABC News, September 5, 2011 (http://abcnews.go.com/blogs/politics/2011/09/demint-says-hell-likely-skip-obamas-econ-speech/; accessed December 18, 2011).

12. As reported by Patrick Summers, "Sen Vitter Picking Pigskin over Politics," Fox News, September 7, 2011 (http://politics.blogs.foxnews.com/2011/09/07/sen-vitter-picking-pigskin-over-politics-0; accessed December 18, 2011).

13. Quoted in "Presidential Support Background," *2006 CQ Almanac*, ed. Jan Austin, 62nd ed. (Washington: CQ-Roll Call Group, 2006), B-19.

14. The regression used for these calculations are reported in table 8.B, which is parallel to table 8.A, though the dependent variable is now presidential support scores

rather than confirmation ideology. While the triple interaction is not statistically significant, the variables comprising it are jointly significant. The simulated effect presented in table 8.5 demonstrates a real Gingrich Senator Effect.

15. For more on this fascinating subject, see Koger (2010) and Sarah Binder's testimony to the Senate Rules and Administration Committee (www.brookings.edu/research/testimony/2010/04/22-filibuster-binder; accessed September 6, 2012). Furthermore, the previous question was not used as an instrument to end debate until 1811. See "The Rules of the House of Representatives," 111th Congress, House Document 111–157, 799.

16. Data on cloture votes taken from the Senate's official website (see http://www.senate.gov/pagelayout/reference/cloture_motions/clotureCounts.htm; accessed March 24, 2012).

17. Koger (2010) shows that the number of filibusters from the 102nd to the 108th Congresses (1990–2004) did not change much. Regrettably, his filibuster count stops before the 110th Congress (2007–2008), so we can determine only if the number of votes has increased or the number of actual filibusters has likewise increased, though the subject matter of the votes hints toward an answer. Of the 91 votes that the Senate took on cloture in the 111th Congress, only four of them were repeats—i.e., 86 of the cloture votes were on at least unique parts of legislation. Using a stricter standard, the 91 cloture votes were taken on 56 unique pieces of legislation. In comparison, when Koger counted 38 filibusters in the 103rd Congress (1993–1994), they involved only 24 different pieces of legislation.

18. The numbers have a correlation coefficient of -0.953 in the 111th Congress, which is statistically significant at the 0.0000 level.

19. The results for the sophisticated model are in table 8.C.

9 THE GINGRICH SENATORS AS PARTISAN WARRIORS BEYOND ROLL-CALL VOTES

1. President Jimmy Carter used the Saxbe Fix to install Senator Edmund Muskie as secretary of state and President Bill Clinton used it to install Lloyd Bentsen as secretary of the treasury.

2. From a Vitter press release (http://vitter.senate.gov/public/index.cfm?FuseAction=PressRoom.PressReleases&ContentRecord_id=1e453722-cbf2-c8f2-461c-11474e0559a6; accessed December 18, 2011). The "boot on the neck" quote is the same one that Salazar used in reference to BP as it started cleaning up the Gulf.

3. As quoted in Amanda Becker, "Reid Faults Vitter, Presses for Raise for Salazar," *Roll Call*, May 25, 2011 (http://www.rollcall.com/news/reid_faults_vitter_salazar_raise_gulf-205980-1.html ; accessed January 13, 2013).

4. Ibid.

5. Ibid.

6. A Senate Ethics Committee, in dismissing a complaint by the Citizens for Responsibility and Ethics in Washington, chastised Vitter in a letter written by Chair Barbara Boxer (D-California) and Vice Chair Johnny Isakson: "While the committee found that there was no substantial credible evidence that you violated the law or Senate rules, it did conclude that it is inappropriate to condition support for a Secretary's personal salary increase directly on his or her performance of a specific official act." Quoted in Darren Goode, "After Ethics Ruling, David Vitter Vows to Keep Blocking Ken Salazar's Pay Raise," politico.com, March 30, 2012 (http://www.politico.com/news/stories/0312/74689.html; accessed April 22, 2012).

7. Transcripts for the episode are at http://www.msnbc.msn.com/id/15330717/ns/msnbc_tv-hardball_with_chris_matthews/t/hardballs-college-tour-john-mccain/#.TvDdZJiQs-c; accessed December 20, 2011.

8. The Zogby International Poll results, as published in "Opinions of Military Personnel on Sexual Minorities in the Military" can be downloaded: http://www.palmcenter.org/files/active/0/ZogbyReport.pdf; accessed December 20, 2011.

9. As reported in an editorial, "Old Prejudice Dishonors New Military Generation," *USA Today*, March 14, 2007, 10A.

10. As reported in Elisabeth Bumiller, "A Call to Topple Policy for Gays in Armed Forces," *New York Times*, February 3, 2010, 1.

11. See Dana Milibank, "Give Mullen a Medal for Bravery in Hostile Senate Territory," *Washington Post*, February 3, 2010, 2.

12. McCain early voiced support for waiting until the survey was released, but this particular quote comes from Joe Davidson, "A Senate Vote Could Go a Long Way to Ending 'Don't Ask, Don't Tell,'" *Washington Post*, September 21, 2010, B3.

13. As quoted in Elisabeth Bumiller, "Service Chiefs Seek to Delay Vote on Gays," *New York Times*, May 27, 2010, 19.

14. As quoted in David M. Herszenhorn, "Hoping to Keep Majority, Democrats Wield It," *New York Times*, September 17, 2010, 15.

15. See Elisabeth Bumiller, "Top Brass and McCain Square Off Over Gays," *New York Times*, December 3, 2010, 16.

16. See Ed O'Keefe, "McCain Wants More Time before End of 'Don't Ask,'" *Washington Post*, November 15, 2010, A19. Also, see Ed O'Keefe, "Pentagon Worries That Congress Won't End 'Don't Ask, Don't Tell,'" *Washington Post*, December 3, 2010, A8.

17. For a more pointed criticism of McCain's role in the debate see Dana Milbank, "After McCain Flares Up, Senate's Cooler Heads Prevail," *Washington Post*, December 19, 2010, A8.

18. The data and quote come from Emily Cadei, "For GOP, A Cold War Vet Is Not Hawk Enough," *CQ Weekly*, May 17, 2010, 1191.

19. As quoted in Emily Cadei, "Measuring Kyl's Clout," *CQ Weekly*, December 6, 2010, 2800.

20. Ibid., 2803.

21. As quoted in Peter Baker, "Obama Rallying Support for Arms Pact with Russia," *New York Times*, December 2, 2010, 25.

22. As quoted in Cadei, "Measuring Kyl's Clout," 2806.

23. Ibid.

24. Quoted in David M. Drucker, "Kyl: GOP Can Play More Than Just Defense," *Roll Call*, January 10, 2011, 4.

25. Senator Kyl (AZ). "Budget Negotiations." *Congressional Record* 157, no. 51 (April 8, 2011): S2289.

26. As quoted in Jason Linkins, "Jon Kyl Now Says He 'Misspoke' on Planned Parenthood So Everyone Should Please Stop Making Fun of Him," *Huffington Post*, April 15, 2011 (http://www.huffingtonpost.com/2011/04/15/jon-kyl-planned-parenthood-factual-statement_n_849658.html; accessed December 20, 2011).

27. Ibid.

28. As quoted in Jackie Calmes, "'Gang of Six' in the Senate Seeking a Plan on Debt," *New York Times*, April 16, 2011.

29. Hutchison challenged incumbent Governor Rick Perry, but lost in the primary. Bennett was seeking reelection, though the convention process, which Utah uses, denied him renomination.

30. The floor mechanics on this amendment are a bit tricky. Instead of subjecting Democrats to an explicit vote on the amendment, Senator Max Baucus (D-Montana) offered a motion to table Coburn's amendment. Fifty-five out of 57 Democrats voted for that motion, thus the amendment was tabled, which in this instance is equivalent to defeating the amendment.

31. As quoted in Chris Casteel, "U.S. Sen. Tom Coburn's Viagra Amendment Fails," NewsOK, March 25, 2010 (http://newsok.com/u.s.-sen.-tom-coburns-viagra-amendment-fails/article/3449000; accessed December 20, 2011).

32. The regressions used to derive the simulated results are reported in table 9.A.

33. In the previous chapter, I argued that including ideology was inappropriate both theoretically and empirically. Because the new dependent variable is not based on roll-call votes, I offer the analysis including ideology in this footnote even though it still violates my theoretical concern (see table 9.B and column C of table 9.A).

34. McConnell, incidentally, ranked 74th in offering only 26 amendments. He ranked 79th in only introducing 19 bills.

35. This correlation is statistically significant at the 0.0001 level.

36. This correlation is not statistically significant ($p = 0.71$).

37. The other senators in the top ten were Finance Committee Chair Baucus (D-Montana; ranked 5th with 17), Majority Leader Reid (D-Nevada; 7th, 15), and Sessions (10th, 12).

38. The results for the sophisticated model are in table 9.C.

39. Again, with much hesitancy, I offer the analysis including ideology (see table 9.D and column C of table 9.C).

Table 9.A Predicting Amendment Introductions in the 111th Congress (2009–2010)

Independent Variables	(A)	(B)	(C)
Republican	9.080	4.053	−32.234
	(32.34)	(36.71)	(47.65)
Former House Member	15.672	14.695	13.985
	(23.96)	(24.32)	(27.65)
Post-96th Congress	8.666	2.833	2.345
	(23.36)	(24.56)	(29.38)
Republican * Former House Member	2.730	9.554	8.033
	(34.89)	(36.91)	(37.30)
Republican * Post-96th Congress	−4.931	0.274	−4.362
	(34.03)	(35.16)	(37.04)
Former House Member * Post-96th Congress	1.800	5.050	7.296
	(26.34)	(27.14)	(29.75)
Republican * Former House Member * Post-96th Congress (Gingrich Senators)	30.352	27.524	17.301
	(37.47)	(39.67)	(40.70)
Republican Presidential Vote Advantage (RPVA)		70.412	12.684
		(78.17)	(90.22)
South		2.643	−1.526
		(23.15)	(23.51)
Republican * South		−24.465	−27.374
		(27.81)	(28.09)
State Population		1.994	2.665
		(5.82)	(5.89)
DW-NOMINATE			64.237
			(48.74)
Constant	23.052	30.135	52.914
	(22.11)	(24.29)	(34.24)
N	109	109	109
R^2	0.132	0.152	0.165

*Statistically Significant at 0.05.

Table 9.B The Gingrich Senator Effect on Amendments Offered, Taking into Consideration Constituency Factors and Ideology, 111th Congress (2009–2010)

Republicans			Democrats		
	No House Experience	House Experience		No House Experience	House Experience
Pre-1978	11.39	33.41	Pre-1978	49.79	63.78
Post-1978	9.37	55.99	Post-1978	52.14	73.42
Gingrich Senator Effect		2.10	Gephardt Senator Effect		0.33

Table 9.C Predicting Roll-Call Votes on Amendments,
111th Congress (2009–2010)

Independent Variables	(A)	(B)	(C)
Republican	−0.162	−2.996	−11.512
	(3.50)	(3.95)	(4.97)
Former House Member	2.755	2.375	1.872
	(2.59)	(2.62)	(2.88)
Post–96th Congress	−0.438	−1.178	−1.700
	(2.53)	(2.64)	(3.06)
Republican * Former House Member	−1.425	0.050	−0.228
	(3.77)	(3.97)	(3.89)
Republican * Post–96th Congress	2.769	3.927	3.156
	(3.68)	(3.79)	(3.86)
Former House Member *	−1.235	−0.532	0.293
Post–96th Congress	(2.85)	(2.92)	(3.10)
Republican * Former House Member *	7.503*	5.389	3.030
Post–96th Congress (Gingrich Senators)	(4.05)	(4.27)	(4.24)
Republican Presidential Vote Advantage		9.694	−3.503
(RPVA)		(8.42)	(9.41)
South		−1.897	−2.841
		(2.49)	(2.45)
Republican * South		3.607	2.990
		(2.99)	(2.93)
State Population		−0.222	−0.103
		(0.63)	(0.61)
DW–NOMINATE			14.541***
			(5.08)
Constant	1.497	2.711	8.286**
	(2.39)	(2.62)	(3.57)
N	109	109	109
R^2	0.296	0.319	0.371

***Statistically Significant at 0.001; **Statistically Significant at 0.01; *Statistically Significant at 0.05.

40. The difference in appearances between the Gingrich Senators and the other Republicans is not statistically significant ($p = 0.317$). When McConnell is deleted from the analysis, the difference nears statistical significance ($p = 0.113$).
41. The Democratic senators' approval numbers are similar to the Republicans. Their fellow partisans gave them a net approval of 51 percentage points and their Republican constituents gave them a net disapproval of 7 percentage points, which is just about halfway in between the Gingrich Senators and the other Republicans.
42. The correlation of the approval numbers for own-party and other-party constituents is statistically significant ($p = 0.000$).

Table 9.D The Gingrich Senator Effect on the Number of Amendment Roll-Call Votes Taking into Consideration Constituency Factors and Ideology, 111th Congress (2009–2010)

Republicans			Democrats		
	No House Experience	House Experience		No House Experience	House Experience
Pre-1978	4.09	5.74	Pre-1978	3.30	5.17
Post-1978	5.55	10.52	Post-1978	1.60	3.76
Gingrich Senator Effect		1.05	Gephardt Senator Effect		0.12

10 THE 2010 ELECTIONS, THE 112TH CONGRESS, THE TEA PARTY SENATORS, AND GINGRICH'S PRESIDENTIAL CAMPAIGN

1. Data taken from a Gallup Poll as reported by "The American Presidency Project" (http://www.presidency.ucsb.edu/data/popularity.php; accessed March 10, 2012).

2. See http://cookpolitical.com/charts/senate/raceratings_2009–07–15_13–59–09.php; accessed March 10, 2012.

3. See http://cookpolitical.com/charts/senate/raceratings_2010–01–14_14–48–48.php; accessed March 10, 2012.

4. See Kate Zernike, "Tea Party Set to Win Enough Races for Wide Influence," *New York Times*, October 14, 2010 (http://www.nytimes.com/2010/10/15/us/politics/15teaparty.html?_r=0; accessed January 13, 2013).

5. See Timothy P. Carney, "Did DeMint's Endorsement of Toomey Set Off Specter?" *Washington Examiner*, April 2009 (http://washingtonexaminer.com/politics/beltway-confidential/2009/04/did-demints-endorsement-toomey-set-specter/136018; accessed March 10, 2012).

6. As reported by Manu Raju, "Jim DeMint Backs Marco Rubio in Florida Governor Race," Politico, June 15, 2009 (http://www.politico.com/news/stories/0609/23754.html; accessed March 12, 2012). Incidentally, the headline of this article is inaccurate—the endorsement was in the Senate race.

7. As reported by Reid Wilson, "Senator DeMint Bucks Republican Party, Backs Conservative in California Race," *The Hill*, November 4, 2009, (http://thehill.com/homenews/campaign/66169-demint-bucks-party-backs-conservative-in-california; accessed March 10, 2012).

8. The SCF claimed that DeMint was responsible for raising more than $9.3 million in the 2010 cycle (see http://senateconservatives.com/site/post/692/release-scf-raises-100000-for-mandel; accessed March 31, 2012). The records filed with the FEC show that DeMint raised less than that amount. As such, it is not clear for whom

he raised that much and how it was distributed. In an earlier SCF press release (http://senateconservatives.com/site/post/366/scf-tops-5-million-candidate-goal; accessed April 3, 2012), $5.2 million of the $9.3 million is accounted. This includes $554,000 to candidates that lost in the primary (the FEC only reports $156,709 of that amount). It also includes $1,856,000 in donations to state GOP victory committees. The same press release announced that he had raised more than $7 million.

9. See Alexander Bolton, "DeMint's Leadership PAC Battles Leaders in Fight for Future of Senate GOP Caucus," *The Hill*, August 4, 2011 (http://thehill.com/homenews/senate/175397-demints-leadership-pac-battles-leaders-in-fight-for-future-of-senate; accessed January 13, 2013). .

10. See http://www.heritage.org/events/2010/11/mitch-mcconnell; accessed March 13, 2012.

11. *Congressional Record*, 111th Congress, 2nd Session, November 15, 2010, S7872.

12. The roll-call votes of the Gingrich Senators and the other Republicans are statistically significantly different from one another (p = 0.010).

13. The roll-call votes among the Tea Party Senators, the Gingrich Senators, and the other Republicans are statistically significantly different from one another (p = 0.042 for Gingrich Senators and other Republicans; 0.013 for Gingrich Senators and Tea Party Senators; and 0.000 for Tea Party Senators and other Republicans).

14. Extremism scores for 2011 are based on the DW-NOMINATE estimates for all roll-call votes from the 1st Congress through the first session of the 112th Congress as calculated by Keith Poole. These data are not available on Poole's website.

15. Not all the Gingrich Senators greeted the Tea Party Senators with open arms. In separate incidents, McCain, on the Senate floor, went after Paul on his foreign policy views and Toomey on his budget views. For the former, see Halimah Abdullah, "D.C. Is Big Tea Party for Rand Paul," *Houston Chronicle*, December 11, 2011, A38. For the latter, see David M. Drucker, "McCain Spars with Activists on Debt," *Roll Call*, July 29, 2011, 3. On the other hand, McCain has become a mentor to Portman, a fellow Gingrich Senator. See David M. Drucker, "McCain Coaches Portman," *Roll Call*, September 13, 201, 1.

16. This assessment is based on an average polarizing score of the Tea Party Senators of 0.80 multiplied by the five senators giving them a total polarizing effect of 3.98. The 22 Gingrich Senators had an average polarizing score of 0.53, giving them a polarizing effect of 12.15, which is more than three times larger than the effect of the Tea Party Senators.

17. See Richard Shelby, "The Danger of an Unaccountable 'Consumer-Protection' Czar," *Wall Street Journal*, July 21, 2011, 17.

18. While Collins switched her vote to uphold the filibuster even though she voted for the initial legislation, Snowe voted "present" to avoid a potential conflict with her husband's business involving student loans that are regulated by the agency.

19. The roll-call votes among the Tea Party Senators, the Gingrich Senators, and the other Republicans are statistically significantly different from one another (p = 0.063 for Gingrich Senators and other Republicans; 0.000 for Gingrich Senators and Tea Party Senators; and 0.000 for Tea Party Senators and other Republicans).

20. As quoted in Jennifer Steinhauer, "Secret Santa in the Senate," *New York Times*, November 30, 2011 (http://thecaucus.blogs.nytimes.com/2011/11/30/secret-santa-in-the-senate/; accessed January 13, 2013).

21. On the day of the drawing, 58 senators participated. On the day of the gift exchange, news accounts indicated that as many as 61 senators exchanged gifts. All news accounts said that either 21 or 22 Republicans participated. Through an extensive search of the Internet, including news articles, press releases, and blogs, 21 Republican senators and 29 Democratic senators could be identified.

22. The proportions are statistically significantly different from one another (p = 0.015).

23. The Tea Party Senators who participated were Rubio and Lee. The Gingrich Senators who participated were Boozman, Crapo, Portman, Vitter, and Wicker. The differences in proportions between the Gingrich Senators and the other Republicans is statistically significant (p = 0.001). The difference in proportions involving the Tea Party Senators is not (p = 0.767 with the Gingrich Senators and p = 0.135 with the other Republicans).

24. See http://dailycaller.com/2011/12/24/sen-toomey-on-his-secret-santa-gift-for-sen-reid-video/#ixzz1pNuuu000; accessed March 17, 2012.

25. To learn more about the gifts given and received, see Ann Gerhart, "Senate's Secret Santas Make Their Rounds," *Washington Post*, December 13, 2011 (http://articles.washingtonpost.com/2011-12-13/lifestyle/35285223_1_secret-santa-republican-senators-gifts; accessed January 13, 2013. Interestingly, the article was published in the Style section, not on the front page.

26. The difference in appearances between the Gingrich Senators and the other Republicans is not quite statistically significant (p = 0.141), unless McConnell is deleted from the analysis (p = 0.051). The differences in appearances between the Tea Party Senators and the other Republicans (p = 0.185) or between the Tea Party Senators and the Gingrich Senators (p = 0.438) are not statistically significant.

27. Through the 2010 elections, the Gingrich Senators not only transformed the Senate but also, as it turns out, the Republican Conference in the Kansas Legislature. Brownback, who was elected its governor in 2010, took the lessons of the Gingrich Senators to the state legislature. When Republican moderates, in the tradition of Senators Bob Dole and Nancy Kassebaum, dared to cross him, he vowed revenge: "We cannot continue on this path and hope we can move forward and win the future. It won't work. We have to change course, and we're going to have to be aggressive about it or we are doomed to a slow decline." Nine of them faced primary challengers in 2012. Quote from Annie Gowen, "In Kansas, Gov. Sam Brownback Puts Tea Party Tenets into Action with Sharp Cuts," *Washington Post*, December 21,

2011 (http://articles.washingtonpost.com/2011–12–21/politics/35286057_1_sa m-brownback-state-pensions-repealer; access January 13, 2013).

28. Quoted in Paul West, "Gingrich's Record Belies His Conservative Image," *Los Angeles Times*, December 8, 2011 (http://articles.latimes.com/2011/dec/08/nation/ la-na-1209-gingrich-conservative-20111209; accessed January 13, 2013).

29. Coburn was on *Fox News Sunday* on December 4, 2011. His appearance was reported in Kathleen Hennessey, "Tom Coburn Takes Dim View of Newt Gingrich as President," *Los Angeles Times*, December 4, 2011 (http://articles.latimes. com/2011/dec/04/news/la-pn-coburn-gingrich-20111204; accessed January 13, 2013).

30. Quoted in David M. Drucker, "Lack of Discipline Could Bite Gingrich," *Roll Call*, December 6, 2011, 3.

31. Reported in Josiah Ryan, "Coburn: Gingrich Lacks 'Moral Rudder,'" *The Hill*, December 6, 2012 (http://thehill.com/blogs/floor-action/senate/208809-coburn-gi ngrich-lacks-moral-rudder-; accessed January 13, 2013).

32. As reported by Arlette Saenz, "John McCain: Send Newt Gingrich to the Moon!" ABC News' "The Note," January 27, 2012 (http://abcnews.go.com/blogs/politics/2012/01/ john-mccain-send-newt-gingrich-to-the-moon/; accessed March 13, 2012).

33. As quoted in Steven T. Dennis, "Fracturing GOP Positions on War in Afghanistan," *Roll Call*, March 14, 2012, 6.

34. Quotes from David M. Drucker, "Alexander Takes a Step Back," *Roll Call*, September 21, 2011, 1.

35. As quoted in David M. Drucker, "Independence Could Stall Alexander's Rise," *Roll Call*, September 19, 2011, 1 and 12.

11 THE FUTURE OF THE U.S. SENATE

1. John McCain and Lincoln Chafee (R-Rhode Island) voted against the bill. Pete Domenici (R-New Mexico) and Mike Enzi (R-Wyoming) did not vote.

2. The Republican Conferences in the 65th through 69th Congresses (1917–1926) were more polarized than in the 107th.

3. As quoted in Louis Romano, "Newt Gingrich, Maverick on the Hill; The New Right's Abrasive Point Man Talks of Changing His Tone and Tactics," *Washington Post*, January 3, 1985, B1.

4. As quoted in Strahan (2007, 127). The quote originated from Gingrich's (1998) book, *Lessons Learned the Hard Way*.

5. As quoted in DeMint (2011, 23).

6. Harold Meyerson, "The Do-Nothing Senate," *Washington Post*, November 11, 2009, A25.

7. Quoted in "Snowe, Kerrey Complicate GOP Goals," March 5, 2012, *CQ Weekly*, 450.

8. From an interview by Bob Schieffer on *Face the Nation*, March 7, 2010.

9. Quoted in Alec MacGillis, "Is the South Too Republican for Republicans?" *New Republic*, March 12, 2012 (http://www.tnr.com/blog/the-stump/101634/the-south -too-republican-republicans; accessed April 22, 2012). Voinovich didn't label the group of DeMints and Coburns as the "Gingrich Senators" but as Southerners. The analysis in chapter 3 and throughout this book suggests that the Gingrich Senators are more distinctive than even the Southern Republicans.

10. Quoted in John Stanton, "GOP Whip Swipes at Senate," *Roll Call*, March 21, 2012, 1.

11. Ben Nelson (D-Nebraska) and Jim Webb (D-Virginia) retired. Bill Nelson (D-Florida) and Claire McCaskill (D-Missouri) both did better on election night than many political observers thought they would, in part, because of the ineptness of their Republican opponents.

Bibliography

Abramowitz, Alan I. 2010. *The Disappearing Center: Engaged Citizens, Polarization and American Democracy.* New Haven: Yale University Press.

Asher, Herbert B. 1973. "The Learning of Legislative Norms." *American Political Science Review* 67 (June): 499–513.

Balz, Dan, and Ronald Brownstein. 1996. *Storming the Gates: Protest Politics and the Republican Revival.* New York: Little, Brown.

Binder, Sarah A., and Forrest Maltzman. 2009. *Advice and Dissent: The Struggle to Shape the Federal Judiciary.* Washington, DC: Brookings Institution Press.

Bishop, Bill. 2008. *The Big Sort: Why the Clustering of Like-Minded America Is Tearing Us Apart.* New York: Houghton Mifflin.

Black, Earl, and Merle Black. 2002. *The Rise of Southern Republicans.* Cambridge, MA: Harvard University Press.

Bond, Jon R., Richard Fleisher, and Glen S. Krutz. 2009. "Malign Neglect: Evidence that Delay Has Become the Primary Method of Defeating Presidential Appointments." *Congress and the Presidency.* 36, no. 3: 226–43.

Brady, David W., Hahrie Han, and Jeremy C. Pope. 2007. "Primary Elections and Candidate Ideology: Out of Step with the Primary Electorate?" *Legislative Studies Quarterly* 32, no. 2: 59–78.

Browne, William P. 1985. "Multiple Sponsorship and Bill Success in the U.S. State Legislatures." *Legislative Studies Quarterly* 10, no. 3: 483–88.

Browne, William P., and Delbert J. Ringquist. 1985. "Sponsoring and Enactment: State Lawmakers and Aging Legislation, 1956–1978." *American Politics Quarterly* 13, no. 4: 447–66.

Burden, Barry C. 2007. *The Personal Roots of Representation.* Princeton, NJ: Princeton University Press.

Cain, Bruce, John Ferejohn, and Morris Fiorina. 1987. *The Personal Vote: Constituency Service and Electoral Independence.* Cambridge, MA: Harvard University Press.

Carney, Timothy P. 2009. "Did DeMint's Endorsement of Toomey Set Off Specter?" *Washington Examiner*, April 27.

Carson, Jamie, Charles Finocchiaro, and David Rohde. 2007. "Redistricting and Party Polarization in the U.S. House of Representatives." *American Politics Research* 35, no. 6: 878–904.

Collie, Melissa P., and John Lyman Mason. 2000. "The Electoral Connection between Party and Constituency Reconsidered: Evidence from the U.S. House of Representatives, 1972–1994." In *Continuity and Change in House Elections*, ed. David W. Brady, John F. Cogan, and Morris P. Fiorina. Stanford, CA: Stanford University Press.

Corkery, William Bernard, III. 2011. "Newt Gingrich and GOPAC: Training the Farm Team That Helped Win the Republican Revolution in 1994." Unpublished thesis, College of William and Mary.

Davidson, Roger H. 1990. "The Advent of the Modern Congress: The Legislative Reorganization Act of 1946." *Legislative Studies Quarterly* 15, no. 8: 357–73.

Davis, Christopher M. 2011. "Invoking Cloture in the Senate." *CRS Report*, February 25, 98–425.

DeMint, Jim. 2011. *The Great American Awakening: Two Years That Changed America, Washington, and Me*. Nashville, TN: B&H Publishing.

Downs, Anthony. 1957. *An Economic Theory of Democracy*. New York: Harper & Row.

Edsall, Thomas Byrne, and Mary Edsall. 1992. *Chain Reaction: The Impact of Race, Rights, and Taxes on American Politics*. New York: W. W. Norton.

Fenno, Richard F. 1989. *The Making of a Senator: Dan Quayle*. Washington, DC: CQ Press.

Fenno, Richard F. 1990. *The Presidential Odyssey of John Glenn*. Washington, DC: CQ Press.

Fenno, Richard F. 1991a. *The Emergence of a Senate Leader: Pete Domenici and the Reagan Budget*. Washington, DC: CQ Press.

Fenno, Richard F. 1991b. *Learning to Legislate: The Senate Education of Arlen Specter*. Washington, DC: CQ Press.

Fenno, Richard F. 1992. *When Incumbency Fails: The Senate Career of Mark Andrews*. Washington, DC: CQ Press.

Fiorina, Morris P. 2010. *Culture War? The Myth of a Polarized America*. New York: Longman.

Fleisher, Richard, and Jon R. Bond. 2004. "The Shrinking Middle in Congress." *British Journal of Politics* 34: 429–51.

Fowler, James H. 2006a. "Connecting the Congress: A Study of Cosponsorship Networks." *Political Analysis* 14, no. 4: 456–87.

Fowler, James H. 2006b. "Legislative Cosponsorship Networks in the U.S. House and Senate." *Social Networks* 28, no. 4: 454–65.

Galloway, George B. 1951. "The Operation of the Legislative Reorganization Act of 1946." *American Political Science Review* 45, no. 1: 41–68.

Gamm, Gerald, and Steven S. Smith. 2002. "Emergence of Senate Party Leadership." In *U.S. Senate Exceptionalism, ed.* Bruce I. Oppenheimer. Columbus: Ohio State University Press, 105–34.

Gilmour, John, and Paul Rothstein. 1994. "Term Limitations in a Dynamic Model of Partisan Balance." *American Journal of Political Science* 38: 770–96.

Gingrich, Newt. 1998. *Lessons Learned the Hard Way*. New York: HarperCollins.

Harris, Douglas B. 2006. "Legislative Parties and Leadership Choice: Confrontation or Accommodation in the 1989 Gingrich-Madigan Whip Race." *American Politics Research* 34, no. 3: 189–222.

Heniff, Bill, Jr. 2008. "Legislative Procedures for Adjusting the Public Debt Limit: A Brief Overview." CRS Report RS21519.

Hetherington, Marc J. 2001. "Resurgent Mass Partisanship: The Role of Elite Polarization." *American Political Science Review* 95, no. 9: 619–31.

Hetherington, Marc J., and Jonathan D. Weiler. 2009. *Authoritarianism and Polarization in American Politics*. New York: Cambridge University Press.

Highton, Benjamin, and Michael S. Rocca. 2005. "Beyond the Roll-Call Arena: The Determinants of Position Taking in Congress." *Political Research Quarterly* 58 (June): 303–16.

Hirsch, Sam. 2003. "The United States of Unrepresentatives: What Went Wrong in the Latest Round of Congressional Redistricting." *Election Law Journal* 2, no. 11: 179–216.

Huitt, Ralph K. 1961. "The Outsider in the Senate: An Alternative Role." *American Political Science Review* 55, no. 9: 566–75.

Jacobson, Gary C. 2000. "Party Polarization in National Politics: The Electoral Connection." In *Polarized Politics: Congress and the President in a Partisan Era*, ed. Jon R. Bond and Richard Fleisher. Washington, DC: CQ Press.

Jacobson, Gary C. 2012. *The Politics of Congressional Elections*. 8th ed. Upper Saddle River, NJ: Pearson.

Jenkins, Jeffery A., Michael H. Crespin, and Jamie L. Carson. 2005. "Parties as Procedural Coalitions in Congress: An Examination of Differing Career Tracks." *Legislative Studies Quarterly* 30, no. 8: 365–90.

Harris, Douglas B. 2006. "Legislative Parties and Leadership Choice: Confrontation or Accommodation in the 1989 Gingrich-Madigan Whip Race." *American Politics Research* 34, no. 2: 189–222.

Kessler, Daniel, and Keih Krehbiel, 1996. "Dynamics of Cosponsorship." *American Political Science Review* 90, no. 3: 555–66.

Koger, Gregory. 2003. "Position Taking and Cosponsorship in the U.S. House." *Legislative Studies Quarterly* 28, no. 8: 225–46.

Koger, Gregory. 2010. *Filibustering: A Political History of Obstruction in the House and Senate*. Chicago: University of Chicago Press.

Krehbiel, Keith. 1995. "Cosponsors and Wafflers from A to Z." *American Journal of Political Science* 39: 906–23.

Krutz, Glen S. 2005. "Issues and Institutions: 'Winnowing' in the U.S. Congress." *American Journal of Political Science* 49, no. 4: 313–24.

Lee, Frances. 2009. *Beyond Ideology: Politics, Principles, and Partisanship in the U.S. Senate*. Chicago: University of Chicago Press.

Light, Paul. 1992. *Forging Legislation: Building the Department of Veterans Affairs*. New York: W. W. Norton.

Lott, Trent. 2005. *Herding Cats: A Life in Politics.* New York: HarperCollins.

Mann, Thomas E., and Norman J. Ornstein. 2006. *The Broken Branch: How Congress is Failing America and How to Get It Back on Track.* New York: Oxford University Press.

Matthews, Donald R. 1960. *U.S. Senators and Their World.* Chapel Hill: University of North Carolina Press.

McCarty, Nolan M., Keith T. Poole, and Howard Rosenthal. 2006. *Polarized America: The Dance of Ideology and Unequal Riches.* Cambridge: Massachusetts Institute of Technology Press.

Nokken, Timothy P., and Keith Poole. 2004. "Congressional Party Defection in American History." *Legislative Studies Quarterly* 29: 545–68.

Oppenheimer, Bruce I. 2005. "Deep Red and Blue Congressional Districts." In *Congress Reconsidered,* ed. Lawrence C. Dodd and Bruce I. Oppenheimer. 8th ed. Washington, DC: CQ Press, 135–57.

Ornstein, Norman. 2008. "Our Broken Senate." *The American.* March/April. Available at: http://www.american.com/archive/2008/march-april-magazine-contents/our-broken-senate; accessed January 13, 2013.

Ornstein, Norman J., and Thomas E. Mann, eds. 2000. *The Permanent Campaign and Its Future.* Washington, DC: AEI Brookings Press.

Panning, William H. 1982. "Blockmodels: From Relations to Configurations." *American Journal of Political Science* 26, no. 3: 585–608.

Peterson, Merrill D. 1987. *The Great Triumvirate: Webster, Clay, and Calhoun.* New York: Oxford University Press.

Pierson, Paul. 1994. *Dismantling the Welfare State? Reagan, Thatcher, and the Politics of Retrenchment.* New York: Cambridge University Press.

Poole, Keith T., and Howard Rosenthal. 1997. *Congress: A Political-Economic History of Roll Call Voting.* New York: Oxford University Press.

Rae, Nicol. 1989. *The Decline and Fall of the Liberal Republicans: From 1952 to the Present.* New York: Oxford University Press.

Roberts, Jason M., and Steven S. Smith. 2003. "Procedural Contexts, Party Strategy, and Conditional Party Voting in the U.S. House of Representatives, 1971–2000." *American Journal of Political Science* 47, no. 4: 305–17.

Rocca, Michael S. 2007. "Non-Legislative Debate in the House of Representatives." *American Politics Research* 35: 489–505.

Rocca, Michael S., and Benjamin Highton. 2005. "Beyond the Roll Call Arena: The Determinants of Position Taking in Congress." *Political Research Quarterly* 58: 303–16.

Rohde, David W. 1979. "Risk-Bearing and Progressive Ambition: The Case of Members of the United States House of Representatives." *American Journal of Political Science* 23, no. 2: 1–26.

Rohde, David W., and John Aldrich. 2010. "Consequences of Electoral and Institutional Change: The Evolution of Conditional Party Government in the U.S. House of

Representatives." In *New Directions in American Political Parties*, ed. Jeffrey M. Stonecash. New York: Routledge, 234–50.

Rothman, David J. 1966. *Politics and Power: The United States Senate, 1869–1901*. Cambridge, MA: Harvard University Press.

Schickler, Eric, Eric McGhee, and John Sides. 2003. "Remaking the House and Senate: Personal Power, Ideology, and the 1970s Reforms." *Legislative Studies Quarterly* 28, no. 3: 297–333.

Schiller, Wendy. 2000. *Partners and Rivals: Representation in U.S. Senate Delegations*. Princeton, NJ: Princeton University Press.

Schiller, Wendy J. 1995. "Senators and Political Entrepreneurs: Using Bill Sponsorship to Shape Legislative Agendas." *American Journal of Political Science* 39, no. 1: 186–203.

Sharlet, Jeff. 2008. *The Family: The Secret Fundamentalism at the Heart of American Power*. New York: Harper Perennial.

Sharlet, Jeff. 2010. *C Street: The Fundamentalist Threat to American Democracy*. New York: Harper Perennial.

Shepsle, Kenneth A. 1989. "The Changing Textbook Congress." In *Can the Government Govern?* ed. John E. Chubb and Paul E. Peterson. Washington, DC: Brookings Institution Press, 355–68.

Sinclair, Barbara. 1989. *The Transformation of the U.S. Senate*. Baltimore: Johns Hopkins University Press.

Sinclair, Barbara. 2006. *Party Wars: Polarization and the Politics of National Policy Making*. Norman: University of Oklahoma Press.

Smith, Steven S. 1989. *Call to Order: Floor Politics in the House and Senate*. Washington, DC: Brookings Institution Press.

Stonecash, Jeffrey M., Mark D. Brewer, and Mark D. Mariani. 2003. *Diverging Parties: Social Change, Realignment, and Party Polarization*. Boulder, CO: Westview Press.

Strahan, Randall W. 2007. *Leading Representatives: The Agency of Leaders in the Politics of the U.S. House*. Baltimore: Johns Hopkins University Press.

Talbert, Jeffery C., and Matthew Potoski. 2002. "Setting the Legislative Agenda: The Dimensional Structure of Bill Cosponsoring and Floor Voting." *Journal of Politics* 64, no. 8: 864–91.

Theriault, Sean M. 2005. *The Power of the People: Congressional Competition, Public Attention, and Voter Retribution*. Columbus: Ohio State University Press.

Theriault, Sean M. 2006. "Party Polarization in the U.S. Congress: Member Replacement and Member Adaptation." *Party Politics* 12, no. 4: 483–503.

Theriault, Sean M. 2008. *Party Polarization in Congress*. New York: Cambridge University Press.

White, William S. 1956. *Citadel: The Story of the U.S. Senate*. New York: Harper & Bros.

Wilson, Reid. 2009. "Senator DeMint Bucks Republican Party, Backs Conservative in California Race." *The Hill*, November 4.

Wilson, Rick K., and Cheryl D. Young. 1997. "Cosponsorship in the U.S. Congress." *Legislative Studies Quarterly* 22: 25–44.

Woon, Jonathan. 2008. "Bill Sponsorship in Congress: The Moderating Effect of Agenda Positions on Legislative Proposals." *Journal of Politics* 70, no. 1: 201–16.

Index

Abdnor, James, 194n11
age, 65
Aldrich, Nelson W., 73
Alexander, Lamar, 170, 173–74
Allard, Wayne, 78
Allen, George, 15
Allison, William B., 73
amendments for nonlegislative purposes
    Baucus on Coburn's health care
        reform, 142
    Gingrich Senator Effect on, 144–45,
        144t, 147–48, 148t, 214t
    Gingrich Senators and, 141–48, 143f
    of Gingrich Senators compared to
        Democrats, 143–44, 143f
    Gingrich Senators roll-call voting on,
        145–48, 146f, 148t
    growing number of, 142–45, 143f,
        144t
    obstructionism from, 145, 147
    111th Congress predicting, 214t
    Reid and, 144–45
    Senate delays from, 145
    strategies for, 145
amendment voting. See also "Death by
        Amendment" strategy
    Gingrich Senators roll-call votes for,
        145–48, 146f, 148t, 216t
    legislative process slowed by, 94
    in 111th Congress, 202t
    pack mentality of Gingrich Senators
        on, 94–96, 95t

roll-call votes in 111th Congress for,
    215t
of Tea Party Senators in 112th
    Congress, 164
Andrews, Mark, 194n11
Angle, Sharon, 158
anti-Federalists, 6
approval ratings, Gingrich Senator Effect,
    149–50
Armey, Dick, 156, 169
Ayotte, Kelly, 157–58

Bacon, Perry, 111–12
Baird, David, Jr., 82
Baker, Gilbert, 203n14
Baker, Howard, 20
Baker, Jim, 137
Balanced Budget Amendment of 1994
    Dole, Bob, switching vote on, 201n1
    public support of, 91
Barrasso, John, 54
Baucus, Max, 4, 213n30
    on Coburn's health care amendment,
        142
Bayh, Evan, 6, 11, 153, 189n2
    partisan warfare complaints of, 13,
        129, 173
Begich, Mark, 35
Bennett, Michael, 157
Bennett, Robert, 140–41, 157, 175
Bentsen, Lloyd, 212n1
Biden, Joe, 136, 139

Bingaman, Jeff, 4

Bipartisan Task Force for Responsible
    Fiscal Action, 140

Blagojevich, Rod, 97

Blue Dog Democrats, 98

Blunt, Roy, 160

Boehner, John, 120, 139, 166, 169

Bond, Kit, 3–4, 13

Boozman, John, 160, 203n14

Bowles, Erskine, 51

Boxer, Barbara, 156, 212n6

Bradley, Bill, 77

Bridgewater, Tim, 157

Brown, Hank, 113

Brown, Scott, 15, 67, 94, 104
    election of, 155

Brownback, Sam, 16, 53, 78, 136, 140, 162
    as governor, 219n27

Broyhill, James, 82, 194n11

Buck, Ken, 157

Buechner, Jack, 26

Bunning, Jim
    criticism against, 111–12
    Federal unemployment benefits
        extension battle with, 109, 111
    McConnell criticized by, 111

Burden, Barry, 189n12

Burns, Conrad, 150

Burr, Aaron, 123

Burr, Richard, 135, 169
    bills introduced by, 145
    Dole, Elizabeth's, extremism score
        compared to, 52
    Edwards' extremism score compared
        to, 53
    elections of, 51

Burris, Roland, 97–98, 189n4

Bush, George H. W., 24, 107
    "No New Taxes" pledge of, 25–26
    presidential nomination success rate
        of, 115f–116f, 117, 118t

Bush, George W., 37, 109

majority support of, 171
    presidential nomination success rate
        of, 114, 115f–116f, 118–19, 118t

Byrd, Harry, Jr., 183n2

Calhoun, John C., 73

campaign fundraising
    DeMint's 2010 contributions to, 158,
        159t, 217n8
    of Gephardt Senators, 79, 80t
    Gingrich Senator Effect on, 79, 80t
    Gingrich Senators and, 77–79,
        80t, 87
    in Kirk's election, 98
    1996 Republican success with, 78
    "permanent campaign" reality with,
        141
    Republicans 1984–2010–, predicting,
        197n6, 198t
    state disparity with, 79
    of would-be Gingrich Senators, 79

Campbell, Ben Nighthorse, 183n3

Campbell, Tom, 157

Carnahan, Jean, 189n4

Carter, Jimmy, 20
    "Saxbie Fix" used by, 212n1

Case, Clifford, 46

Castle, Mike, 101, 158, 175

CFPB. *See* Consumer Financial
        Protection Bureau

Chafee, John, 81

Chafee, Lincoln, 150

Chambliss, Saxby, 16, 53, 134, 138–40

Cheney, Dick, 24, 157, 171

The Citadel (White), 9

Citizens for Responsibility and Ethics in
        Washington, 212n6

Clay, Henry, 52, 73

Cleland, Max, 53

Clinton, Bill, 51, 91
    debt-limit ceiling fights between
        Gingrich and, 107–8

presidential nomination success
  rates of, 114, 115*f*–116*f*, 116–17,
  117*t*–118*t*
presidential support scores for,
  121–23, 121*f*, 122*t*–123*t*
"Saxbie Fix" used by, 212n1
Surgeon General nomination struggles
  of, 113–14
Clinton, Hillary, 19, 130
cloture, 109. *See also* filibusters
  Gingrich Senator Effect on ideology
    with, 128*t*
  ideology based on, 125–27, 126*t*–
    127*t*, 211*t*
  majority party invoking, 125, 125*t*
  obstructionism with, 124
  Tea Party Senators in 112th Congress
    effect on, 164–65
Club for Growth, 103
Coats, Dan, 22, 37, 101, 157, 189n2
  Elders disapproved by, 113
Coburn, Tom, 15, 138–40, 145, 158
  Baucus on health care amendment of,
    142
  earmark ban efforts of, 161–62
  Gingrich criticized by, 169
Cochran, Thad, 35
Coleman, Norm, 150
Collins, Susan, 15, 103, 111, 135, 171
  approval ratings of, 149
  extremism score of, 54
Compromise of 1850, 7, 73
Conrad, Kent, 4, 138, 140
conservatism
  by constituencies, 57
  Gingrich Senator Effect durability
    with, 48–49, 49*f*
  of Gingrich supporters, 29–30, 29*f*
  of Gramm compared to
    McCain, 82
  Reagan casting new light on, 29
Conservative Coalition, 43

Conservative Opportunity Society
  (COS)
  core members of, 69
  Democrat confrontations with, 22–23
  founding of, 21–22
  legislative strategy of, 23–24
  membership in, 180n22
  Special Orders speeches strategy
    adopted by, 30–31, 30*f*
constituencies
  conservatism by, 57
  of Gephardt Senators, 57
  Gephardt Senators impact lessened by
    variable of, 63
  Gingrich Senator Effect and effect of,
    59, 61–63, 62*t*, 191*t*–192*t*
  of Gingrich Senators, 51–63
  partisan tilt variable of, 61
  regional variable on, 61
  state size variable on, 62
Consumer Financial Protection Bureau
  (CFPB), 165–66
Contract with America, 26
Cook, Charlie, 155, 158
Coons, Chris, 158
Cordray, Richard, 165
Corker, Bob, 136–37
Cornyn, John, 149, 156
COS. *See* Conservative Opportunity
  Society
cosponsorship activity, 71
  of Gingrich Senators, 93–94
  of Gingrich Senators and Democrats,
    132–33, 132*t*
  literature on, 202n8
  pack mentality of Gingrich Senators
    on, 96–97, 97*t*
  roll-call votes compared to, 96
Craig, Larry, 15
Crapo, Mike, 139–40, 142
Crist, Charlie, 156, 175
Curtis, Carl, 46

DADT. *See* "Don't Ask, Don't Tell"
Daschle, Tom, 179n22
Davis, Jefferson, 52
"Death by Amendment" strategy
  Obama confronted with, 94
  of Republicans, 94–95
debt-limit ceiling
  bipartisan consensus on raising,
    106–7
  Clinton, Bill, and Gingrich fights over,
    107–8
  Democrat strategies with, 105–6
  Gephardt Rule on, 105
  Gingrich Senators transforming
    debate on, 105–8, 106*f*
  key changes, 19792011–, 204*t*–206*t*
  partisan warfare with, 107–8
  prisoner's dilemma of, 105
  2011 crisis with, 166
DeLay, Tom, 169
DeMint, Jim, 13, 16, 79, 136, 161
  Buck endorsed by, 157
  DeVore endorsed by, 156–57
  Lamontagne endorsed by, 157–58
  Leadership PAC of, 158
  Lee, Mike, endorsed by, 157
  McConnell on Senate changing efforts
    of, 172
  Obama attacked on health care reform
    by, 3–5, 12, 155
  Obama frustration of, 120
  Obama opposition of, 122–23, 122*t*
  O'Donnell endorsed by, 158
  Paul endorsed by, 157
  Rubio endorsed by, 156
  Senate influence of, 172
  Stutzman endorsed by, 157
  Tea Party movement endorsements of,
    156–58
  Tea Party movement importance of,
    155–56, 170
  Toomey aided by, 104, 156

2010 campaign fundraising
  contributions of, 158, 159*t*, 217n8
Democrats. *See also* Gephardt Senators
  amendments for nonlegislative
    purposes of Gingrich Senators
    compared to, 143–44, 143*f*
  Blue Dog, 98
  COS confrontations with, 22–23
  debt-limit ceiling strategies of, 105–6
  Gingrich Senators cosponsorship
    activity with, 132–33, 132*t*
  Gingrich Senators succeeding, 53
  Gingrich Senators views of, 149–50
  104th Congress (1995–1996) losses
    of, 77
  partisan warfare causing retirement
    of, 174
  Reagan agenda blocked by, 21
  Republicans and Gingrich Senators
    compared to Northern and
    Southern, 42–45, 44*f*
  Senate electoral dynamics with
    former House members of, 74–77,
    75*f*, 77*t*
  state population represented by,
    190n17
desk seating traditions, in Senate, 52–53,
  189n1
DeVore, Chuck, 156–57
DeWine, Mike, 15, 39–40, 85, 165,
  189n4
  Santorum endorsed by, 169
Diggs, Charles, C., Jr., 22
Dodd-Frank Wall Street Reform Act,
  165
Dole, Bob, 3, 53, 219n27
  Balanced Budget Amendment vote
    switching of, 201n1
  Hatfield's resignation refused by, 91
Dole, Elizabeth, 51, 150
  Burr, Richard's, extremism score
    compared to, 52

"Don't Ask, Don't Tell" (DADT),
    133–35
Downs, Anthony
    electoral security logic of, 85
    on median voters, 78
DuPont, Pete, 23
Durbin, Dick, 111, 138
    Sunday morning talk show
        appearances of, 149
Durenburger, David, 54
DW-NOMINATE scores, 27–28, 28*f*,
    178n21, 184n4
    extremism score based on, 185n10
    Gingrich Senator Effect baseline
        model for, 185*t*

Eagleburger, Lawrence, 137
earmark ban, in 112th Congress,
    161–62
Edwards, John, 51
    Burr, Richard's, extremism score
        compared to, 53
Elders, Jocelyn, 113
electoral security
    Down's logic on, 85
    of Gingrich Senators, 85–87,
        86*f*, 86*t*
Emolument Clause, 130
Ensign, John, 15, 68, 135, 140, 142
Enzi, Mike, 4, 54, 192n9
extremism score
    of Burr, Richard, compared to Dole,
        Elizabeth, 52
    of Burr, Richard, compared to
        Edwards, 53
    of Collins and Snowe, 54
    definition of, 41
    DW-NOMINATE scores as basis for,
        185n10
    of Gephardt Senators compared to
        Gingrich Senators, 38–39, 39*t*,
        41–42, 42*t*

Gingrich proximity effect on, 195*t*–196*t*
    of Gingrich Senators compared to
        other Republicans, 38, 39*f*, 78
    personal characteristics of Republicans
        in 111th Congress and, 193*t*–194*t*
    of Tea Party Senators in 112th
        Congress, 162–63, 163*f*, 164*t*

Face the Nation, 148
FEC. *See* Federal Election Commission
Federal Election Commission (FEC), 98
Federalists, 6
Federal unemployment benefits
    Bunning's battle over extension of,
        109, 111
    economic downturn impact on, 108–9
    Gingrich Senators transforming
        debate on extension of, 108–9,
        110*t*, 111–12
    key votes on extension of, 110*t*
"Fellowship," 67–68
Fenno, Richard, 141
filibusters, 9–10. *See also* cloture
    criticism of, 123–24
    growing use of, 124, 127
    Senate creation of, 123
Finance Committee, 4–5
Fiorina, Carly, 156–57
Flake, Jeff, 175
Ford, Gerald R., 178n17
Foster, Henry, 113
Fowler, James, 96
Fox News Sunday, 148
Frahm, Sheila, 53
Franken, Al, 94
    Secret Santa plan of, 167
fraternity, 67
fundraising. *See* campaign fundraising

Gang of Six
    forming of, 138–39
    negotiation difficulties with, 138–40

Gang of Six (*Cont.*)
  revenue issues dividing, 139
  2011 debt-limit crisis and, 166
Gates, Robert M., 134, 137
gays in military, 133–35
Gephardt, Richard, 16
  debt-limit ceiling rule of, 105
  election of, 179n22
Gephardt Senators. *See also* Democrats
  campaign fundraising of, 79, 80*t*
  constituencies of, 57
  constituencies' variables lessening
    impact of, 63
  Gingrich Senators compared to, 16
  Gingrich Senators extremism score
    compared to, 38–39, 39*t*, 41–42,
    42*t*
  would-be, 76, 79
Giffords, Gabrielle, 120
"Gilded Age," 7
Gingrich, Newt, 13, 17
  ambition of, 171
  Coburn criticizing, 169
  conservatism of supporters of, 29–30,
    29*f*
  debt-limit ceiling fights between
    Clinton, Bill, and, 107–8
  Diggs investigated and pressured by,
    22
  extremism score and proximity to,
    195*t*–196*t*
  Gingrich Senators opposing
    presidential run of, 168–70
  GOPAC audio tapes produced by,
    23–24
  House of Representatives influence of,
    27–31, 28*f*–30*f*, 171–72
  Michel's leadership compared to, 27
  Minority Whip election of, 24–25
  moon colony promise of, 169
  O'Neill confrontations with, 23
  proximity to, 68–71

  Senate influence of, 33
  Speaker tenure of, 26–27
  Special Orders speeches of, 22–23,
    179n9
  supporters of, 180n23
  tax increases fought by, 25–26
  Vander Jagt supporting rise of, 21
  Wright confrontations with, 24–25,
    179n23
Gingrich Senator Effect, 39, 42
  on amendments for nonlegislative
    purposes, 144–45, 144*t*, 147–48,
    148*t*, 214*t*
  on approval ratings, 149–50
  on campaign fundraising, 79, 80*t*
  on cloture ideology, 128*t*
  conservatism durability in,
    48–49, 49*f*
  constituencies' effect on, 59, 61–63,
    62*t*, 191*t*–192*t*
  DW-NOMINATE score baseline
    model for, 185*t*
  electoral influence of, predicting,
    76–77, 77*t*
  Gingrich's presidential run opposed
    by, 168–70
  personal characteristics in, 66*t*
  Reagan's effect on Republicans
    compared to, 45
  term length and, 187*t*–188*t*
  triple interaction needed for, 184n4
  variables in, 184n4
Gingrich Senators. *See also* pack
    mentality of Gingrich Senators;
    Republicans; Tea Party Senators;
    would-be Gingrich Senators
  age of, 65
  amendments for nonlegislative
    purposes and, 141–48, 143*f*
  amendments for nonlegislative
    purposes of Democrats compared
    to, 143–44, 143*f*

bills introduced by, 145
birth and growth of, 37–38, 38*f*
campaign fundraising and, 77–79,
    80*t*, 87
characteristics of, 13
constituencies of, 51–63
cosponsorship activity of, 93–94
debt-limit ceiling debate transformed
    by, 105–8, 106*f*
definition of, 50
Democrats cosponsorship activity
    with, 132–33, 132*t*
Democrats succeeded by, 53
Democrats view of, 149–50
differences amongst, 13, 15
dividing line for, 46
electoral dynamics of, 74–77, 75*f*
electoral security of, 85–87, 86*f*, 86*t*
extremism score of Republicans
    compared to, 38, 39*f*, 78
as face of partisan warfare, 148–49
Federal unemployment benefits debate
    transformed by, 108–9, 110*t*,
    111–12
"Fellowship" and, 67–68
former House of Representatives
    serving as, 45–49, 47*f*
fraternity of, 67
future of, 153
Gephardt Senators compared to, 16
Gephardt Senators extremism
    compared to, 38–39, 39*t*, 41–42,
    42*t*
Gramm argument for being, 183n3
growth of, 73–74
House arrival compared to Senate
    arrival for, 48
ideology of, 38–40
list of, 14*t*–15*t*
longevity of, 83–87
military service of, 67
negotiation difficulties with, 133–41

Northern and Southern Democrats
    split compared to Republicans and,
    42–45, 44*f*
obstructionism of, 126
occupation of, 66–67
pack mentality of, 42–45, 93–104
pairs of, 54, 57–59, 60*t*, 61*f*
Partisan Senate era responsibility of,
    50
as partisan warriors, 89
as partisan warriors on roll-call votes,
    113–29
party polarization and, 16, 33, 40–42,
    40*f*, 41*f*
personal characteristics of, 64–68, 66*t*
predecessors of, 52–54, 55*t*–56*t*
presidential nominations and, 114,
    115*f*–116*f*, 116–19, 117*t*–119*t*
presidential support scores and, 119–
    23, 121*f*, 122*t*
proximity to Gingrich of, 68–71
religion of, 65–66
Republican Conference transformed
    by, 104–12, 106*f*, 110*t*
Republican inundation of, 81–83, 81*f*,
    83*f*, 84*f*
Republicans recruited by, 93
Republicans succeeded by, 53–54
roll-call votes on amendments by,
    145–48, 146*f*, 148*t*, 216*t*
Romney endorsed by, 169
Senate unable to change, 87
Southern Democrats compared to,
    44–45
state population represented by,
    190n17
Sunday morning talk shows
    participation in 112th Congress
    of, 168
Tea Party Senators impact compared
    to, 160
term length of, 84–85

Gingrich Senators (*Cont.*)
  transformational force of, 16–17
  would-be Gingrich Senators compared
    to, 80–81
  would-be Gingrich Senators
    Leadership PAC contributions
    from, 100–101, 102*t*, 103, 160
Giuliani, Rudy, 157
Goldwater, Barry, 21, 54, 82
GOPAC, 23–24
Gottemoeller, Rose, 137
Graham, Lindsey, 15, 67, 169
  approval ratings of, 149
  bills introduced by, 145
Gramm, Phil, 16, 40, 99
  election of, 74
  Gingrich Senator argument for, 183n3
  McCain's conservatism compared to,
    82
  party affiliation changes of, 37
Grams, Rod, 15, 54, 85
Grassley, Chuck, 101, 192n9, 194n11,
    203n14
  health care reform opposition
    of, 4–5
Grayson, Trey, 157, 175
Great Triumvirate, 73
Gregg, Judd, 15, 22, 101, 140, 158
  Elders disapproved by, 113

Harding, Warren G., 178n17
Harkin, Tom, 77
Hatfield, Mark
  Dole, Bob, refusing resignation of, 91
  retirement of, 93
  Santorum criticizing, 91–92
health care reform
  Baucus on Coburn's amendment for,
    142
  DeMint attacking Obama on, 3–5,
    12, 155
  Grassley's opposition to, 4–5

  Obama on need for, 3
  Republican opposition of, 4–5
Heinz, John, 81
Helms, Jesse, 51, 82
Herding Cats (Lott), 151
Hostettler, John, 157
House of Representatives, 7
  design of, 19
  disjuncture in ideology of, 181*t*–183*t*
  Gingrich Senators arrival in Senate
    compared to, 48
  Gingrich Senators as former members
    of, 45–49, 47*f*
  Gingrich's influence on, 27–31, 28*f*–
    30*f*, 171–72
  in 1980s, 20–27
  Senate electoral dynamics with former
    members of, 74–77, 75*f*, 77*t*
  Senate friction with, 19
Hutchinson, Tim, 15, 78
Hutchison, Kay Bailey, 140–41

ideology
  cloture and, 125–27, 126*t*–127*t*, 211*t*
  Downs on median voters, 78
  Gingrich Senator Effect on cloture,
    128*t*
  of Gingrich Senators, 38–40
  House Republicans disjuncture in,
    181*t*–183*t*
  presidential nominations and
    confirmation, 207n8, 208*t*
  in presidential support score
    predictions, 210*t*
  Senate dividing line for, 186*t*–187*t*
Individualized Senate era, 9–10
Inhofe, Jim, 67, 140, 162
Inner Club, of Senate, 8–10
Isakson, Johnny, 67, 136–37, 212n6

Javits, Jacob, 36, 46
Jeffords, Jim, 194n11

Johanns, Mike, 167
Johnson, Ron, 158
Johnson, Tim, 58

Kansas Legislature, 219n27
Kansas-Nebraska Act of 1854, 7
Kassebaum, Nancy, 219n27
Kennedy, Ted, 94, 155
Kirk, Mark, 67, 79, 101, 135, 160, 189n4
  campaign fundraising in election of,
    98
Kissinger, Henry, 137
Kyl, Jon, 4, 22, 92, 166
  New START negotiation difficulties
    with, 135–37
  Planned Parenthood funding
    negotiation difficulties with, 138
  retirement of, 170

Lamontagne, Ovide, 157–58
Leadership PACs
  of DeMint, 158
  Gingrich Senators contributing to
    would-be Gingrich Senators, 100–
    101, 102t, 103, 160
  growth of, 98–99, 99f
  of McCain, 99
  original purpose of, 98
  pack mentality of Gingrich Senators
    on, 97–103, 99f, 100t, 102t
  runoff elections and, 203n13
  Specter compared to Toomey on
    money from, 203n16
Lee, Frances, 12, 141
Lee, Mike, 160
  DeMint endorsing, 157
Legislative Reorganization Act of 1946, 8
LeMieux, George, 101
Lieberman, Joe, 135
Lightfoot, Jim Ross, 77
Lincoln, Blanche, 175
Lott, Trent, 17, 85, 151, 194n11

Lowden, Sue, 158
Lugar, Dick, 136, 192n9
Lungren, Dan, 22

Mack, Connie, 22, 37
Madigan, Ed, 25, 29–30
Maine voting slants, 57
Manchin, Joe, 168
Martinez, Mel, 5
Mathias, Charles, 36
Matthews, Chris, 133, 135
McCain, John, 5, 15, 54, 140–41,
    156, 158
  approval ratings of, 149
  bills introduced by, 145
  DADT negotiation difficulties with,
    133–35
  Gramm's conservatism compared to,
    82
  Leadership PACs of, 99
  military service of, 67
  Senate career beginning of, 37
  Tea Party Senators friction with,
    217n15
  2008 election state results
    for, 57–58
McCarthy, Kevin, 173
McCaskill, Claire, 162, 220n11
McConnell, Mitch, 5, 82, 109, 130, 145,
    156, 158
  Baker campaign contributions of,
    203n14
  Bunning criticizing, 111
  on DeMint's efforts to change Senate,
    172
  earmark ban criticized by, 161
  Sunday morning talk show
    appearances of, 149
  "Super Committee" appointments of,
    166
median voters, Downs on ideologies
    of, 78

Meek, Kendrick, 156
Meet the Press, 148
Menendez, Bob, 149
Merkley, Jeff, 111
Metzenbaum, Howard, 189n4
Michel, Bob, 20
    Gingrich's leadership compared to, 27
    Madigan backed by, 25
    Republican Conference united by, 21
    retirement of, 26, 31
Milibank, Dana, 134
military service, 67
    DADT and, 133–35
Miller, Joe, 158
Missouri Compromise of 1820, 7, 73
moon colony promise, of Gingrich, 169
Moran, Jerry, 101, 160
    general election opposition of, 203n12
Mullen, Mike, 134
Murkowski, Lisa, 140, 158
Muskie, Edmund, 212n1

National Prayer Breakfast, 68
National Republican Senatorial
    Committee (NRSC), 156
negotiation difficulties
    changing positions and, 140–41
    with Gang of Six, 138–40
    with Gingrich Senators, 133–41
    with Kyl and Planned Parenthood
        funding, 138
    with Kyl in New START, 135–37
    with McCain on DADT, 133–35
Nelson, Ben, 220n11
Nelson, Bill, 179n22, 192n9, 220n11
New STrategic Arms Reduction Treaty
    (New START), 135–37
Nixon, Richard M., 36, 178n17
    Emolument Clause worked around
        by, 130
nominations. *See* presidential
    nominations

Northern Democrats, 42–45, 44*f*
Norton, Joe, 157
NRSC. *See* National Republican
    Senatorial Committee
Nunn-Lugar Act of 1991, 136

Obama, Barack, 57–58, 79, 139, 166
    Bipartisan Task Force for Responsible
        Fiscal Action endorsed by, 140
    CFPB nomination challenges of,
        165–66
    "Death by Amendment" strategy to
        fight, 94
    DeMint attacking Obama on health
        care reform, 3–5, 12, 155
    DeMint's frustration with, 120
    DeMint's opposition of, 122–23, 122*t*
    first term popularity of, 3
    on health care reform's need, 3
    joint session jobs address of, 120–21
    party polarization under, 36
    presidential nomination success rate
        of, 114, 115*f*–116*f*, 117, 117*t*–118*t*
    presidential support scores for, 120–
        23, 121*f*, 122*t*–123*t*
    Senate successor controversy with,
        97–98
Obamacare, 5, 142. *See also* health care
    reform
obstructionism
    from amendments for nonlegislative
        purposes, 145, 147
    cloture and, 124
    of Gingrich Senators, 126
occupation, 66–67
O'Donnell, Christine, 101
    DeMint endorsing, 158
Oleszek, Walter, 180n22
111th Congress
    amendments for nonlegislative
        purposes in, 214*t*
    amendment voting in, 202*t*

extremism score and personal
   characteristics of Republicans in,
   193*t*–194*t*
roll-call votes on amendments in, 215*t*
112th Congress
   amendment voting of Tea Party
      Senators in, 164
   cloture effect of Tea Party Senators in,
      164–65
   earmark ban in, 161–62
   presidential nominations and Tea
      Party Senators in, 165–66
   presidential support scores of Tea
      Party Senators in, 165
   Republican gains in, 160
   roll-call votes of Tea Party Senators in,
      162–63, 163*f*
   Senate frustrations with, 167
   Sunday morning talk shows
      participation during, 168
O'Neill, Tip, 20, 105
   Gingrich confrontations with, 23
Ornstein, Norman, 5

pack mentality of Gingrich Senators,
   42–45, 93–104
   on amendment voting, 94–96, 95*t*
   on cosponsorship activity,
      96–97, 97*t*
   on Leadership PACs, 97–103, 99*f*,
      100*t*, 102*t*
   Toomey and, 103–4
pairs, of Gingrich Senators, 54, 57–59,
   60*t*, 61*f*
Palin, Sarah, 156, 158
partisan bickering, 12
Partisan Senate era, 10–13, 36, 153,
   172–73
   Gingrich Senators responsibility for,
      50
partisan tilt variable, of constituencies, 61
partisan warfare, 12

approval ratings price of, 149
Bayh complaining about, 13, 129, 173
cost of, 173
with debt-limit ceiling, 107–8
Democrats retiring from, 174
Gingrich Senators and, 89
Gingrich Senators as face of, 148–49
of Gingrich Senators on roll-call votes,
   113–29
motivation from, 175
Senate changed by, 129
Snowe complaining about, 13, 129,
   173
party polarization
   electoral victories and, 53
   electorate encouraging, 178n20
   Gingrich Senators and, 16, 33, 40–42,
      40*f*, 41*f*
   under Obama, 36
   in Senate, 35–42, 37*f*
Paul, Rand
   DeMint endorsing, 157
   press received by, 160
"permanent campaign," 141
Perry, Rick, 213n29
personal characteristics
   age, 65
   extremism score of Republicans in
      111th Congress and, 193*t*–194*t*
   "Fellowship," 67–68
   fraternity, 67
   full model of, 68
   Gingrich Senator Effect and, 66*t*
   of Gingrich Senators, 64–68, 66*t*
   military service, 67
   occupation, 66–67
   religion, 65–66
The Personal Roots of Representation
   (Burden), 189n12
Pickering, Chip, 68
Planned Parenthood funding, 138
Portman, Rob, 160, 166

Powell, Colin, 134, 137
presidential nominations
  Bush, George W., success rate with,
    114, 115*f*–116*f*, 118–19, 118*t*
  CFPB challenges for, 165–66
  Clinton, Bill, success rates with, 114,
    115*f*–116*f*, 116–17, 117*t*–118*t*
  of Clinton, Bill, for Surgeon General,
    113–14
  confirmation ideology in,
    207n8, 208*t*
  Gingrich Senators and, 114,
    115*f*–116*f*, 116–19, 117*t*–119*t*
  Obama success rate with, 114,
    115*f*–116*f*, 117, 117*t*–118*t*
  Reagan success rate with, 114,
    115*f*–116*f*
  roll-call votes increases on, 114
  Tea Party Senators in 112th Congress
    effect on, 165–66
presidential support scores
  for Clinton, Bill, 121–23, 121*f*,
    122*t*–123*t*
  components of, 121
  Gingrich Senators and, 119–23, 121*f*,
    122*t*
  ideology predictions for, 210*t*
  for Obama, 120–23, 121*f*, 122*t*–123*t*
  of Tea Party Senators in 112th
    Congress, 165
proximity to Gingrich, 68–71
Pryor, Mark, 192n9

Quayle, Dan, 37, 189n2, 194n11

Raese, John, 158
Reagan, Ronald, 25
  conservatism cast in new light by, 29
  Democrats blocking agenda of, 21
  election of, 20, 29
  Gingrich Senator Effect on
    Republicans compared to, 45

presidential nomination success rate
  of, 114, 115*f*–116*f*
redistricting, 10
regional variable, on constituencies, 61
Reid, Harry, 109, 130, 151
  amendments for nonlegislative
    purposes and, 144–45
  bills introduced by, 145
  Vitter criticized by, 131
religion, 65–66
Republican Conference, 17
  Gingrich Senators transforming,
    104–12, 106*f*, 110*t*
  Michel's retirement as final step in
    transforming, 26, 31
  Michel uniting, 21
Republican In Name Only (RINO), 103
Republican Presidential Vote Advantage
  (RPVA), 61, 76
  basis for, 189n7
Republicans. *See also* Gingrich Senators;
    Tea Party Senators
  campaign fundraising predictions
    1984–2010 for, 197n6, 198*t*
  campaign fundraising success in 1996
    of, 78
  "Death by Amendment" strategy of,
    94–95
  disjuncture in ideology of House,
    181*t*–183*t*
  extremism score of Gingrich Senators
    compared to, 38, 39*f*, 78
  Gingrich Senator Effect compared to
    Reagan's effect on, 45
  Gingrich Senators increasing
    proportion of, 81–83, 81*f*, 83*f*, 84*f*
  Gingrich Senators recruiting, 93
  Gingrich Senators succeeding, 53–54
  health care reform opposition of, 4–5
  incumbent re-election 1974–2010
    predictions for, 199n11, 199*t*–201*t*,
    200n11

Northern and Southern Democrats compared to Gingrich Senators and, 42–45, 44*f*
112th Congress gains of, 160
personal characteristics effect on extremism score of 111th Congress, 193*t*–194*t*
Romney's success in 2012 compared to Senate candidates of, 175
Senate elections predicting two-party vote for, 197*t*
Senate electoral dynamics with former House members of, 74–77, 75*f*, 77*t*
state population represented by, 190n17
Sunday morning talk shows as outlet for, 148–49
responsible parties, 17
Rhodes, John, 22
RINO. *See* Republican In Name Only
Roberts, Pat, 15, 67, 78, 101
roll-call votes. *See also* filibusters; presidential nominations; presidential support scores
on amendments in 111th Congress, 215*t*
cosponsorship activity compared to, 96
Gingrich Senators as partisan warriors on, 113–29
of Gingrich Senators on amendments, 145–48, 146*f*, 148*t*, 216*t*
presidential nominations increasing number of, 114
of Tea Party Senators in 112th Congress, 162–63, 163*f*
Romney, Mitt, 3
Gingrich Senators endorsing, 169
2012 Republican Senate candidates success compared to, 175
Roosevelt, Franklin D., 7
Rossi, Dino, 158

RPVA. *See* Republican Presidential Vote Advantage
Rubin, Robert, 108
Rubio, Marco
DeMint endorsing, 156
press received by, 160
Rudman, Warren, 59, 158
runoff elections, Leadership PACs and, 203n13

Salazar, Ken, 130, 157
Sanford, Mark, 68
Santorum, Rick, 16, 24, 189n4
DeWine endorsing, 169
Hatfield criticized by, 91–92
on Senate transformation, 92–93
Specter's individual experiences different from, 189n12
Satcher, David, 114
Saxbe, William, 130
"Saxbe Fix," 130, 212n1
Schultz, George, 137
Schumer, Chuck, 168
Scott, Hugh, 46
seating traditions, in Senate, 52–53, 189n1
Secret Santa plan, in Senate, 167–68
Senate. *See also* Gephardt Senators; Gingrich Senators; Tea Party Senators
amendments for nonlegislative purposes delaying, 145
DeMint's influence on, 172
desk seating traditions in, 52–53, 189n1
developmental phases of, 6–13
filibuster creation in, 123
former House members electoral dynamics with, 74–77, 75*f*, 77*t*
future of, 171–75
Gingrich Senators arrival in House compared to, 48

Senate (*Cont.*)
    Gingrich Senators unchanged by, 87
    Gingrich's influence on, 33
    Great Triumvirate in, 73
    House of Representatives friction
        with, 19
    ideology dividing line for, 186t–187t
    Individualized era of, 9–10
    Inner Club of, 8–10
    McCain starting career in, 37
    McConnell on DeMint's efforts to
        change, 172
    Obama's successor controversy in,
        97–98
    112th Congress frustrations in, 167
    Partisan era of, 10–13, 36, 50, 153,
        172–73
    partisan warfare changing, 129
    party polarization in, 35–42, 37f
    polarization theories in, 10–11
    presidents visiting, 178n17
    public approval ratings of, 5–6
    Republicans two-party vote
        predictions for elections to, 197t
    Romney's success in 2012 compared to
        Republican candidates for, 175
    Santorum on transformation of,
        92–93
    Secret Santa plan in, 167
    Textbook era of, 7–9
    Washington's battles with, 6–7
"Senate type," 8
Sessions, Jeff, 134, 192n9
Sestak, Joe, 175
Seventeenth Amendment, 7
sex offenders, 142
Sharlet, Jeff, 67
Shelby, Richard, 165–66, 179n22,
    183n3
Simpson, Alan, 35
Smith, Bob, 53–54, 59, 169
Smith, Gordon, 150

Snowe, Olympia, 4, 46, 103, 153, 156,
    194n11
    approval ratings of, 149
    extremism score of, 54
    partisan warfare complaints of, 13,
        129, 173
    retirement of, 6, 11, 174
Souder, Mark, 157
South Dakota voting slants, 58
Southern Democrats, 42–45, 44f
Special Orders speeches
    COS adoption of, 30–31, 30f
    of Gingrich, 22–23, 179n9
Specter, Arlen, 81, 94, 156
    party switch of, 104
    Santorum's individual experiences
        different from, 189n12
    Toomey challenging, 103–4
    Toomey's Leadership PAC money
        compared to, 203n16
Stafford, Robert, 81
State of the Union, 148
state size variable, on constituencies, 62
Stewart, Jon, 138
STOCK Act, 162
Strategic Offensive Reductions Treaty,
    136
Stutzman, Marlin, 157
Sunday morning talk shows, 148–49, 168
Sununu, John, 53–54
"Super Committee," 139, 166
Surgeon General nominations, 113–14
Swift, Al, 179n1
Symms, Steve, 194n11

Talent, Jim, 40, 169
"Taxation Protection Pledge," 139
tax increases, Gingrich fighting, 25–26
Taylor, Glen, 82
Tea Party movement
    DeMint's endorsements for, 156–58
    DeMint's importance to, 155–56, 170

motivation from, 175

overzealousness hurting, 160

Tea Party Senators, 153. *See also*
  Republicans

  amendment voting in 112th Congress
    of, 164

  cloture effect in 112th Congress of,
    164–65

  earmark ban and, 161–62

  extremism scores in 112th Congress
    of, 162–63, 163*f*, 164*t*

  Gingrich Senators impact compared
    to, 160

  McCain's friction with, 217n15

  presidential nominations in 112th
    Congress and, 165–66

  presidential support scores in 112th
    Congress of, 165

  roll-call votes in 112th Congress of,
    162–63, 163*f*

  STOCK Act and, 162

  on Sunday morning talk shows in
    112th Congress, 168

  2011 debt-limit crisis and, 166

term length

  Gingrich Senator Effect and, 187*t*–188*t*

  of Gingrich Senators, 84–85

Textbook Senate era, 7–9

Thomas, Clarence, 167

Thomas, Craig, 16, 54

  death of, 85

Thomas, Ginni, 167–68

Thune, John, 58, 136

Tiahrt, Todd, 101, 203n12

Toomey, Pat, 160, 162, 166

  DeMint aiding, 104, 156

  pack mentality of Gingrich Senators
    and, 103–4

  Secret Santa plan ridiculed by, 167–68

  Specter challenged by, 103–4

  Specter's Leadership PAC money
    compared to, 203n16

Torricelli, Bob, 77

Trible, Paul, 194n11

Truman, Harry S., 178n17

Twain, Mark, 7

2010 elections, 156–58, 159*t*, 160

2011 debt-limit crisis, 166

unemployment benefits. *See* Federal
  unemployment benefits

U.S. Taxpayer Party, 169

Vander Jagt, Guy, 20

  Gingrich's rise supported by, 21

Vereide, Abraham, 67

Versailles Treaty, 178n17

Viagra, 142, 145

Vitter, David, 15, 16, 120, 212n6

  approval ratings of, 149

  pay raise objections of, 130–31

  Reid criticizing, 131

Voinovich, George, 4, 13, 35, 173

Walker, Robert, 21–22, 23, 169

Wallop, Malcolm, 54

Walsh, Joe, 120

Warner, Mark, 138

Warren, Elizabeth, 165

Washington, George, 6–7

Watergate Babies, 36

Watergate scandal, 36

Watts, J. C., 169

Webb, Jim, 220n11

Weber, Vin, 22

Webster, Daniel, 52, 73

This Week, 148

White, William, 9

Wicker, Roger, 67, 134, 136

Wilson, Woodrow, 178n17

Wofford, Harris, 189n4

would-be Gephardt Senators,
  76, 79. *See also* Gephardt
  Senators

would-be Gingrich Senators, 76. *See also* Gingrich Senators
    campaign fundraising of, 79
    Gingrich Senators compared to, 80–81
    Leadership PAC contributions of Gingrich Senators to, 100–101, 102*t*, 103, 160

Wright, Jim, 22
    Gingrich confrontations with, 24–25, 179n23
    resignation of, 25
Wyoming voting slants, 57

Zimmer, Dick, 77

CPSIA information can be obtained at www.ICGtesting.com
Printed in the USA
BVOW02s2113201113

336884BV00001B/5/P